Inside Cisco IOS Software Architecture

Vijay Bollapragada, CCIE #1606,
Curtis Murphy, CCIE #1521, & Russ White, CCIE #2635

Cisco Press
201 W 103rd Street
Indianapolis, IN 46290 USA

Inside Cisco IOS Software Architecture

Vijay Bollapragada, Curtis Murphy, & Russ White

Copyright© 2000 Cisco Systems, Inc.

Cisco Press logo is a trademark of Cisco Systems, Inc.

Published by:
Cisco Press
201 West 103rd Street
Indianapolis, IN 46290 USA

Printed in the United States of America 1 2 3 4 5 6 7 8 9 0

Library of Congress Cataloging-in-Publication Number: 99-64092

ISBN: 1-57870-181-3

Warning and Disclaimer

This book is designed to provide information about Cisco's proprietary Internetwork Operating System (IOS) software architecture. Every effort has been made to make this book as complete and as accurate as possible, but no warranty or fitness is implied.

The information is provided on an "as is" basis. The author, Cisco Press, and Cisco Systems, Inc., shall have neither liability nor responsibility to any person or entity with respect to any loss or damages arising from the information contained in this book or from the use of the discs or programs that may accompany it.

The opinions expressed in this book belong to the author and are not necessarily those of Cisco Systems, Inc.

Trademark Acknowledgments

All terms mentioned in this book that are known to be trademarks or service marks have been appropriately capitalized. Cisco Press or Cisco Systems, Inc. cannot attest to the accuracy of this information. Use of a term in this book should not be regarded as affecting the validity of any trademark or service mark.

Feedback Information

At Cisco Press, our goal is to create in-depth technical books of the highest quality and value. Each book is crafted with care and precision, undergoing rigorous development that involves the unique expertise of members from the professional technical community.

Readers' feedback is a natural continuation of this process. If you have any comments regarding how we could improve the quality of this book, or otherwise alter it to better suit your needs, you can contact us through e-mail at ciscopress@mcp.com. Please make sure to include the book title and ISBN in your message.

We greatly appreciate your assistance.

Publisher	John Wait
Editor-In-Chief	John Kane
Cisco Systems Program Manager	Jim LeValley
Managing Editor	Patrick Kanouse
Senior Acquisitions Editor	Brett Bartow
Development Editor	Christopher Cleveland
Project Editor	Jennifer Nuckles
Copy Editor	Theresa Wehrle
Technical Editors	Mike Brown, Jennifer DeHaven Carroll, Ron Long, Alexander Marhold
Team Coordinator	Amy Lewis
Book Designer	Gina Rexrode
Cover Designer	Louisa Klucznik
Production Team	Argosy
Indexer	Kevin Fulcher

CISCO SYSTEMS

CISCO PRESS

Corporate Headquarters
Cisco Systems, Inc.
170 West Tasman Drive
San Jose, CA 95134-1706
USA
http://www.cisco.com
Tel: 408 526-4000
    800 553-NETS (6387)
Fax: 408 526-4100

European Headquarters
Cisco Systems Europe s.a.r.l.
Parc Evolic, Batiment L1/L2
16 Avenue du Quebec
Villebon, BP 706
91961 Courtaboeuf Cedex
France
http://www-europe.cisco.com
Tel: 33 1 69 18 61 00
Fax: 33 1 69 28 83 26

**American
Headquarters**
Cisco Systems, Inc.
170 West Tasman Drive
San Jose, CA 95134-1706
USA
http://www.cisco.com
Tel: 408 526-7660
Fax: 408 527-0883

Asia Headquarters
Nihon Cisco Systems K.K.
Fuji Building, 9th Floor
3-2-3 Marunouchi
Chiyoda-ku, Tokyo 100
Japan
http://www.cisco.com
Tel: 81 3 5219 6250
Fax: 81 3 5219 6001

Cisco Systems has more than 200 offices in the following countries. Addresses, phone numbers, and fax numbers are listed on
the Cisco Connection Online Web site at http://www.cisco.com/offices.

Argentina • Australia • Austria • Belgium • Brazil • Canada • Chile • China • Colombia • Costa Rica • Croatia • Czech Republic
• Denmark • Dubai, UAE Finland • France • Germany • Greece • Hong Kong • Hungary • India • Indonesia • Ireland • Israel
• Italy • Japan • Korea • Luxembourg • Malaysia • Mexico • The Netherlands • New Zealand • Norway • Peru • Philippines •
Poland • Portugal • Puerto Rico • Romania • Russia • Saudi Arabia • Singapore • Slovakia • Slovenia • South Africa • Spain •
Sweden • Switzerland • Taiwan • Thailand • Turkey • Ukraine • United Kingdom • United States • Venezuela

About the Authors

Vijay Bollapragada, CCIE #1606, is currently a manager in the Solution Engineering team at Cisco, where he works on new world network solutions and resolves complex software and hardware problems with Cisco equipment. Vijay also teaches Cisco engineers and customers several courses, including Cisco Router Architecture, IP Multicast, Internet Quality of Service, and Internet Routing Architectures. He is also an adjunct professor in Duke University's electrical engineering department.

Curtis Murphy, CCIE #1521, is an engineer in Cisco's Serviceability Design Department in Research Triangle Park, specializing in IOS software products. He has worked in the networking industry since 1989 and at Cisco since 1994. While at Cisco, he has worked both as an IBM protocols specialist in the Technical Assistance Center and as a software engineer in IOS Software Development for mid-range and high-end routers.

Russ White, CCIE #2635, currently is working on the IOS Network Protocols Deployment and Scalability Team, where he is involved in the design and implementation of routing protocols and scalable network design. Russ is the co-author of the Cisco Press title *CCIE Professional Development: Advanced IP Network Design* (ISBN: 1-57870-097-3), published in June 1999.

About the Technical Reviewers

Michael Brown, CCIE #2249, is an ISP Support engineer for Cisco Systems. He earned his bachelor of science degree in electrical engineering from North Carolina State University. In the 11 years he has worked in the networking industry, he has supported a variety of customer networks and technologies. He spent three and half years supporting customers in the Cisco Technical Assistance Center in Brussels, Belgium, before joining the Cisco ISP Support team in Research Triangle Park, NC. He has taught several router architecture courses to Cisco internal audiences and to Cisco customers.

Jennifer DeHaven Carroll, CCIE #1402, is a principal consultant for Lucent Technologies, NetworkCare Professional Services. She earned her bachelor of science degree in computer science from University of California, Santa Barbara. In the past 11 years, Jennifer has planned, designed, and implemented many Cisco-based networks, utilizing all the various IOS switching and packet queuing methods.

Ron Long is the Director of Internet Development for a large, southwestern integrated communications provider. He is responsible for the planning, extension, development, and implementation of Internet services and Layer 2-3 access. Ron entered the networking industry in 1995 when he co-founded an ISP in a small town in Texas. Since then, Ron has provided consulting services and has implemented Cisco solutions to Fortune 1000 companies across the globe.

Alexander Marhold, CCIE #3324, holds an MSC degree in industrial electronics and an MBA. He works as Senior Consultant and Manager at PROIN, a leading European training and consulting company. His focus areas are core routing and service provider issues, such as MPLS, Local Loop, Network Design, and Implementation. Beside his works as a consultant, Alexander is also a CCSI and develops and holds specialized trainings in the service provider area. His previous working experiences also include academic teaching at a polytechnical university for telecommunications, as well as working as CIM-Project Manager in the chemical industry.

Dedications

Vijay Bollapragada:

To my best friend and wife, Leena, for her love and support and sacrifice to let me write this book; to my two lovely children, Amita and Abhishek; to my parents; and to all my friends.

Curtis Murphy:

To my darling wife, Ann, for her ever cheerful smile, her loving support, and her willingness to sacrifice some of our quiet time together to allow me to write this book.

Russ White:

To my wife, Lori, who supports me through the trials and tribulations of book writing, and my daughter Rebekah, who's learning not to play with the mouse and keyboard while I'm working. (I'll install some software for you soon.) I would like to thank God for giving me the opportunity, time, and talent to embark on these bold ventures.

Acknowledgments

This book would have not been possible without the help of many people whose many comments and suggestions improved the end result. First, we want to thank the technical reviewers for the book: Mike Brown, Chris Shaker, Derek Iverson, Alexander Marhold, Jennifer Carroll, and Ron Long. Thanks also to Bob Olsen, Eric Osborne, Siva Valliappan, Ruchi Kapoor, and Lance McCallum for valuable feedback. Finally, we want to thank Brett Bartow, Chris Cleveland, as well as the other people at Cisco Press for keeping us on track and for getting the book published.

Contents at a Glance

Contents

Introduction

Venture into any bookstore today and you can find numerous books on internetworking covering a wide range of topics from protocols to network design techniques. There's no question that internetworking has become a popular field with the enormous growth of the Internet and the increasing convergence of voice, video, and data. Cisco has built a very successful business selling the equipment that forms the network infrastructure—by some accounts, Cisco has more than 85 percent of the market—and at the same time has seen its Cisco IOS Software become a *de facto* industry standard. Yet, although plenty of material is written about network design and the protocols IOS supports, very little information is available from sources other than Cisco.

This lack of information is understandable—IOS is proprietary, after all—but it nevertheless leaves network implementers at a disadvantage. During our experience helping design and troubleshoot IOS-based networks, we've seen many cases where limited IOS architectural knowledge either contributed to a problem or made it more difficult to solve. In addition, we collectively have answered countless numbers of questions (and dispelled some myths) from bewildered Cisco customers about the workings of various IOS features.

This book is an attempt to bring together, in one place, the wealth of information about the architecture and the operation of IOS. Some of this information has been made public previously through forums, Cisco presentations, and the Cisco Technical Assistance Center. Most of the information you cannot find in the Cisco IOS documentation.

Objectives

Inside Cisco IOS Software Architecture is intended to be an IOS "shop manual" for network designers, implementers, and administrators. The objective of this book is to describe key parts of the architecture and the operation of the IOS software. This book also covers the architecture of some of Cisco's hardware platforms. Because IOS is a specialized embedded operating system tightly coupled to the underlying hardware, it's difficult to describe the software without also considering the hardware architecture. Note, however, that this book is not meant to be an exhaustive manual for Cisco hardware. The hardware descriptions are provided only to help illustrate unique features in the IOS software. You might notice that this book does not cover many of the Cisco platforms; in particular, this book does not cover any of the Catalyst switch products, and it omits many of the access routers. In most cases, the missing platforms either are similar to ones that are covered or, in the case of the Catalyst switches, would be best treated in a separate text of their own.

Organization

The book is divided into three general sections. The first covers the general architecture of IOS, including its software infrastructure and packet switching architecture. The second section, beginning with Chapter 3, examines the IOS implementations on a few selected Cisco hardware platforms, covering the design and operation of the platform-specific features. Finally, Chapter 8 describes how IOS implements select Quality of Service (QoS) mechanisms. The book is organized into the following chapters:

- **Chapter 1, "Fundamental IOS Software Architecture"**—Provides an introduction to operating system concepts and then covers the IOS software infrastructure, including processes, memory management, CPU scheduling, packet buffers, and device drivers.

- **Chapter 2, "Packet Switching Architecture"**—Gives an overview of the switching architecture and describes the theory of operation of several platform-independent switching methods, including process switching, fast switching, optimum switching, and Cisco Express Forwarding.

- **Chapter 3, "Shared Memory Routers"**—Shows how the features discussed in Chapter 1 and Chapter 2 actually are implemented on a platform using the relatively simple shared memory routers as an example.

- **Chapter 4, "Early Cbus Routers"**—Covers platform-specific switching features in the IOS implementation for the early Cbus routers. Describes the architecture of the AGS+ and Cisco 7000 routers.

- **Chapter 5, "Particle-Based Systems"**—Describes the particle-based packet buffering scheme using the Cisco 7200 router IOS implementation example. Covers the packet switching implementation on the Cisco 7200.

- **Chapter 6, "Cisco 7500 Routers"**—Continues the description of the Cbus architecture focusing on the Cisco 7500 router IOS implementation. Also examines the IOS distributed switching implementation on the Versatile Interface Processor (VIP).

- **Chapter 7, "The Cisco Gigabit Switch Router: 12000"**—Covers the IOS implementation on the Cisco 12000 series routers.

- **Chapter 8, "Quality of Service"**—Gives an overview of IOS Quality of Service (QoS) and describes several QoS methods, including priority queuing, custom queuing, weighted fair queuing, and modified deficit round robin.

- **Appendix A, "NetFlow Switching"**—Covers the NetFlow feature in IOS used for traffic monitoring and billing.

This chapter covers the following key topics:

- Operating Systems Basics
- IOS Architecture Overview
- Memory Organization
- IOS Processes
- IOS Kernel
- Packet Buffer Management
- Device Drivers

CHAPTER 1

Fundamental IOS Software Architecture

If you were naming the most popular and widely used computer operating systems, which ones would you choose? Most likely, your list would contain names like UNIX, MS-DOS, Microsoft Windows, or even IBM's MVS for mainframes. These are all well-known operating systems—you might even be using one on a computer at home. Now, think for a minute; are there any others? Would your list contain Cisco IOS? No, it probably wouldn't, even though IOS is one of the most widely deployed operating systems in use today.

Unlike the general-purpose operating systems just mentioned, many people never encounter IOS directly. Most who use a computer to access the Internet aren't even aware IOS is behind the scenes. Even those who are aware of IOS, people who use it directly, often don't consider it to be an operating system but instead just the software that runs Cisco routers.

IOS might not run word processors or accounting applications like others on the list but it is still, in fact, an operating system—albeit, one specialized for switching data packets. As you will see, much of the IOS architecture is focused on switching packets as quickly and efficiently as possible.

Although IOS is constructed of many of the same fundamental components found in general-purpose operating systems, the components often contain key differences due to the design goals for IOS. This chapter covers these fundamental operating system components—the *software infrastructure* of IOS—and explores the rationale behind their design.

This chapter begins by introducing a few basic operating system concepts and terms that are useful in understanding the IOS architecture. If you already have a thorough understanding of operating systems, you might want to skip this first section and continue with the section, "IOS Architecture Overview." The remainder of this chapter deals with the major elements of the IOS architecture.

Operating Systems Basics

Modern operating systems provide two primary functions: hardware abstraction and resource management. Hardware abstraction gives software developers a common interface between their application programs and the computer's hardware so each individual programmer doesn't need to deal with the hardware's intricacies. Instead, the hardware-specific programming is developed once, in the operating system, and everyone shares.

The second function that operating systems provide is managing the computer's resources (CPU cycles, memory, and disk drive space, for example) so they can be shared efficiently among multiple applications. Like hardware abstraction, building resource management into the operating system keeps each application programmer from writing resource management code for every program.

CPU Resource Management and Multitasking

Although some operating systems only allow one program to run at a time (most versions of MS-DOS operate this way, for example), it's more common to find operating systems managing multiple programs concurrently. Running multiple programs at once is called *multitasking* and operating systems that support it are typically called *multitasking operating systems*.

Computer programs written for multitasking operating systems themselves often contain multiple independent tasks that run concurrently. These little subprograms are called *threads* because they form a single thread of instruction execution within the program. Threads each have their own set of CPU register values, called a *context*, but can share the same memory address space with other threads in the same program. A group of threads that share a common memory space, share a common purpose, and collectively control a set of operating system resources is called a *process*. On operating systems and CPUs that support virtual memory, each process might run in a separate address space that is protected from other processes.

Because a processor can execute instructions for only one program at a time, the operating system must manage which set of program instructions (which thread) is allowed to run. Deciding which process should run is called *scheduling* and is usually performed by a core piece of the operating system called the *kernel*. An operating system can use one of several methods to schedule threads, depending on the type of applications the operating system has been optimized to support. Different types of applications (batch, interactive, transactional, real-time, and others) have different CPU utilization characteristics, and their overall performance is affected by the scheduling method used.

The simplest scheduling method is to assign each thread to the processor in the order its run request is received and let each thread run to completion. This method is called *FIFO* (first-in, first-out) *run-to-completion* scheduling. FIFO's advantages are: It is easy to implement, it has very low overhead, and it's "fair"—all threads are treated equally, first come, first served.

FIFO with run-to-completion scheduling is good for batch applications and some transactional applications that perform serial processing and then exit, but it doesn't work well for interactive or real-time applications. Interactive applications need relatively fast, short duration access to the CPU so they can return a quick response to a user or service some external device.

One possible solution for these applications is to assign priorities to each thread. Threads with a critical need for fast access to the CPU, such as real-time threads, can be assigned a higher priority than other less critical threads, such as batch. The high priority threads can jump to the head of the line and quickly run on the CPU. If multiple threads are waiting with the same priority, they are processed in the order in which they're received (just like basic FIFO). This method is called *run-to-completion priority scheduling*.

Run-to-completion priority scheduling, though an improvement over FIFO, still has one drawback that makes it unsuitable for interactive and real-time applications—it's easy for one thread to monopolize the processor. High priority threads can get stuck behind a long-running, low-priority thread already running on the processor. To solve this problem, a method is needed to temporarily suspend or *preempt* a running thread so other threads can access the CPU.

Thread Preemption

Involuntarily suspending one thread to schedule another is called *preemption*. Scheduling methods that utilize preemption instead of run to completion are said to be *preemptive*, and operating systems that employ these methods are called *preemptive multitasking* operating systems. Preemption relies on the kernel to periodically change the currently running thread via a *context switch*. The trigger for a context switch can be either a system timer (each thread is assigned a time slice) or a function call to the kernel itself. When a context switch is triggered, the kernel selects the next thread to run and the preempted thread is put back in line to run again at its next opportunity based on the scheduling method being used.

NOTE   A *context switch* occurs when an operating system's kernel removes one thread from the CPU and places another thread on the CPU. In other words, context switches occur when the computer changes the task on which it is currently working. Context switches can be quite expensive in terms of CPU time because all of the processor's registers must be saved for the thread being taken off the CPU and restored for the thread being put on the CPU. The context is essential for the preempted thread to know where it left off, and for the thread being run to know where it was the last time it ran.

There are several advantages to preemptive multitasking, including the following:

- **It's predictable**—A thread can, within limits, know when it will likely run again. For instance, given the limits of kernel implementations, a thread can be set up to run once a second and the programmer can be reasonably certain that the thread will be scheduled to run at that interval.

- **It's difficult to break**—No single thread can monopolize the CPU for long periods of time. A single thread falling into an endless loop cannot stop other threads from running.

Of course, there are also disadvantages to preemptive multitasking, such as:

- **It's less efficient than run-to-completion methods**—In general, preemptive multitasking systems tend to switch contexts more often, which means the CPU spends more time scheduling threads and switching between them than it does with run to completion.

- **It adds complexity to application software**—A thread running on a preemptive system can be interrupted anywhere. Programmers must design and write their applications to protect critical data structures from being changed by other threads when preempted.

Memory Resource Management

Operating systems also manage the computer's memory, typically dividing it into various parts for storing actual computer instructions (code), data variables, and the *heap*. The heap is a section of memory from which processes can allocate and free memory dynamically.

Some operating systems provide a means for processes to address more memory than is physically present as RAM, a concept called *virtual memory*. With virtual memory, the computer's memory can be expanded to include secondary storage, such as a disk drive, in a way that's transparent to the processes. Operating systems create virtual memory using a hardware feature, available on some processors, called a *memory map unit* (MMU). MMU automatically remaps memory address requests to either physical memory (RAM) or secondary storage (disk) depending on where the contents actually reside. The MMU also allows some address ranges to be protected (marked read-only) or to be left totally unmapped.

Virtual memory also has another benefit: In operating systems that support it, an MMU can be programmed to create a separate address space for each process. Each process can have a memory space all to itself and can be prevented from accessing memory in the address space of other processes.

Although it has many benefits, virtual memory does not come for free. There are resource requirements and performance penalties—some of them significant—associated with its use. For this reason, as you will see, IOS does not employ a full virtual memory scheme.

Interrupts

Operating systems usually provide support for CPU interrupts. Interrupts are a hardware feature that cause the CPU to temporarily suspend its current instruction sequence and to transfer control to a special program. The special program, called an *interrupt handler*, performs operations to respond to the event that caused the interrupt, and then returns the CPU to the original instruction sequence. Interrupts often are generated by external hardware, such as a media controller requesting attention, but they also can be generated by the CPU itself. Operating systems support the interrupts by providing a set of interrupt handlers for all possible interrupt types.

IOS Architecture Overview

IOS was originally designed to be a small, embedded system for early Cisco routers. At that time, routers themselves were viewed mostly as hardware appliances—little distinction was made between the hardware and software. In fact, initially IOS wasn't even called "IOS"; it was just referred to as "the OS" that ran a Cisco router.

As routed networks gained popularity, demand rose for routers to support an increasing number of protocols and to provide other functionality, such as bridging. Cisco responded to this enormous demand by adding new features into the router software, resulting in the multi-functional routing and bridging software IOS is today. Interestingly, although the functionality of IOS has grown considerably, the basic operating system architecture has remained mostly the same.

Compared to other operating systems, IOS has a fairly simple architecture. Like most small, embedded systems, IOS was designed to be lean and mean to stay within the memory and speed constraints of the original platforms.

Early routers had limited amounts of memory to share between the software and data (such as routing tables). To limit the size of the executable image, IOS was designed to provide only essential services.

Speed was also a major consideration in the design. To maximize the router's capability to quickly switch packets, a conscious effort was made to design the operating system with a minimum of operational overhead and to allow maximum CPU bandwidth for packet switching. Many safeguards, such as inter-thread memory protection mechanisms, found in other operating systems are missing from IOS because of the CPU and the memory overhead they introduce. In general, the IOS design emphasizes speed at the expense of extra fault protection.

Figure 1-1 shows a conceptual diagram of the IOS architecture.

Figure 1-1   *IOS Architecture*

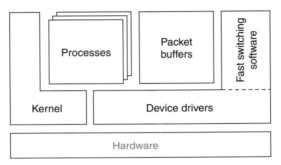

As Figure 1-1 illustrates, IOS has five major elements:

- **Processes**—Individual threads and associated data that perform tasks, such as system maintenance, switching packets, and implementing routing protocols.

- **Kernel**—Provides basic system services to the rest of IOS, such as memory management and process scheduling. It provides hardware (CPU and memory) resource management to processes.

- **Packet Buffers**—Global memory buffers and their associated management functions used to hold packets being switched.

- **Device Drivers**—Functions that control network interface hardware and peripherals (such as a flash card). Device drivers interface between the IOS processes, the IOS kernel, and the hardware. They also interface to the fast switching software.

- **Fast Switching Software**—Highly optimized packet switching functions.

Each of these elements, except fast switching software, is discussed in more detail in the following sections. The fast switching software is discussed later in Chapter 2, "Packet Switching Architecture." Before we investigate these architectural elements, let's first look at how IOS organizes memory.

Memory Organization

IOS maps the entire physical memory into one large flat virtual address space. The CPU's MMU is used when available to create the virtual address space even though IOS doesn't employ a full virtual memory scheme. To reduce overhead, the kernel does not perform any memory paging or swapping, so virtual address space is limited to the bounds of the physical memory available.

IOS divides this address space into areas of memory called *regions,* which mostly correspond to the various types of physical memory. For example, SRAM might be present for storing packets and DRAM might be present for storing software and data on a given type of router. Classifying memory into regions allows IOS to group various types of memory so software needn't know about the specifics of memory on every platform.

Memory regions are classified into one of eight categories, which are listed in Table 1-1.

Table 1-1   *Memory Region Classes*

Memory Region Class	Characteristics
Local	Normal run-time data structures and local heaps; often DRAM.
Iomem	Shared memory that is visible to both the CPU and the network media controllers over a data bus. Often is SRAM.
Fast	Fast memory, such as SRAM, used for special-purpose and speed-critical tasks.
IText	Executable IOS code.
IData	Initialized variables.
IBss	Uninitialized variables.
PCI	PCI bus memory; visible to all devices on the PCI buses.
Flash	Flash memory. This region class can be used to store run-from-Flash or run-from-RAM IOS images. It often also can be used to store backups of the router configuration and other data, such as crash data. Typically, a file system is built in the Flash memory region.

Memory regions also can be nested in a parent-child relationship. Although there is no imposed limit on the depth of nesting, only one level is really used. Regions nested in this manner form *subregions* of the parent region. Figure 1-2 shows a typical platform virtual memory layout and the regions and subregions IOS might create.

Figure 1-2   *Memory Regions*

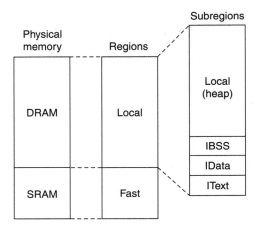

The IOS EXEC command **show region** can be used to display the regions defined on a particular system as demonstrated in Example 1-1 (taken from a Cisco 7206 router).

Example 1-1   **show region** *Command Output*

```
router#show region
Region Manager:
      Start          End       Size(b)  Class  Media  Name
 0x01A00000   0x01FFFFFF      6291456  Iomem  R/W    iomem
 0x31A00000   0x31FFFFFF      6291456  Iomem  R/W    iomem:(iomem_cwt)
 0x4B000000   0x4B0FFFFF      1048576  PCI    R/W    pcimem
 0x60000000   0x619FFFFF     27262976  Local  R/W    main
 0x600088F8   0x61073609     17214738  IText  R/O    main:text
 0x61074000   0x611000FF       573696  IData  R/W    main:data
 0x61100100   0x6128153F      1578048  IBss   R/W    main:bss
 0x61281540   0x619FFFFF      7858880  Local  R/W    main:heap
 0x7B000000   0x7B0FFFFF      1048576  PCI    R/W    pcimem:(pcimem_cwt)
 0x80000000   0x819FFFFF     27262976  Local  R/W    main:(main_k0)
 0xA0000000   0xA19FFFFF     27262976  Local  R/W    main:(main_k1)
```

On the left, the **Start** and **End** addresses correspond to parts of the platform virtual memory map. On the right are the regions and subregions. Subregions are denoted by a name with the **:** separator and no parentheses.

Figure 1-3 illustrates this memory map and its regions.

Figure 1-3   *Memory Map and Regions*

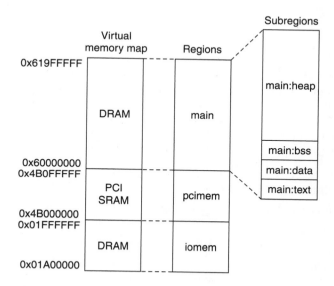

The gaps between the address ranges—for example, **pcimem** ends at **0x4B0FFFFF** and **main** begins at **0x60000000**—are intentional. These gaps allow for expansion of the regions and provide a measure of protection against errant threads. If a runaway thread is advancing through memory writing garbage, it is forced to stop when it hits a gap.

From the output in Example 1-1 and Figure 1-3, you see that the entire DRAM area from 0x60000000 to 0x619FFFFF has been classified as a **local** region and further divided into subregions. These subregions correspond to the various parts of the IOS image itself (text, BSS, and data) and the heap. The heap fills all the local memory area left over after the image is loaded.

Some regions appear to be duplicates, only with a different address range, such as **iomem:(iomem cwt)**:

```
       Start          End      Size(b)  Class  Media  Name
  0x01A00000    0x01FFFFFF     6291456  Iomem  R/W    iomem
  0x31A00000    0x31FFFFFF     6291456  Iomem  R/W    iomem:(iomem_cwt)
  ....
```

These duplicate regions are called *aliases*. Some Cisco platforms have multiple *physical* address ranges that point to the same block of physical memory. These different ranges are used to provide alternate data access methods or automatic data translation in hardware. For example, one address range might provide cached access to an area of physical memory while another might provide uncached access to the same memory.

The duplicate ranges are mapped as alternate views during system initialization and IOS creates alias regions for them. Aliased regions don't count toward the memory total on a platform (because they aren't really separate memory), so they allow IOS to provide a separate region for alternate memory views without artificially inflating the total memory calculation.

Memory Pools

IOS manages available free memory via a series of *memory pools,* which are essentially heaps in the generic sense; each pool is a collection of memory blocks that can be allocated and deallocated as needed. Memory pools are built out of regions and are managed by the kernel. Often, the pools correspond one-to-one to particular regions, but they are not required to. A memory pool can be built from memory spanning several regions, allowing memory to be allocated and reclaimed from various areas for maximum efficiency.

You can obtain information on IOS memory pools by using the **show memory** command as demonstrated by Example 1-2.

Example 1-2   *IOS Memory Pool Information in* **show memory** *Command Output*

```
router#show memory
                Head     Total(b)    Used(b)    Free(b)   Lowest(b)  Largest(b)
Processor   61281540    7858880    3314128    4544752    4377808    4485428
      I/O    1A00000    6291456    1326936    4964520    4951276    4964476
      PCI   4B000000    1048576     407320     641256     641256     641212
 ...
```

NOTE   The output from **show memory** can be very long. It should *not* be issued while console output paging is disabled (the terminal length set to 0) because there is no way to stop or pause the output until it completes.

In Example 1-2, there are three memory pools: **Processor**, **I/O**, and **PCI**. Comparing the **Head** column in this output with the **Start** column from the output of **show region** in Example 1-3 allows you to see which regions are contained within each memory pool.

Example 1-3   **show region** *Command Output*

```
router#show region
Region Manager:
      Start          End      Size(b)  Class  Media  Name
   0x01A00000   0x01FFFFFF    6291456  Iomem  R/W    iomem
   0x31A00000   0x31FFFFFF    6291456  Iomem  R/W    iomem:(iomem_cwt)
   0x4B000000   0x4B0FFFFF    1048576  PCI    R/W    pcimem
   0x60000000   0x619FFFFF   27262976  Local  R/W    main
   0x600088F8   0x61073609   17214738  IText  R/O    main:text
   0x61074000   0x611000FF     573696  IData  R/W    main:data
   0x61100100   0x6128153F    1578048  IBss   R/W    main:bss
   0x61281540   0x619FFFFF    7858880  Local  R/W    main:heap
 ....
```

From Example 1-3, you can see the Processor memory pool contains memory from the subregion of **main**, called **heap**, which is in class **Local**. The Processor memory pool is common to all IOS systems and always resides in local memory. This is the general memory pool from which data is allocated (such as routing tables).

The **I/O** pool is managing memory from the **iomem** region and the **PCI** pool is managing memory from the **pcimem** region.

The remaining fields in the **show memory** output in Example 1-2 provide useful statistics about the pools as documented in the following list. All units are in bytes.

- **Total**—Total size of the pool.
- **Used**—Current amount of memory allocated.
- **Free**—Current amount of memory available.
- **Lowest**—The least amount of memory ever available since the pool was created.
- **Largest**—The size of the largest contiguous block of memory currently available.

The **show memory** command can also display the blocks within each memory pool, as you'll see later in this chapter.

IOS Processes

IOS processes are essentially equivalent to a single thread in other operating systems—IOS processes have one and only one thread each. Each process has its own stack space, its own CPU context, and can control such resources as memory and a console device (more about that later). To minimize overhead, IOS does not employ virtual memory protection between processes. No memory management is performed during context switches. As a result, although each process receives its own memory allocation, other processes can freely access that same memory.

IOS uses a priority run-to-completion model for executing processes. Initially, it might appear that this non-preemptive model is a poor choice for an operating system that must process incoming packets quickly. In some ways, this is an accurate observation; IOS switching needs quickly outgrew the real-time response limitations of its process model, and in Chapter 2, "Packet Switching Architectures," you'll see how this apparent problem was solved. However, this model still holds some advantages that make it a good fit for support processes that remain outside the critical switching path. Some of these advantages are as follows:

- **Low overhead**—Cooperative multitasking generally results in fewer context switches between threads, reducing the total CPU overhead contributed by scheduling.
- **Less complexity for the programmer**—Because the programmer can control where a process is suspended, it's easy to limit context switches to places where shared data isn't being changed, reducing the possibility for side effects and deadlocks between threads.

Process Life Cycle

Processes can be created and terminated at any time while IOS is operating except during an *interrupt*. A process can be created or terminated by the kernel (during IOS initialization) or by another running process.

NOTE	The term *interrupt* used here refers to a hardware interrupt. When the CPU is interrupted, it temporarily suspends the current thread and begins running an interrupt handler function. New processes cannot be created while the CPU is running the interrupt handler.

One component in particular is responsible for creating many of the processes in IOS: the *parser*. The parser is a set of functions that interprets IOS configuration and EXEC commands. The parser is invoked by the kernel during IOS initialization and EXEC processes that are providing a command-line interface (CLI) to the console and Telnet sessions.

Any time a command is entered by a user or a configuration line is read from a file, the parser interprets the text and takes immediate action. Some configuration commands result in the setting of a value, such as an IP address, while others turn on complicated functionality, such as routing or event monitoring.

Some commands result in the parser starting a new process. For example, when the configuration command **router eigrp** is entered via the CLI, the parser starts a new process, called *ipigrp* (if the *ipigrp* process hasn't already been started), to begin processing EIGRP IP packets. If the configuration command **no router eigrp** is entered, the parser terminates the ipigrp process and effectively disables any EIGRP IP routing functionality.

IOS processes actually go through several stages during their existence. Figure 1-4 shows these stages and their corresponding states.

Figure 1-4   *Process Life Cycle*

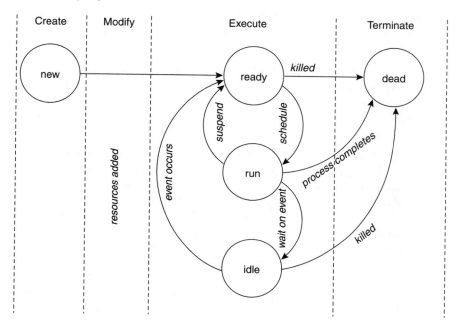

Creation Stage

When a new process is created, it receives its own stack area and enters the *new* state. The process can then move to the modification stage. If no modification is necessary, the process moves to the execution stage.

Modification Stage

Unlike most operating systems, IOS doesn't automatically pass startup parameters or assign a console to a new process when it is created, because it's assumed most processes don't need these resources. If a process does need either of these resources, the thread that created it can *modify* it to add them.

Execution Stage

After a new process is successfully created and modified, it transitions to the *ready* state and enters the execution stage. During this stage, a process can gain access to the CPU and run.

During the execution stage, a process can be in one of three states: ready, run, or idle. A process in the *ready* state is waiting its turn to access the CPU and to begin executing instructions. A process in the *run* state is in control of the CPU and is actively executing instructions. An *idle* process is asleep, waiting on external events to occur before it can be eligible to run.

A process transitions from the ready state to the run state when it's scheduled to run. With non-preemptive multitasking, a scheduled process continues to run on the CPU until it either suspends or terminates. A process can suspend in one of two ways. It can explicitly suspend itself by telling the kernel it wants to relinquish the CPU, transition to the ready state, and wait its next turn to run. A process can also suspend by waiting for an external event to occur. When a process begins waiting on an event, the kernel implicitly suspends it by transitioning it to the idle state, where it remains until the event occurs. After the event occurs, the kernel transitions the process back to the ready state to await its next turn to run.

Termination Stage

The final stage in the process life cycle is the termination stage. A process enters the termination stage when it completes its function and shuts down (called *self termination*) or when another process kills it. When a process is killed or self terminates, the process transitions to the *dead* state. A terminated process remains in the dead state, inactive, until the kernel reclaims all of its resources. The kernel might also record statistics about the process' stack when it terminates. After its resources are reclaimed, the terminated process transitions out of the dead state and is totally removed from the system.

IOS Process Priorities

IOS employs a priority scheme to schedule processes on the CPU. At creation time, every process is assigned one of four priorities based on the process' purpose. The priorities are static; that is, they're assigned when a process is created and never changed. The IOS process priorities are:

- **Critical**—Reserved for essential system processes that resolve resource allocation problems.

- **High**—Assigned to processes that provide a quick response time, such as a process that receives packets directly from a network interface.

- **Medium**—The default priority used by most IOS processes.
- **Low**—Assigned to processes providing periodic background tasks, such as logging messages.

Process priorities provide a mechanism to give some processes preferential access to the CPU based on their relative importance to the entire system. Remember though, IOS doesn't employ preemption, so a higher priority process can't interrupt a lower priority process. Instead, having a higher priority in IOS gives a process more *opportunities* to access the CPU, as you'll see later when you investigate the operation of the kernel's scheduler.

Process Examples

You can use the **show process** command to see a list of all the processes in a system along with some run-time data about each one, as demonstrated in Example 1-4.

Example 1-4 **show process** *Command Output*

```
router#show process
CPU utilization for five seconds: 0%/0%; one minute: 0%; five minutes: 0%
 PID QTy       PC Runtime (ms)    Invoked    uSecs    Stacks TTY Process
   1 M*         0          400         55  727210020/12000  0 Exec
   2 Lst 6024E528      201172      33945     5926 5752/6000  0 Check heaps
   3 Cwe 602355E0           0          1        0 5672/6000  0 Pool Manager
   4 Mst 6027E128           0          2        0 5632/6000  0 Timers
   5 Mwe 602F3E60           0          1        0 5656/6000  0 OIR Handler
   6 Msi 602FA560      290744    1013776      286 5628/6000  0 EnvMon
   7 Lwe 60302944          92      17588        5 5140/6000  0 ARP Input
   8 Mwe 6031C188           0          1        0 5680/6000  0 RARP Input
   9 Mwe 60308FEC       15200     112763  13410748/12000  0 IP Input
  10 Mwe 6033ADC4         420     202811        2 5384/6000  0 TCP Timer
  11 Lwe 6033D1E0           0          1     011644/12000  0 TCP Protocols
  12 Mwe 60389D6C       10204     135198       75 5392/6000  0 CDP Protocol
  13 Mwe 6035BF28       66836    1030665  6411200/12000  0 IP Background
  14 Lsi 60373950           0      16902        0 5748/6000  0 IP Cache Ager
  15 Cwe 6023DD60           0          1        0 5692/6000  0 Critical Bkgnd
  16 Mwe 6023DB80           0         13        0 4656/6000  0 Net Background
  17 Lwe 6027456C           0         11     011512/12000  0 Logger
  18 Msp 6026B0CC         100    1013812        0 5488/6000  0 TTY Background
  19 Msp 6023D8F8           8    1013813        0 5768/6000  0 Per-Second Jobs
  20 Msp 6023D854      405700    1013812      400 4680/6000  0 Net Periodic
  21 Hwe 6023D9BC        5016     101411       49 5672/6000  0 Net Input
  22 Msp 6023D934      135232      16902     8000 5640/6000  0 Per-minute Jobs
```

The following list describes each of the **show process** command output fields found in Example 1-4.

- **PID**—Process identifier. Each process has a unique process identifier number to distinguish it from other processes.
- **Qty**—Process priority and process state. The first character represents the process' priority as follows:
    - **K**—No priority, process has been killed.
    - **D**—No priority, process has crashed.
    - **X**—No priority, process is corrupted.
    - **C**—Critical priority.
    - **H**—High priority.
    - **M**—Medium priority.
    - **L**—Low priority.

    The remaining two characters in this field represent the current state of the process as follows:
    - *****—Process is currently running on the CPU.
    - **E**—Process is waiting for an event (event dismiss).
    - **S**—Process is suspended.
    - **rd**—Process is ready to run.
    - **we**—Process is idle, waiting on an event.
    - **sa**—Process is idle, waiting until a specific absolute time occurs.
    - **si**—Process is idle, waiting for a specific time interval to elapse.
    - **sp**—Process is idle, waiting for a specific time interval to elapse (periodic).
    - **st**—Process is idle, waiting for a timer to expire.
    - **hg**—Process is hung.
    - **xx**—Process is dead.
- **PC**—Contents of the CPU program counter register when the process last relinquished the CPU. This field is a memory address that indicates where the process begins executing the next time it gets the CPU. A value of zero means the process is currently running.
- **Runtime**—Cumulative amount of time (in milliseconds) the process has used the CPU.
- **Invoked**—Total number of times the process has run on the CPU since it was created.

- **uSecs**—Average amount of CPU time (in microseconds) used each time the process is invoked.

- **Stacks**—Stack space usage statistic. The number on the right of the slash (/) shows the total size of the stack space. The number on the left indicates the low water mark for the amount of free stack space available.

- **TTY**—Console device associated with this process. Zero indicates the process does not own a console or communicates with the main system console.

- **Process**—Name of the process. Process names need not be unique (multiple copies of a process can be active simultaneously). However, process IDs are always unique.

If you issue the **show process** command on several different IOS systems, you'll notice some processes appear on every one. Most of these are processes that perform housekeeping or provide services to other processes. Table 1-2 describes the most common of these processes and the tasks they perform.

Table 1-2   *Common System Processes and Their Functions*

System Process	Function
EXEC	Command-line interface (CLI) for the console and directly connected asynchronous TTY lines. The EXEC process accepts user input and provides an interface to the parser.
Pool manager	Manages buffer pools (more on this in the "Packet Buffer Management" section in this chapter).
Check heaps	Periodically validates the integrity of the runtime IOS code and the structure of the memory heap.
Per-minute jobs	Generic system process that runs every 60 seconds performing background maintenance, such as checking the integrity of process stacks.
Per-second jobs	Generic system process that performs tasks that need to be repeated every second.
Critical background	Critical priority process that performs essential system services, such as allocating additional IOS queue elements when they run out.
Net background	Sends interface keepalive packets, unthrottles interfaces, and processes interface state changes.
Logger	Looks for messages (debug, error, and informational) queued via the kernel by other processes and outputs them to the console and, optionally, to a remote syslog server.
TTY background	Monitors directly connected asynchronous TTY lines for activity and starts "EXEC" processes for them when they go active.

All the processes in Table 1-2, except EXEC, are created by the kernel during system initialization and normally persist until IOS is shut down.

IOS Kernel

When used within the context of operating systems, the word *kernel* usually conjures pictures of an operating system core that runs in a special protected CPU mode and manages system resources. Although the IOS kernel does help manage system resources, its architecture differs from those in other operating systems. The IOS kernel is not a single unit but rather a loose collection of components and functions linked with the rest of IOS as a peer rather than a supervisor. There's no special kernel mode. Everything, including the kernel, runs in user mode on the CPU and has full access to system resources.

The kernel schedules processes, manages memory, provides service routines to trap and handle hardware interrupts, maintains timers, and traps software exceptions. The major functions of the kernel are described in more detail in the following sections.

The Scheduler

The actual task of scheduling processes is performed by the *scheduler*. The IOS scheduler manages all the processes in the system using a series of *process queues* that represent each process state. The queues hold context information for processes in that state. Processes transition from one state to another as the scheduler moves their context from one process queue to another. In all, there are six process queues:

- **Idle queue**—Contains processes that are still active but are waiting on an event to occur before they can run.

- **Dead queue**—Contains processes that have terminated but need to have their resources reclaimed before they can be totally removed from the system.

- **Ready queues**—Contain processes that are eligible to run. There are four ready queues, one for each process priority:
    - Critical
    - High
    - Medium
    - Low

When a running process suspends, the scheduler regains control of the CPU and uses an algorithm to select the next process from one of its four ready queues. The steps for this algorithm are as follows:

Step 1 The scheduler first checks for processes waiting in the critical priority ready queue. It runs each critical process, one by one, until all have had a chance to run.

Step 2 After all critical processes have had a chance to run, the scheduler checks the high priority queue. If there are no high priority processes ready, the scheduler skips to Step 3 and checks the medium priority queue.

Otherwise, the scheduler removes each high priority process from the queue and allows it to run. Between each high priority process, the scheduler checks for any critical processes that are ready and runs all of them before proceeding to the next high priority process. After all high priority processes have had their chance, the scheduler skips the medium and low process queues and starts over at Step 1.

Step 3   After there are no high priority processes waiting to run, the scheduler checks the medium priority queue. If there are no medium priority processes ready, the scheduler skips to Step 4 and checks the low priority queue. Otherwise, the scheduler removes each medium priority process from the queue and allows it to run. Between each medium priority process, the scheduler checks for any high priority processes that are ready and runs all of them (interleaved with any critical priority processes) before proceeding to the next medium priority process. After all medium priority processes have had their chance, the scheduler skips over the low priority queue and starts over at Step 1 again. The scheduler skips the low priority queue a maximum of 15 times before proceeding to Step 4. This threshold is a failsafe mechanism to prevent the low priority processes from being starved.

Step 4   After there are no medium or high priority processes waiting to run (or the low priority queue has been skipped 15 times) the scheduler checks the low priority queue. The scheduler removes each low priority process from the queue and allows it to run. Between each low priority process, the scheduler checks for any ready medium priority processes and runs them (interleaved with any high and critical priority processes) before proceeding to the next low priority process.

Step 5   The scheduler finally returns to Step 1 and starts over.

The scheduling algorithm works similar to the operation of a stopwatch. Think of the seconds as representing the critical processes, the minutes as representing the high priority processes, the hours as representing medium processes, and the days as representing the low priority processes. Each pass of the second hand covers all the seconds on the dial. Each pass of the minute hand covers all the minutes on the dial, including a complete pass of all seconds for each minute passed, and so on.

Like a stopwatch, the scheduling algorithm also has a built-in reset feature. The algorithm doesn't advance to check the medium priority queue until there are no high priority processes waiting to run. As long as it finds high priority processes, it starts over from the beginning, checking for critical processes and then high priority processes like a stopwatch that's reset to zero when it reaches the first hour.

Process CPU Utilization

Although IOS does not provide any statistics on the operation of the scheduler itself, there is a way to see how the processes are sharing the CPU. In an earlier example, you saw how the **show process** command gives general statistics about all active processes. A variant of that command, **show process cpu**, has similar output but focuses more on the CPU utilization by each process. Example 1-5 provides some sample output from the **show process cpu** command.

Example 1-5   **show process cpu** *Command Output*

```
router#show process cpu
CPU utilization for five seconds: 90%/82%; one minute: 60%; five minutes: 40%
PID  Runtime(ms)  Invoked   uSecs   5Sec    1Min    5Min TTY Process
  1         1356  2991560       0   0.00%   0.00%   0.00%   0 BGP Router
  2       100804     7374   13670   0.00%   0.02%   0.00%   0 Check heaps
  3            0        1       0   0.00%   0.00%   0.00%   0 Pool Manager
  4            0        2       0   0.00%   0.00%   0.00%   0 Timers
  5         6044    41511000   0.00%   0.00%   0.00%   0 OIR Handler
  6            0        1       0   0.00%   0.00%   0.00%   0 IPC Zone Manager
  7            0        1       0   0.00%   0.00%   0.00%   0 IPC Realm Manager
  8         7700    36331     211   8.00%   0.00%   0.00%   0 IP Input
...
```

The first line of the **show process cpu** output in Example 1-5 shows the overall CPU utilization for the machine averaged over three different time intervals: 5 seconds, 1 minute, and 5 minutes. The 5 second usage statistic is reported as two numbers separated by a slash. The number on the left of the slash represents the total percentage of available CPU capacity used during the last 5-second interval (total percent CPU busy). The number on the right of the slash represents the total percentage of available CPU capacity used while processing interrupts. The 1-minute usage and the 5-minute usage show the total percent CPU usage as an exponentially decaying average over the last minute and the last 5 minutes, respectively.

Below the general usage statistics, the same three intervals are reported on a per process basis. Note, the scheduler automatically computes all these usage statistics every 5 seconds and stores them internally in case someone issues a **show process cpu** command. So, it's possible to see the exact same statistics twice—not updated—if the command is issued twice within a 5 second period.

Using the **show process cpu** output, it's fairly easy to determine what processes are most active and how much of the CPU capacity they use. In the example, an average of 90 percent of the CPU capacity was being used during the 5-second interval right before the command was issued. An average of 82 percent of capacity was being used by interrupt processing with the other 8 percent being used by scheduled processes (90% − 82% = 8%). Over the last 60 seconds, an average of 60 percent of the CPU capacity was being used, and over the last 5 minutes, 40 percent of the CPU capacity was being used, on average. Looking at the individual scheduled processes, 8 percent of the CPU capacity was being consumed by the **ip_input** process during the last 5 seconds. This accounts for all the process usage; so, the other processes either weren't scheduled on the CPU during that interval or they used less than 0.01 percent of the CPU.

In this example, a relatively large percentage of the CPU capacity is being consumed by interrupt processing. So what is IOS doing during that 82 percent of the time? Unfortunately, there's no detailed account of interrupt processing CPU usage like there is for processes; so, we really can't pinpoint the usage to a specific source. However, we can make a good estimate about how this CPU time is being used. As you'll see in Chapter 2, when Fast Switching is being used for packets, most of the packet switching work is performed during an interrupt. IOS does do some other processing during interrupts, but by far most of the processing time is used for fast packet switching. A high interrupt CPU usage statistic usually just means IOS is fast switching a large volume of packets.

The remaining unused CPU capacity (10 percent in our example) is called *idle* CPU time. "Idle," though, is a somewhat misleading term because a CPU is never really idle while it's running; it's always executing instructions for something. In IOS, that idle time actually represents the time the CPU is spending running the scheduler itself—a very important task indeed. It's important for an IOS system to operate with sufficient idle time. As CPU utilization approaches 100 percent, very little time is left over for the scheduler, creating a potentially serious situation. Because the scheduler is responsible for running all the background critical support processes, if it can't run, neither can the processes and that can lead to system failure.

As you'll see, IOS has watchdog timers to prevent runaway processes from consuming all the CPU capacity. Unfortunately, IOS does not always employ this type of limiting mechanism for interrupts. Although many platforms do support limiting CPU interrupt time through *interrupt throttling*, it's not always enabled by default.

In any event, watchdog timers and interrupt throttling are just safety mechanisms. When planning for a system that might encounter a high rate of packets (many busy high speed network interfaces, for example), it's best to select a sufficiently fast CPU and configure IOS with the most efficient switching methods to avoid CPU starvation problems.

Watchdog Timer

To reduce the impact of runaway processes, IOS employs a process *watchdog* timer to allow the scheduler to periodically poll the current running process. This feature is not the same as preemption but is instead a failsafe mechanism to prevent the system from becoming unresponsive or completely locking up due to a process consuming all of the CPU. If a process appears to be hung (for example, it's been running for a long time), the scheduler can force the process to terminate.

Each time the scheduler allows a process to run on the CPU, it starts a watchdog timer for that process. After a preset period, two seconds by default, if the process is still running, the timer expires and the scheduler regains control. The first time the watchdog expires, the scheduler prints a warning message for the process similar to the following, and then continues the process on the CPU:

```
%SNMP-3-CPUHOG: Processing GetNext of ifEntry.17.6
%SYS-3-CPUHOG: Task ran for 2004 msec (49/46), Process = IP SNMP, PC = 6018EC2C
 -Traceback= 6018EC34 60288548 6017E9C8 6017E9B4
```

If the watchdog expires a second time and the process still hasn't suspended, the scheduler terminates the process.

The Memory Manager

The kernel's memory manager is responsible, at a macro level, for managing all the memory available to IOS, including the memory containing the IOS image itself. The memory manager is actually not one single component but three separate components, each with its own responsibility:

- **Region Manager**—Defines and maintains the various memory regions on a platform.
- **Pool Manager**—Manages the creation of memory pools and the allocation/de-allocation of memory blocks within the pools.
- **Chunk Manager**—Manages the specially allocated memory blocks that contain multiple fixed-sized sub-blocks.

Region Manager

The region manager is responsible for maintaining all the memory regions. It provides services allowing other parts of IOS to create regions and to set their attributes. It also allows others to query the available memory regions, for example, to determine the total amount of memory available on a platform.

Pool Manager

The memory pool manager is a very important component of the kernel. Just as the scheduler manages allocating CPU resources to processes, the pool manager manages memory allocation for processes. All processes must go through the pool manager, directly or indirectly, to allocate memory for their use. The pool manager is invoked each time a process uses the standard system functions *malloc* and *free* to allocate or return memory.

The pool manager operates by maintaining lists of free memory blocks within each pool. Initially, of course, each pool contains just one large free block equal to the size of the pool. As the pool manager services requests for memory, the initial free block gets smaller and smaller. At the same time, processes can release memory back to the pool, creating a number of discontiguous free blocks of varying sizes. This scenario is called *memory fragmentation* and is illustrated in Figure 1-5.

Figure 1-5   *Memory Pool Allocation*

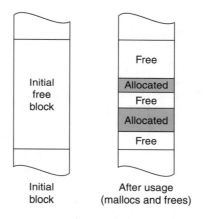

As free blocks are returned to a pool, the pool manager adds their size and starting addresses to one of the pool's free lists for blocks of similar size. By default, the pool manager maintains free lists for each of the following block sizes: 24, 84, 144, 204, 264, 324, 384, 444, 1500, 2000, 3000, 5000, 10,000, 20,000, 32,768, 65,536, 131,072, and 262,144 bytes. Note that these sizes have no relation to the system buffers discussed later in this chapter.

When a process requests memory from a pool, the pool manager first starts with the free list associated with the size of the request. This method helps make efficient use of memory by matching requests to recycled blocks that are close in size. If there are no blocks available on the best-fit list, the pool manager continues with each higher list until a free block is found. If a block is found on one of the higher lists, the pool manager splits the block and puts the unused portion back on the appropriate list of smaller blocks.

The pool manager tries to control fragmentation by coalescing returned blocks that are physically adjacent to one another. When a block is returned and it's next to an existing free block, the pool manager combines the two blocks into one larger block and places the resulting block on the appropriate sized list, as shown in Figure 1-6.

Figure 1-6 *Free Block Coalesce*

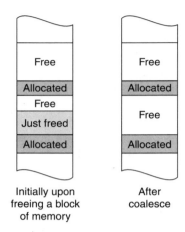

Initially upon
freeing a block
of memory

After
coalesce

Earlier, Example 1-2 demonstrated how the EXEC command **show memory** displays names and statistics for the available memory pools in its summary. The **show memory** command also lists detail about the individual blocks contained in each of the pools. Following the pool summary, the command output lists all the blocks, in order, under each pool, as demonstrated in the output in Example 1-6.

Example 1-6 **show memory** *Command Output with Memory Pool Details*

```
router#show memory
               Head    Total(b)   Used(b)    Free(b)  Lowest(b) Largest(b)
Processor  61281540    7858880    3314128    4544752    4377808    4485428
      I/O  1A00000     6291456    1326936    4964520    4951276    4964476
      PCI  4B000000    1048576     407320     641256     641256     641212


Processor memory

  Address Bytes Prev.     Next     Ref  PrevF    NextF   Alloc PC  What
  61281540 1460 0         61281B20   1                   6035CCB0  List Elements
  61281B20 2960 61281540  612826DC   1                   6035CCDC  List Headers
  612826DC 9000 61281B20  61284A30   1                   60367224  Interrupt Stack
  61284A30   44 612826DC  61284A88   1                   60C8BEEC  *Init*
  61284A88 9000 61284A30  61286DDC   1                   60367224  Interrupt Stack
  61286DDC   44 61284A88  61286E34   1                   60C8BEEC  *Init*
  61286E34 9000 61286DDC  61289188   1                   60367224  Interrupt Stack
  61289188   44 61286E34  612891E0   1                   60C8BEEC  *Init*
  612891E0 4016 61289188  6128A1BC   1                   602F82CC  TTY data
  6128A1BC 2000 612891E0  6128A9B8   1                   602FB7B4  TTY Input Buf
  6128A9B8  512 6128A1BC  6128ABE4   1                   602FB7E8  TTY Output Buf
```

The memory pool detail fields displayed in Example 1-6 are as follows:

- **Address**—Starting address of the block.
- **Bytes**—Size of the block.
- **Prev**—Address of the preceding block in the pool.
- **Next**—Address of the following block in the pool.
- **Ref**—Number of owners of this memory block.
- **PrevF**—For free blocks only, the address of the preceding block in the free list.
- **NextF**—For free blocks only, the address of the next block in the free list.
- **Alloc PC**—Value of the CPU's program counter register when the block was allocated. This value can be used to determine which process allocated the block.
- **What**—Description of how the block is being used.

You can use a variation of this command, **show memory free**, to display the free blocks in each pool, as demonstrated in Example 1-7. The command output lists each free block in order by free list. Empty free lists appear with no memory blocks listed under them.

Example 1-7   **show memory free** *Command Output*

```
router#show memory free
...

Processor memory

Address   Bytes Prev.     Next      Ref  PrevF    NextF    Alloc PC  What
          24       Free list 1
6153E628  52    6153E5F0 6153E688  0    0        615A644  603075D8  Exec
615A6444  44    615A63F8 615A649C  0    6153E62  0        603567F0  (fragment)
          92       Free list 2
          112      Free list 3
          116      Free list 4
          128      Free list 5
61552788  128   6155273C 61552834  0    0        0        603075D8  (coalesced)
          132      Free list 6
          152      Free list 7
          160      Free list 8
          208      Free list 9
          224      Free list 10
          228      Free list 11
6153E460  240   6153E428 6153E57C  0    0        0        6047A960  CDP Protocol
          272      Free list 12
          288      Free list 13
          296      Free list 14
          364      Free list 15
          432      Free list 16
          488      Free list 17
          500      Free list 18
```

continues

Example 1-7   **show memory free** *Command Output (Continued)*

```
6153E6D4     544 6153E69C 6153E920   0  0         0       60362350   (coalesced)
            1500        Free list 19
            2000        Free list 20
6155 2B84    2316 61552954 615534BC   0  0         0       603075D8   (coalesced)
            3000        Free list 21
6153EA14    4960 6153E9D4 6153FDA0   0  0         0       603080BC   (coalesced)
            5000        Free list 22
           10000        Free list 23
61572824   15456 6157106C 615764B0   0  0         0       603080BC   (coalesced)
           20000        Free list 24
           32768        Free list 25
6159BA64   35876 61598B6C 615A46B4   0  0         0       60371508   (fragment)
           65536        Free list 26
          131072        Free list 27
          262144        Free list 28

Total: >    59616
```

Chunk Manager

The pool manager provides a very effective way for managing a collection of random-sized blocks of memory. However, this feature does not come without cost. The pool manager introduces 32 bytes of memory overhead on every block managed. Although this overhead is insignificant for pools with a few hundred large blocks, for a pool with thousands of small blocks, the overhead can quickly become substantial. As an alternative, the kernel provides another memory manager, called the *chunk manager*, that can manage large pools of small blocks without the associated overhead.

Unlike the pool manager, the chunk manager does not create additional memory pools with free lists of varying size. Instead, the chunk manager manages a set of fixed-size blocks subdivided within a larger block that has been allocated from one of the standard memory pools. In some ways, the chunk manager can almost be considered a submemory pool manager.

The strategy most often employed is this: A process requests the allocation of a large memory block from a particular memory pool. The process then calls on the chunk manager to subdivide the block into a series of smaller fixed-size chunks and uses the chunk manager to allocate and free the chunks as needed. The advantage is there are only 32 bytes of overhead (associated with the one large block) and the pool manager is not burdened with allocating and reclaiming thousands of little fragments. So, the potential for memory fragmentation in the pool is greatly reduced.

Process Memory Utilization

IOS has another variation of the **show process** CLI command, **show process memory**, that shows the memory utilization by each process. This command allows you to quickly determine how available memory is being allocated by processes in the system. Example 1-8 provides some sample output from a **show process memory** command.

Example 1-8   **show process memory** *Command Output*

```
router#show process memory
Total: 7858880, Used: 3314424, Free: 4544456
 PID TTY  Allocated      Freed     Holding    Getbufs    Retbufs Process
   0   0      86900       1808     2631752          0          0 *Init*
   0   0        448      55928         448          0          0 *Sched*
   0   0    7633024    2815568        6348     182648          0 *Dead*
   1   0        268        268        3796          0          0 Load Meter
   2   0        228          0        7024          0          0 CEF Scanner
   3   0          0          0        6796          0          0 Check heaps
   4   0         96          0        6892          0          0 Pool Manager
   5   0        268        268        6796          0          0 Timers
...

  65   0          0      14492        6796          0      13248 Per-minute Jobs
  66   0     143740       3740      142508          0          0 CEF process
  67   0          0          0        6796          0          0 xcpa-driver
                                  3314184 Total
```

The first line in Example 1-8 shows the total number of bytes in the pool followed by the amount used and the amount free. The statistics in the first line represent metrics for the Processor memory pool and should match the output of the **show memory** command. The summary line is followed by detail lines for each scheduled process:

- **PID**—Process identifier.

- **TTY**—Console assigned to the process.

- **Allocated**—The total number of bytes this process has allocated since it was created.

- **Freed**—The total number of bytes this process has freed since it was created.

- **Holding**—The number of bytes this process currently has allocated. Note that, because a process can free memory that was allocated by another process, the **allocated**, **freed**, and **holding** numbers might not always balance. In other words, **allocated** minus **freed** does not always equal **holding.**

- **Getbufs**—The total number of bytes for new packet buffers created on behalf of this process. Packet buffer pools are described later in the "Packet Buffer Management" section.

- **Retbufs**—The total number of bytes for packet buffers trimmed on behalf of this process. Packet buffer trims are described later in the "Packet Buffer Management" section.

- **Process**—The name of the process.

Notice there are three processes appearing in the **show process memory** output labeled ***Init***, ***Sched***, and ***Dead***. These are not real processes at all but are actually summary lines showing memory allocated by IOS outside the scheduled processes. The following list describes these summary lines:

- ***Init***—Shows memory allocated for the kernel during system initialization before any processes are created.

- ***Sched***—Shows memory allocated by the scheduler.

- ***Dead***—Shows memory once allocated by scheduled processes that has now entered the dead state. Memory allocated to dead processes is eventually reclaimed by the kernel and returned to the memory pool.

Memory Allocation Problems

In all the examples thus far, we've assumed that when a process requests an allocation of memory its request is granted. However, this might not always be the case. Memory resources, like CPU resources, are limited; there's always the chance that there might not be enough memory to satisfy a request. What happens when a process calls on the pool manager for a memory block and the request fails? Depending on the severity (that is, what the memory is needed for), the process might continue to limp along or it might throw up its hands and quit. In either case, when the pool manager receives a request that it can't satisfy, it prints a warning message to the console similar to the following:

```
%SYS-2-MALLOCFAIL: Memory allocation of 2129940 bytes failed from 0x6024C00C,
  pool I/O, alignment 32
 -Process= "OIR Handler", ipl= 4, pid= 7
 -Traceback= 6024E738 6024FDA0 6024C014 602329C8 60232A40 6025A6C8 60CEA748
  60CDD700 60CDF5F8 60CDF6E8 60CDCB40 60286F1C 602951
```

Basically, there are two reasons why a valid request for memory allocation can fail:

- There isn't enough free memory available.

- Enough memory is available, but it's fragmented so that no contiguous block is available of sufficient size.

Failures due to lack of memory usually occur because there is simply not enough memory on the platform to support all the activities in the system. When this happens, you have two choices: add more memory to the platform, or reduce configured features, interfaces, and so on until the problem goes away. In some rare cases, though, these "out of memory" failures can occur because of a defect called a *memory leak* in one of the processes. The term *memory leak* refers to a scenario where a process continually allocates memory blocks but never frees any of them; eventually it consumes all available memory. Memory leaks usually are caused by software defects.

Allocation failures also can occur when there's seemingly plenty of memory available. For an example, look at the following sample **show memory** output in Example 1-9.

Example 1-9 *Sample **show memory** Command Output*

```
router#show memory
                 Head    Total(b)   Used(b)   Free(b)  Lowest(b)  Largest(b)
Processor  61281540      7858880   4898452   2960428      10507        8426
....
```

This particular system has 2,960,428 bytes of memory free. Yet, what happens when a process tries to allocate just 9000 bytes? The request fails. The clue to why is in the **Largest** field of the **show memory** output. At the time this command was issued, the largest contiguous block of memory available was only 8426 bytes long—not large enough to satisfy a 9000 byte request.

This scenario is indicative of severe memory fragmentation. Severe fragmentation occurs when many small memory blocks are allocated and then returned in such a way that the pool manager can't coalesce them into larger blocks. As this trend continues, the large contiguous blocks in the pool are chipped away until nothing is left but smaller fragments. When all the larger blocks are gone, memory allocation failures start to occur.

The kernel's pool manager is designed to maintain self-healing memory pools that avoid fragmentation, and in most cases this design works without a problem. However, some allocation scenarios can break this design; one example being the pool of many small blocks discussed earlier.

Packet Buffer Management

In packet routing, as in any store-and-forward operation, there must be some place within the system to store the data while it is being routed on its way. The typical strategy is to create memory buffers to hold incoming packets while the switching operation is taking place. Because the capability to route packets is central to the IOS architecture, IOS contains a special component dedicated to managing just such buffers. This component is called the *buffer pool manager* (not to be confused with the memory pool manager discussed earlier). IOS uses this component to create and manage a consistent series of packet buffer pools for switching on every platform. The buffers in these pools are collectively known as the *system buffers*.

The buffer pool manager provides a convenient way to manage a set (or *pool*) of buffers of a particular size. Although it can be used to manage any type of buffer pool, the buffer pool manager is used primarily to manage pools of packet buffers, so that's what we'll focus on here.

Packet buffer pools are created using memory allocated from one of the available memory pools: for example, Processor, I/O, and so on. To create a pool, the packet buffer manager requests a block of memory from the kernel's memory pool manager and divides it into buffers. The packet buffer manager then builds a list of all the free buffers and tracks the allocation and freeing of those buffers.

Packet buffer pools can be either static or dynamic. Static pools are created with a fixed number of buffers—no additional buffers can be added to the pool. Dynamic pools are created with a particular base minimum number of buffers, called *permanent* buffers, but additional buffers can be added or removed on demand. With dynamic buffer pools, if the buffer pool manager receives a request while the pool is empty, it attempts to expand the pool and satisfy the request immediately. If it's not possible to expand the pool within the context of the request, it fails the request and expands the pool later in the **pool manager** background process.

Packet buffer pools are classified as either public or private. Public pools, as the name implies, are available for use by any system process, and private pools are created for (and known only to) a specific subset of processes that use them.

System Buffers

Every IOS system has a predefined set of public buffer pools known as the *system buffers*. These buffer pools are used for process switching packets through the platform and for creating packets that originate in the platform (such as interface keepalive packets and routing updates). IOS provides statistics about these and other buffer pools through the **show buffer** command. For an example, let's examine the **show buffer** output in Example 1-10.

Example 1-10 show buffer *Command Output*

```
router#>show buffer
Buffer elements:
     500 in free list (500 max allowed)
     747314 hits, 0 misses, 0 created

Public buffer pools:
Small buffers, 104 bytes (total 50, permanent 50):
     46 in free list (20 min, 150 max allowed)
     530303 hits, 6 misses, 18 trims, 18 created
     0 failures (0 no memory)
Middle buffers, 600 bytes (total 25, permanent 25):
     25 in free list (10 min, 150 max allowed)
     132918 hits, 3 misses, 9 trims, 9 created
     0 failures (0 no memory)
```

Example 1-10 show buffer *Command Output (Continued)*

```
Big buffers, 1524 bytes (total 50, permanent 50):
     50 in free list (5 min, 150 max allowed)
     47 hits, 0 misses, 0 trims, 0 created
     0 failures (0 no memory)
VeryBig buffers, 4520 bytes (total 10, permanent 10):
     10 in free list (0 min, 100 max allowed)
     26499 hits, 0 misses, 0 trims, 0 created
     0 failures (0 no memory)
Large buffers, 5024 bytes (total 0, permanent 0):
     0 in free list (0 min, 10 max allowed)
     0 hits, 0 misses, 0 trims, 0 created
     0 failures (0 no memory)
Huge buffers, 18024 bytes (total 0, permanent 0):
     0 in free list (0 min, 4 max allowed)
     0 hits, 0 misses, 0 trims, 0 created
     0 failures (0 no memory)
...
```

Notice the list of **Public buffer pools**. These are the standard system buffers for IOS. Each one has a name, such as **Small buffers**, **Middle buffers**, and so on, that identifies the particular pool. Following the pool name is the byte size of the buffers contained in that pool. Each buffer pool contains buffers of one and only one size. The sizes vary from 104 bytes up to 18,024 bytes in order to accommodate the various maximum transmission unit (MTU) sizes encountered on different interface media.

The remainder of the fields in Example 1-10 are as follows:

- **total**—The total number of buffers in the pool (both allocated and free).

- **permanent**—The base number of buffers in the pool. For dynamic pools, the total number of buffers can fluctuate as the pool grows and shrinks. However, there will never be less than the **permanent** number of buffers in the pool.

- **in free list**—Indicates the number of free buffers available.

- **min**—The minimum number of buffers *desired* in the free list. If the number of free buffers drops below **min**, the buffer pool manager attempts to grow the pool and add more buffers until the number of free buffers is greater than **min**.

- **max allowed**—The maximum number of buffers *desired* in the free list. If the number of free buffers increases beyond **max allowed**, the buffer pool manager attempts to shrink the pool, deleting free buffers, until the number of free buffers drops below **max allowed**. Note that the buffer pool manager never shrinks the size of the pool below the **permanent** metric regardless of the value of **max allowed**.

- **hits**—The number of buffers that have been requested from the pool.

- **misses**—The number of times a buffer was requested from the pool when there were fewer than **min** buffers in the free list.

- **trims**—The number of buffers that have been deleted from the pool during pool shrinkage.

- **created**—The number of buffers that have been created and added to the pool during pool growth.

- **failures**—The number of times a buffer was requested from the pool but the request could not be satisfied. Failures can occur for two reasons:

  — A buffer request occurs during an interrupt and there are no free buffers. Pools can't grow during an interrupt.

  — A buffer request occurs, there are no free buffers, and there is no more memory left in the memory pool to grow the buffer pool.

- **no memory**—The number of times a failure occurred because there was no available memory in the memory pool. Note that this counter is no longer used in recent versions of IOS.

To get an understanding of just how the buffer pool manager operates with these system buffers, let's step through a packet-switching scenario and monitor how the **show buffers** counters change for a particular pool. Consider the following example.

Let's start with 16 buffers in the free list, as shown in the following output and illustrated in Figure 1-7.

```
Small buffers, 104 bytes (total 16, permanent 16):
    16 in free list (8 min, 16 max allowed)
    0 hits, 0 misses, 0 trims, 0 created
    0 failures (0 no memory)
```

Figure 1-7   *Beginning with an Empty Buffer*

16 in free list

Now say IOS receives eight packets that fit nicely into the 104-byte small buffers. The packet receive software requests and receives eight buffers from the small buffer pool and copies in the packets. The free list now drops from 16 to 8, resulting in a count of eight free buffers and eight hits, as illustrated in the following output and in Figure 1-8.

```
Small buffers, 104 bytes (total 16, permanent 16):
    8 in free list (8 min, 16 max allowed)
    8 hits, 0 misses, 0 trims, 0 created
    0 failures (0 no memory)
```

Figure 1-8   *Eight Packets Received*

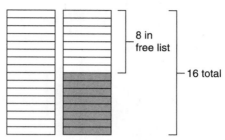

Now IOS receives four more packets before processing any of the eight previously received. The packet receive software requests four more buffers from the **small** pool and copies in the data packets. Figure 1-9 illustrates the pool at this point.

Figure 1-9   *Four More Packets Received*

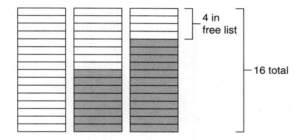

Looking at the output of **show buffers**, we see several counters have incremented. Let's inspect them to see what happened to the pool:

```
Small buffers, 104 bytes (total 16, permanent 16):
    4 in free list (8 min, 16 max allowed)
    12 hits, 4 misses, 0 trims, 0 created
    0 failures (0 no memory)
```

The number in the free list has now dropped to 4 and there are now 12 hits, reflecting the 4 new buffers requested. Why have the misses incremented to four, though? Because each time a buffer is requested from a pool where it causes the free list to drop below the minimum free buffers allowed, a miss is counted. We can see from the output that the minimum free is eight and we now have only four buffers in the free list; so, IOS counted four misses.

Because there are now fewer than **min** buffers in the free list, the buffer pool manager runs the pool manager process to grow the pool and to create more free buffers, as demonstrated in the following output and illustrated in Figure 1-10.

```
Small buffers, 104 bytes (total 20, permanent 16):
    8 in free list (8 min, 16 max allowed)
    12 hits, 4 misses, 0 trims, 4 created
    0 failures (0 no memory)
```

Figure 1-10 *After Pool Manager Creates New Buffers*

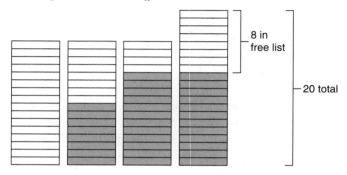

We now see that the pool manager process has created four new buffers to bring the number in the free list back up to a total of eight, the minimum number of buffers desired to be free at any time in this pool.

Now, Figure 1-11 illustrates what happens when IOS tries to request nine more packet buffers from this pool before returning any free buffers.

Figure 1-11 *Storing Nine More Packets*

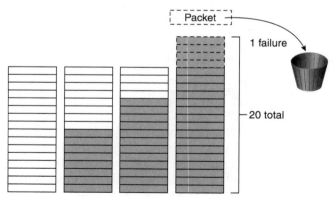

From the following output, we see that the free list has been completely exhausted— 0 buffers remaining—and there have been 20 hits, 13 misses, and 1 failure. The failure accounts for the one request that overran the buffer pool.

```
Small buffers, 104 bytes (total 20, permanent 16):
    0 in free list (8 min, 16 max allowed)
    20 hits, 13 misses, 0 trims, 4 created
    1 failures (0 no memory)
```

Finally, IOS begins processing packets and returning buffers to the pool. IOS processes 17 of the 20 packets and returns the 17 free buffers, as illustrated in Figure 1-12 and the output that follows.

Figure 1-12 *Returning 17 Buffers to the Pool*

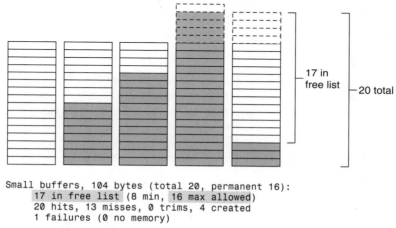

```
Small buffers, 104 bytes (total 20, permanent 16):
    17 in free list (8 min, 16 max allowed)
    20 hits, 13 misses, 0 trims, 4 created
    1 failures (0 no memory)
```

The **small** pool now has 17 in the free list. However, the desired maximum free buffers is only 16. Because the number in the free list exceeds the **max allowed**, the next time the **pool manager** process runs it shrinks the buffer pool to adjust the number of free buffers, causing one to be trimmed, as shown in Figure 1-13 and the output that follows.

Figure 1-13 *Trimming the Extra Buffer*

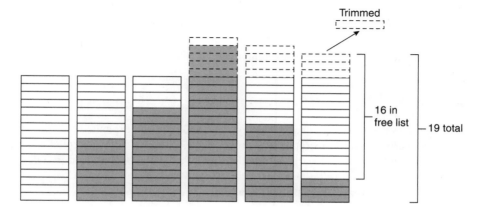

```
Small buffers, 104 bytes (total 20, permanent 16):
    17 in free list (8 min, 16 max allowed)
    20 hits, 13 misses, 1 trims, 4 created
    1 failures (0 no memory)
```

Finally, IOS processes all the remaining packets and returns the buffers to the pool. Eventually, the pool manager process trims all the remaining buffers above the permanent pool size, resulting in the following counts:

```
Small buffers, 104 bytes (total 16, permanent 16):
    16 in free list (8 min, 16 max allowed)
    20 hits, 13 misses, 4 trims, 4 created
    1 failures (0 no memory)
```

Device Drivers

One of the primary functions of an operating system is to provide hardware abstraction between platform hardware and the programs that run on it. This hardware abstraction typically occurs in device drivers that are part of the operating system, making those components an integral part of the system. IOS is no different in that regard. IOS contains device drivers for a range of platform hardware devices, such as Flash cards and NVRAM, but most notable are its device drivers for network interfaces.

IOS network interface device drivers provide the primary intelligence for packet operations in and out of interfaces. Each driver consists of two main components: a control component and a data component. The control component is responsible for managing the state and status of the device (for example, shutting down an interface). The data component is responsible for all data flow operations through the device and contains logic that assists with the packet switching operations. IOS device drivers are very tightly coupled with the packet switching functions, as we discuss in Chapter 2.

IOS device drivers interface with the rest of the IOS system via a special control structure called the *interface descriptor block* (IDB). The IDB contains, among other things, entry points into a device driver's functions and data about a device's state and status. For example, the IP address, the interface state, and the packet statistics are some of the fields that are present in the IDB. IOS maintains an IDB for each interface present on a platform and maintains an IDB for each subinterface.

Summary

Cisco IOS began as a small embedded system and has been expanded over time to become the powerful network operating system it is today. The basic components for IOS are no different than the ones used to build other operating systems. However, in IOS those components are optimized to work within the environment in which IOS is used: limited memory and speed-critical packet switching.

IOS is a cooperative multitasking operating system and operates within a single flat address space. All program code, buffers, routing tables, and other data, reside in the same address space, and all processes can address each other's memory. IOS processes are equivalent to threads in other operating systems.

IOS has a small kernel that provides CPU scheduling services and memory management services to processes. Unlike other operating systems, the IOS kernel runs in "user" mode on the CPU (peer-to-processes) and shares the same address space with the rest of the system.

IOS device drivers provide a hardware abstraction layer between the media hardware and the operating system. The network interface device drivers are tightly coupled to the packet switching software. In Chapter 2, "Packet Switching Architecture," we examine this packet switching software in more detail.

This chapter covers the following key topics:

- Process Switching
- Fast Switching
- Optimum Switching
- Cisco Express Forwarding

CHAPTER 2

Packet Switching Architecture

A multiprotocol router's primary purpose is, of course, to switch packets from one network segment to another. If the scheduler and memory manager are the router's software infrastructure, then the IOS switching architecture is the router's very foundation. The switching methods and structures used by IOS essentially dictate how well the router performs its primary task—so, as you can imagine, a great deal of effort has been put into designing and refining this important part of IOS.

In spite of all the fanfare surrounding packet switching, the operation itself is fairly straightforward:

Step 1 A packet comes into an interface.

Step 2 The packet's destination address is inspected and compared against a list of known destinations.

Step 3 If a match is found, the packet is forwarded out the appropriate interface.

Step 4 If a match is not found, the packet is dropped.

Clearly, this isn't rocket science. Indeed, the problem to be solved isn't so much *how* to switch packets, but how to switch them *quickly*. Switching packets is a data-intensive operation as opposed to a computation-intensive one; speeding up the operation isn't as simple as just using a faster CPU. Other factors, such as I/O bus performance and data memory speed, can have a big impact on switching performance. The challenge for IOS developers is to create the highest possible switching performance given the limits of available CPU, I/O bus, and memory technology.

As the size and number of routed networks grow, IOS developers continuously look for better ways to solve this performance challenge, resulting in a continuous redesign and refinement of IOS switching methods. When IOS was first developed, there was only one switching method, known today as process switching. Later releases introduced newer improved methods of switching; some of these methods rely on hardware-specific optimizations, others use software techniques that work well on many platforms. Today, IOS can switch several hundred thousand packets per second using routing tables containing hundreds of thousands of routes.

The following list summarizes the switching methods developed as of Cisco IOS Release 12.0:

- Process switching
- Fast switching
- Autonomous switching
- Silicon switching engine (SSE) switching
- Optimum switching
- Distributed fast switching
- Cisco Express Forwarding (CEF)
- Distributed Cisco Express Forwarding (dCEF)

This chapter covers in detail four of these methods—process switching, fast switching, optimum switching, and Cisco Express Forwarding (CEF). Autonomous and SSE switching are platform-specific and aren't commonly used in today's networks, so they aren't covered here. Distributed fast switching is actually an implementation of the optimum switching method on intelligent line cards, and isn't covered any further than the coverage provided to optimum switching itself.

It's worth noting that although IP routing examples are used here to illustrate the switching methods, many of these methods also apply to other network protocols, such as IPX and bridging. Although the structures used are often independent for each protocol (for example, there is a separate Fast Cache for IP and IPX), the contents of the switching structures are similar, and switching occurs in essentially the same way for each protocol.

Routing 101: Process Switching

Process switching was the first switching method implemented in IOS. Basically, it uses the brute-force method to switch packets. Although process switching contains the least amount of performance optimizations and can consume large amounts of CPU time, it does have the advantage of being platform-independent, making it universally available across all Cisco IOS-based products. Process switching also provides some traffic load sharing capabilities not found in most of the other switching methods, which are discussed in detail in the section, "Traffic Load Sharing with Process Switching."

To understand just how process switching works, take a look at the steps required to process switch a packet. Figure 2-1 illustrates the process-switched path for an IP packet.

Figure 2-1   *The Process Switched Path*

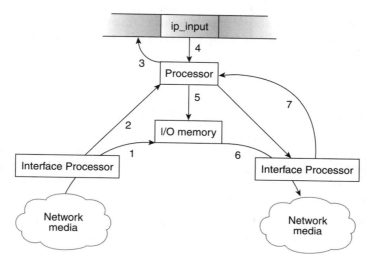

This example begins with the network interface on the router sensing there is a packet on the wire that needs to be processed. The interface hardware receives the packet and transfers it into input/output (I/O) memory—Step 1 in Figure 2-1.

The network interface interrupts the main processor, telling it there is a received packet waiting in I/O memory that needs to be processed; this is called the *receive interrupt*. The IOS interrupt software inspects the packet's header information (encapsulation type, network layer header, and so on), determines that it is an IP packet, and places the packet on the input queue for the appropriate switching process—Step 2 in Figure 2-1. For IP packets, the switching process is named **ip_input**.

After at least one packet is in the input queue of the **ip_input** process, **ip_input** becomes eligible to run—Step 3 in Figure 2-1.

After the **ip_input** process is running (Step 4 in Figure 2-1), the actual packet-forwarding operation can begin. It is here that all the decisions are made about where to direct the received packet. In this example, **ip_input** looks in the routing table to see whether a route exists to the destination IP address. If one is found, it retrieves the address of the next hop (the next router in the path or the final destination) from the routing table entry. It then looks into the ARP cache to retrieve the information needed to build a new Media Access Control (MAC) header for the next hop. The **ip_input** process builds a new MAC header, writing over the old one in the input packet. Finally, the packet is queued for transmission out the outbound network interface—Step 5 in Figure 2-1.

When the outbound interface hardware senses a packet waiting for output, it dequeues the packet from I/O memory and transmits it on to the network—Step 6 in Figure 2-1. After the outbound interface hardware finishes transmitting the packet, it interrupts the main processor to indicate that the packet has been transmitted. IOS then updates its outbound packet counters and frees the space in I/O memory formerly occupied by the packet. This is the final step in Figure 2-1, Step 7.

Traffic Load Sharing with Process Switching

One of the advantages of process switching is its per-packet load sharing capability. Per-packet load sharing provides a relatively simple way to route traffic over multiple links when multiple routes (paths) exist to a destination. When multiple paths exist, process-switched packets are automatically distributed among the available paths based on the routing metric (referred to as the *path cost*) assigned to each path.

The metric or cost of each path in the routing table is used to calculate a *load share* counter, which is actually used to determine which path to take. To better understand how this works, take a look at Figure 2-2.

Figure 2-2 *Traffic Sharing Across Equal Cost Paths*

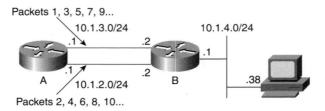

Router A has two paths to the 10.1.4.0/24 network (as illustrated in Figure 2-2). From the output in Example 2-1, you can see these are equal-cost paths.

Example 2-1 *Routing Table for Router A in Figure 2-2*

```
RouterA#show ip route 10.1.4.0 255.255.255.0
Routing entry for 10.1.4.0/24
  Known via "static", distance 1, metric 0
  Routing Descriptor Blocks:
    10.1.2.1
    Route metric is 0, traffic share count is 1
  * 10.1.3.1
    Route metric is 0, traffic share count is 1
```

Note the asterisk (*) next to one of the two network paths in Example 2-1. This indicates the path that will be used for the next packet switched toward 10.1.4.0/24. The traffic-share count on both paths is 1, meaning packets are switched out each path in a round-robin fashion.

In this example, the very next packet arriving for this network will be routed to next hop 10.1.3.1. The second packet arriving will be routed to next hop 10.1.2.1, the third to 10.1.3.1, and so on (as shown by the packet numbers in Figure 2-2).

Some IP routing protocols, in particular Interior Gateway Routing Protocol (IGRP) and Enhanced IGRP (EIGRP), can install unequal cost paths in the routing table; in cases where path costs differ, the traffic-sharing algorithm changes slightly. If a link is changed in the setup in Figure 2-2, for example, so one path has about twice the bandwidth of the other, the resulting network is shown in Figure 2-3.

Figure 2-3   *Traffic Sharing Across Unequal Cost Paths*

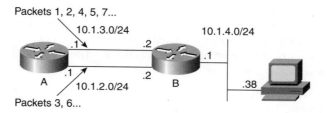

The routing table would look something like Example 2-2.

Example 2-2   *Routing Table for Router A in Figure 2-3*

```
RouterA#show ip route 10.1.4.0 255.255.255.0
Routing entry for 10.1.4.0/24
 Known via "EIGRP", distance 90, metric 284600
 Routing Descriptor Blocks:
   10.1.2.1
   Route metric is 569200, traffic share count is 1
 * 10.1.3.1
   Route metric is 284600, traffic share count is 2
```

Note the traffic share counts in this **show ip route** output. The lower-cost path through 10.1.3.1 has a traffic share count of 2; the higher-cost path through 10.1.2.1 has a traffic share count of 1. Now for every two packets switched out the higher-cost path, one packet is switched out the lower-cost path, as indicated by the packet numbers in Figure 2-3.

NOTE   Although per-packet traffic sharing is very good at balancing traffic load across multiple links, it does have one significant drawback: It can result in packets arriving out of order at the destination. This is especially true if there is a wide variation in latency among the available routes. Out-of-order packet processing can significantly degrade end-station performance.

Disadvantages of Process Switching

As noted before, a key disadvantage of process switching is its speed—or lack thereof. Process switching requires a routing table lookup for every packet; as the size of the routing table grows, so does the time required to perform a lookup (and hence the total switching time). Recursive routes require additional lookups in the routing table (to resolve the recursion), increasing the length of the lookup time.

Longer lookup times also increase the main processor utilization, an effect multiplied by the incoming packet rate. Although this effect might not be noticeable on very small networks with few routes, large networks can have hundreds or even thousands of routes. For these networks, routing table size can significantly impact main processor utilization and routing latency (the delay between the time the packet enters and exits the router).

Another major factor affecting process-switching speed is in-memory data transfer time. On some platforms, process switching requires received packets to be copied from I/O memory to another memory area before they can be switched. After the routing process finishes, the packets must be copied back to I/O memory before being transmitted. Memory data copy operations are very CPU intensive, so on these platforms, process switching can be a very poor performer.

It became quite clear to the early IOS developers that a better switching method would be required if IOS was to be viable in the world of ever-growing routed networks. To understand the solution they devised, take a look at some of the more obvious areas for improvement in process switching.

Looking back at the IP process switching example, the **ip_input** process needs three key pieces of data to switch the packet:

- **Reachability**—Is this destination reachable? If so, what is the IP network address of the next hop toward this destination? This data is in the routing table (also called the forwarding table).

- **Interface**—Which interface should this packet be transmitted on to reach its destination? This data is also stored in the routing table.

- **MAC layer header**—What MAC header needs to be placed on the packet to correctly address the next hop? MAC header data comes from the ARP table for IP or other mapping tables, such as the Frame Relay map table.

Because every incoming packet can be different, **ip_input** must look up these key pieces of data anew each time it switches a packet. It has to search through a potentially huge routing table for reachability and interface data, and then search another potentially large table for a MAC layer header. Wouldn't it be useful if the **ip_input** process could "remember" the results of these lookups for destinations it has already seen before? If it could keep a smaller table of the reachability/interface/MAC combinations for the most popular destinations, it could significantly reduce the lookup time for most of the incoming packets. Furthermore, because looking up the forwarding information is the most intensive part of the switching process, using a smaller table for these lookups could speed up switching enough so the entire operation could be performed during the packet receive interrupt. If the packet can be switched during the receive interrupt, it would also remove the need for in-memory data copying, saving even more time. So how can IOS keep a smaller lookup table and take advantage of these performance savings? The answer is the *Fast Cache*.

Fast Switching: Caching to the Rescue

The term *cache* in the computer industry usually refers to the concept of storing some frequently used subset of a larger data set in a local storage area with very fast access properties. A computer might keep a local copy of frequently accessed parts of a file stored on disk in RAM, for example, or a CPU might prefetch some instructions into a very fast associative memory area to boost performance. The two key characteristics of such a cache are a relatively small size as compared to the entire data space, and the capability to provide very fast access to any addressable member of its contents.

The IOS developers used these concepts when they created the Fast Cache. The Fast Cache quite simply is a data structure in IOS used to keep a copy of the reachability/interface/MAC-header combinations learned while process switching packets.

To understand how the Fast Cache can be helpful, consider the example of process switching a packet discussed earlier in this chapter. Now add a step to the switching operation performed by the **ip_input** process. After **ip_input** looks up the next hop, output interface, and MAC-header data for a packet, add a step that saves this information in a special data structure that allows very fast access to any cache entry based on a destination IP address. This structure is the Fast Cache. Over time, the **ip_input** process builds a large number of frequently used IP destinations into the cache. Now you'll learn how to put this cache to use in switching packets. Figure 2-4 shows the fast-switched path.

Figure 2-4 *The Fast-Switched Path*

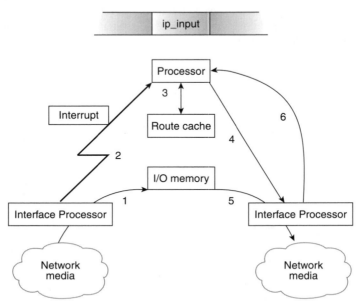

Consider the process switching method again—only this time the newly built Fast Cache is introduced. Again, the switching process begins with the interface hardware sensing there is a packet on the wire. It receives the packet and transfers it to I/O memory—Step 1 in Figure 2-4.

In Step 2, the interface hardware interrupts the main processor to inform it there is a received packet waiting in I/O memory. The IOS interrupt software inspects the packet's header information and determines it is an IP packet. Now, instead of placing the packet in the input queue for **ip_input** as before, the interrupt software consults the Fast Cache directly to determine whether an outbound interface and a MAC header have been cached for this destination. Assuming there is a cache entry, the interrupt software reads the MAC header from the entry and writes it into the packet. It also reads a pointer to the appropriate outbound interface from the cache entry. Step 3 in Figure 2-4 illustrates the cache read and MAC rewrite.

The main processor (still within the same interrupt) then notifies the outbound interface hardware that a packet in I/O memory is ready to transmit and dismisses the interrupt so other processes can continue—Step 4 in Figure 2-4.

The interface hardware dequeues the packet from I/O memory and transmits it in Step 5, and then interrupts the main processor to update its counters and release the I/O memory, Step 6.

The example just described illustrates how the fast switching method works. Notice the **ip_input** process never gets involved in switching this packet; in fact, no scheduled process gets involved when a packet is fast switched as long as a cache entry exists. With the introduction of the Fast Cache, IOS can now perform the entire packet switching operation within the very brief period of an interrupt! Caching has enabled IOS to separate the resource-intensive task of making a routing decision from the relatively easy task of forwarding a packet. Thus, fast switching introduced the concept of "route once, forward many times."

An important implication of the fast switching process should be noted. As you've seen, Fast Cache entries are built while packets are process switched. Because the process switching operation builds the cache entries, the first packet sent to any given destination *will always be process switched* even when fast switching is enabled. As long as the cache entry exists, future packets to the destination can be fast switched.

This method of using the process switching operation to populate the Fast Cache works well as long as certain assumptions are met: The network must be generally stable with few routes changing and traffic must tend to flow between a particular subset of destinations. These assumptions are true in most cases. In some network environments, however, particularly the Internet backbone, they are not true. In those environments, network conditions can cause an increased number of cache *misses* (an instance where no cache entry matches a packet) and can result in a high number of packets being process switched. It's also possible for a certain set of conditions to cause *cache thrashing*, where older cache entries are continually overwritten with newer cache entries because there just isn't enough room in the cache for all the entries required. Such environments are discussed later in this chapter.

Fast Cache Organization

How does a Fast Cache actually work? How can it provide forwarding data so quickly? For the answer, look at how a typical Fast Cache is organized.

First, to get an idea of exactly what's in the Fast Cache, take a look at the output of the **show ip cache verbose** command in Example 2-3.

Example 2-3 *Displaying Fast Cache Contents*

```
router#show ip cache verbose
IP routing cache 1 entry, 172 bytes
  124 adds, 123 invalidates, 0 refcounts
Minimum invalidation interval 2 seconds, maximum interval 5 seconds,
  quiet interval 3 seconds, threshold 0 requests
Invalidation rate 0 in last second, 0 in last 3 seconds

Prefix/Length    Age    Interface    Next Hop
10.1.1.16/32-24  1w4d   Ethernet0    10.1.1.16
          14 00403337E5350060474FB47B0800
```

From the output in Example 2-3, it's obvious the router keeps the destination prefix, the length of the prefix, the outbound interface, the next hop IP address, and a MAC header—just what you'd expect. All the data necessary to switch a packet to a particular destination is contained in this one entry.

Another characteristic of the cache is not evident from **show** command output. Unlike the master tables used to build them, which are basically just big lists, caches are implemented using special data structures, which allow any particular member to be retrieved with a minimal amount of searching. With the master tables, the searching time increases proportionately with the size of the table. With the cache data structures, because of the way they are organized, the searching time can be kept small and fairly constant regardless of the total number of entries.

Fast Cache Data Structures: Hash Tables and Radix Trees

The IP Fast Cache was originally implemented as a data structure called a *hash table*; Figure 2-5 illustrates.

Figure 2-5   *Fast Cache Organization*

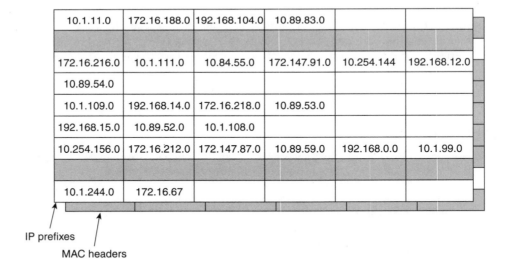

In the hash table, each IP prefix points to a particular place in the table. A particular hash table entry is found by computing some XOR operations on the upper and lower 16 bits of the 32-bit IP address being searched. The result of the calculation points to the desired hash table location, called a *hash bucket*. Each hash bucket contains a cache entry, including a pre-built MAC header for the next hop.

A hash calculation (or just *hash*) does not always produce a unique hash bucket address for every IP address. The case where more than one IP address points to the same hash location is called a *collision*. When collisions occur, IOS links each of the colliding cache entries together in a list within the bucket up to a maximum of six entries. This way, no more than six entries in the cache need to be searched to find a particular match.

In Cisco IOS Release 10.2, the hash table was replaced with another data structure called a *2-way radix tree* (a form of a binary tree). The MAC headers are still stored as part of the cache in this implementation.

The radix tree, like the hash table, is another special data structure used to improve retrieval time of the member data.

A radix tree gets its name from the way in which data is stored—by its *radix*. In practice, this means the information is stored in a tree structure based on the binary representation of the key (the unique field that uniquely identifies each set of data). For example, to store the following numbers:

- 10, which is 1010 in binary

- 7, which is 0111 in binary

- 2, which is 0010 in binary

you could store them in a radix tree structure, as shown in Figure 2-6.

Figure 2-6   *A Radix Tree*

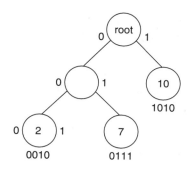

The tree branches are based on the binary digits within the number at any given level. To store, or find, the number 10, for example, you begin at the root with the first bit in 1010, which is 1.

This first 1 causes you to choose the right branch, which takes you to a node on the tree. You find this node doesn't have any children, so you compare the number in the node to the number you are searching for to see whether you have a match. In this case, there is a match.

To find or store 7, you begin at the root of the tree again. The first bit in the binary representation of the number 7 is a 0, so you take the left branch. You find yourself at a node with children, so you branch based on the second digit in the number, which is 1. This causes you to branch right.

As another example, let's work through finding or storing the number 2. The first binary digit in the number is 0, so you branch left. The second binary digit is 0 as well, so the second branch is to the left as well. At this point, you find yourself at a node with no children, so you compare the number the node represents with the number you are searching for, and find a match.

Fast Cache Limitations for IP Routing

There is one major limitation on the way the Fast Cache stores IP prefixes: Overlapping cache entries are not possible. For example, consider building cache entries for the following IP prefixes:

- 172.31.46.0/24
- 172.31.46.128/25
- 172.31.46.129/32

Because the Fast Cache doesn't use the subnet mask, or prefix length, when looking up routing information, there isn't any way to know that the entry for 172.31.46.129 uses a 32-bit prefix, and the 172.31.46.128 entry uses a 25-bit prefix.

A simple way to overcome this limitation is to build a cache entry for each destination host. This is impractical for several reasons, including the processing required to build this many cache entries and the amount of memory a cache containing all this information would consume.

So how does IOS solve this problem? It builds cache entries according to the following set of rules:

- If the destination is directly attached, cache with a 32-bit prefix length.
- If there are multiple equal-cost paths for this destination, cache with a 32-bit prefix length.
- If it's a supernet, cache using the prefix length of the supernet.
- If it's a major network with no subnets, cache using the prefix length of the major network.
- If it's a major network with subnets, cache using the longest length prefix in this major network.

Given the snippet of an IP routing table from a Cisco router in Example 2-4, you could determine what prefix lengths the router would use for various destinations.

Example 2-4 *Determining Destination Prefix Lengths Used by a Router*

```
router#show ip route
....
O    172.31.0.0 [110/11] via 172.25.10.210, 2d01h, Ethernet0
         [110/11] via 172.25.10.215, 2d01h, Ethernet0
     172.16.0.0/16 is variably subnetted, 2 subnets, 2 masks
D EX  172.16.180.0/25 [170/281600] via 172.25.10.210, 3d20h, Ethernet0
D EX  172.16.180.24/32 [170/281600] via 172.25.10.210, 3d20h, Ethernet0
O     10.0.0.0 [110/11] via 172.25.10.210, 2d01h, Ethernet0
O     192.168.0.0/16 [110/11] via 172.25.10.210, 2d18h, Ethernet0
     172.25.0.0/24 is subnetted, 1 subnet
C     172.25.10.0 [0/0] via connected, Ethernet0
```

The following list explains how the destination prefix lengths that appear in Example 2-4 will be cached:

- Every destination in the 172.31.0.0/16 network will be cached with a 32-bit prefix length because there are two equal-cost paths for this network installed in the routing table.

- Every destination in the 172.16.0.0/16 network will be cached with a 32-bit prefix length because there is a host route within this range.

- Network 10.0.0.0/8 will have one cache entry, because it is a major network route with no subnets, host routes, equal-cost paths, and so on.

- 192.168.0.0/16 will have one cache entry because it is a supernet route with no subnets.

- All destinations within the 172.25.10.0/24 network will be cached using a 32-bit prefix because this destination is directly connected to the router.

Maintaining the Cache

Any time data is cached, it's important to somehow maintain the cached data so it doesn't become outdated or out of sync with the master data used to build the cache in the first place. There are two issues to address in this area: cache invalidation and cache aging.

In the case of fast switching, the issue is how to keep the Fast Cache updated so it contains the same information as the routing table and the ARP cache (or other tables from which the MAC headers are built).

Cache Invalidation

The problem of keeping the route cache synchronized with the routing table is complicated when switching IP packets because of recursion or dependencies within the routing table.

Because recursion is such an important concept when considering the operation of route caches, it's helpful to walk through an example of recursive routing. Figure 2-7 provides an example of what recursion looks like in a network.

Figure 2-7   *A Recursive Route*

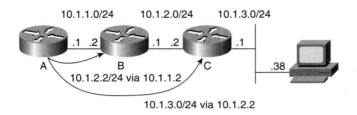

In Figure 2-7, Router A needs to look up a route for the host 10.1.3.38 and find out what next hop and MAC header to use. When Router A examines its routing table, it finds this destination is reachable through 10.1.2.2.

This destination isn't directly attached to Router A, so it needs to look into the routing table again to determine how to reach the next hop. Router A looks up the route to 10.1.2.2, and discovers it is reachable through 10.1.1.2, which is directly connected.

Router A will send all traffic destined to 10.1.3.38 to 10.1.1.2 for further processing.

In fast switching, recursion is resolved when the cache entry is built rather than when the packet is switched. So, the route cache contains the MAC header and outbound interface of the actual next hop toward the destination being cached. This disconnects the cache entry from both the routing table entry and the ARP cache (or other MAC-layer table) entry.

Because recursion is resolved when a cache entry is built, there is no direct correlation between the Fast Cache and the routing table or the ARP cache. So, how can the cache be kept synchronized with the data in the original tables? The best way to solve this problem is to just invalidate, or remove, cache entries when any corresponding data changes in the master tables.

Cache entries can be removed from the Fast Cache, for example, because:

- The ARP cache entry for the next hop changes, is removed, or times out.
- The routing table entry for the prefix changes or is removed.
- The routing table entry for the next hop to this destination changes.

Cache Aging

IOS also ages entries in the Fast Cache periodically. A small portion of the Fast Cache is invalidated every minute to make certain the cache doesn't grow out of bounds, and to resynchronize entries with the routing and ARP tables periodically. When the amount of available memory is greater than 200 KB, the *cache ager* process randomly invalidates 1/20th of the cache entries every minute. If free memory is lower than 200 KB, the cache ager process starts aging entries more aggressively—1/5th of the cache entries are invalidated every minute.

Traffic Load Sharing Considerations with Fast Switching

Unlike process switching, fast switching does not support load sharing on a per-packet basis. This restriction can lead to uneven link utilization in some situations where multiple paths exist between two destinations. The reason for this restriction has to do with the separation of routing and forwarding that occurs when fast switching. To understand this reason and the possible disadvantages, consider the example illustrated in Figure 2-8.

Figure 2-8   *Load Sharing Using the Fast Cache*

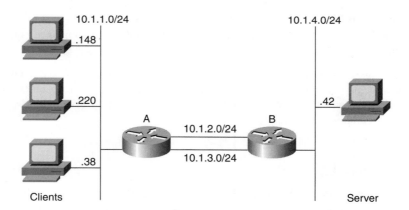

In Figure 2-8, several workstations are connected to a network segment attached to Router A. Each workstation communicates with a single server on another network segment attached to Router B. Router A has multiple parallel paths to Router B. Assume both parallel paths have the same cost in this example. You would like the traffic between the client and the server networks to be evenly distributed over those two paths. Now, check out what happens.

Starting with an empty Fast Cache, Router A receives a packet from client 10.1.1.220, destined toward the server, 10.1.4.42. As you've seen, this first packet will be process switched and Router A will build a Fast Cache entry for the 10.1.4.42 destination. Because there are two equal-cost paths to the 10.1.4.42 destination (via Router B), Router A will have to choose one of these when it builds the cache entry. It will use the per-packet, load-balancing algorithm described earlier for process switching to make the decision.

Next, Router A receives another client packet destined to server 10.1.4.42. This time the packet is fast switched because there is already an entry in the Fast Cache. Because the transmit interface pointer is built in to the cache entry, Router A switches this second packet through the same path as the first. As you can see, Router A will continue to send all packets destined for the 10.1.4.42 server through this same path until the cache entry either ages out or is invalidated for some reason. If the cache entry does happen to get removed, the other path might be chosen—but packets will still only be forwarded out one path for the 10.1.4.42 server.

If there happened to be multiple servers on the 10.1.4.0/24 network, this same process would apply to each of them. The path cached for each server might vary, but for any given server all packets coming from the clients would take the same path.

Now consider traffic originating from the other direction. Router B will also cache destinations on the client network in the same manner Router A did. In this case, Router B will build two cache entries along one path, and the third along the other path. It could turn out Router B will choose to send the traffic for two clients along the path not chosen by Router A. This would result in a fairly well distributed traffic load on the parallel paths. It's just as likely Router B will choose to cache two client entries along the same path Router A chose for the server traffic, however, resulting in unbalanced utilization of the paths.

This lack of a deterministic load-balancing scheme is an area of concern for many network designers. In response, newer switching methods now support load-balancing schemes that help overcome this problem. One such method, Cisco Express Forwarding (CEF), is covered later in this chapter.

Optimum Switching

Optimum switching is essentially fast switching with some caching optimizations. Like fast switching, optimum switching accomplishes the entire task of switching a packet during a single interrupt. The primary difference between optimum and fast switching is in the way the route cache is accessed. The optimum switching software is also crafted to take advantage of specific processor architectures. The fast switching code is generic, and is not optimized for any specific processor. Unlike fast switching, optimum switching is available only for the IP protocol.

Earlier in this chapter, you learned the Fast Cache is accessed using a hash table in earlier releases, and is accessed via a two-way radix tree in later releases. The optimum cache is accessed via a *256-way multiway tree* (mtree). Figure 2-9 provides an illustration of a 256-way mtree.

Figure 2-9   *The Optimum Cache*

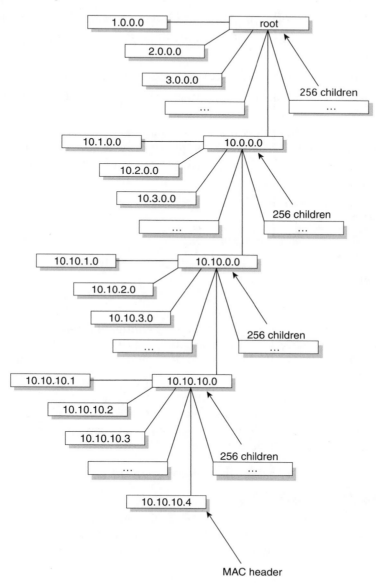

Reachability information is stored as a set of nodes, each with 256 children, and the pre-built MAC headers are stored in the nodes. Although this provides faster lookups than the Fast Cache's two-way radix tree, it still has the same limitations as the Fast Cache.

Optimum switching is still similar to fast switching in many ways, including:

- Cache entries are built when the first packet is process switched toward a destination.
- Cache entries are aged and invalidated as the routing table or other cache information changes.
- Load sharing still occurs based strictly on the destination address.
- The same rules are still used to decide what cache entry to build for each particular destination.

The output of **show ip cache optimum**, shown in Example 2-5, is very similar to the output of **show ip cache verbose** in Example 2-3. The primary differences are in the first few lines of output, which provide information about the mtree in which the information is stored.

Example 2-5 *Displaying Optimum Cache Entries*

```
router#show ip cache optimum
Optimum Route Cache
 1 prefixes, 1 nodes, 0 leaf refcount, 8K bytes
 0 nodes pending, 0 node alloc failures
 8 prefix updates, 4 prefix invalidations

Prefix/Length      Age      Interface      Next Hop
10.1.1.16/32-24    1w4d     Ethernet0      10.1.1.16
```

The first few lines of information, under the heading **Optimum Route Cache**, note the number of nodes in the mtree, the number of leaf nodes that are referred to by other nodes (because of recursive routing), the memory allocation information, and the number of times the mtree has been updated.

The Optimum Cache mtree doesn't start with all its nodes populated; most of the children under each node will be NULL (or lead to nowhere). As the cache is built through the process switching of packets, it fills up, although you would probably never encounter an Optimum Cache mtree with all the nodes filled.

Cisco Express Forwarding

Cisco Express Forwarding (CEF) is the newest, and fastest, switching method available in IOS. CEF was invented to help overcome the major deficiencies of the fast switching method. Reviewing the description of fast switching for a moment, the major deficiencies noted were:

- Lack of support for overlapping cache entries.
- Any change in the routing table or ARP cache results in the invalidation of large sections of the route cache, because there is little or no correlation between the route cache and the tables on which the cache is based.

- The first packet to any given destination must be process switched to build a route cache entry.
- Inefficient load balancing in some situations (primarily in cases where many hosts are transacting with one server).

Most of these deficiencies do not pose a problem in the average enterprise network because routes don't change often and routing tables aren't extremely large. However, there is one environment where these shortcomings *do* become a problem: the Internet backbone.

Internet backbone routers have extremely large routing tables, about 56,000 routes in early 1999 and still growing. Some Internet backbone routers actually carry more than 100,000 routes. The routing table also changes constantly, causing cache entries to be invalidated frequently. In fact, entries are invalidated often enough to cause a significant portion of traffic through some Internet routers to be process switched. CEF was developed specifically to improve routing performance in these types of environments.

CEF was initially tested in the large-scale network environment of the Internet. Internet service providers were given a series of special IOS software images (nicknamed the *ISP Geeks images*) with CEF to see how it operated under extreme conditions. The technology proved itself capable of handling the Internet backbone workload and was eventually integrated into the Cisco IOS product, becoming the default switching mode in Cisco IOS Release 12.0. It is now the only switching mode available on some platforms—in particular, the Cisco 12000 and the Catalyst 8500.

How CEF Works

Unlike fast switching, which builds a cached subset of the routing table and MAC address tables, CEF builds its own structures that mirror the entire routing and MAC address tables. There are two major structures maintained by CEF. These structures collectively can be considered the CEF "Fast Cache":

- CEF table
- Adjacency table

The CEF Table

The CEF table is a "stripped-down" version of the routing table, implemented as a 256-way mtrie data structure for optimum retrieval performance. You can display the size of the CEF table (and other general information about the table) by using the command **show ip cef summary**, as demonstrated in Example 2-6.

Example 2-6   *Displaying CEF Table Information*

```
router#show ip cef summary
IP Distributed CEF with switching (Table Version 96)
   33 routes, 0 reresolve, 0 unresolved (0 old, 0 new)
   33 leaves, 31 nodes, 36256 bytes, 96 inserts, 63 invalidations
   1 load sharing elements, 328 bytes, 2 references
   1 CEF resets, 8 revisions of existing leaves
   refcounts:  8226 leaf, 8192 node

The adjacency table has five adjacencies.
```

In a 256-way mtrie structure, each node in the structure can have up to 256 children. In the CEF table, each child (or link) is used to represent a different address in one octet of an IP address, as shown in Figure 2-10.

For example, given the IP address 10.10.10.4, you would locate the data by choosing the tenth child off the root, the tenth child off that node, the tenth child off that node, and then, finally, the fourth child off the last node. This final node, or *end node*, contains a pointer to an entry in another table outside the CEF, called the *adjacency table*. The adjacency table actually contains the MAC header and other information needed to switch the packet.

NOTE   An *mtree* data structure stores the actual data within the tree structure itself; for example, in the optimum switching mtree cache, the MAC header data used for forwarding packets is actually stored inside the mtree. In an *mtrie* data structure, the tree structure is used to locate the desired data, but the data itself is stored elsewhere.

Figure 2-10 *CEF mtrie and Adjacency Table*

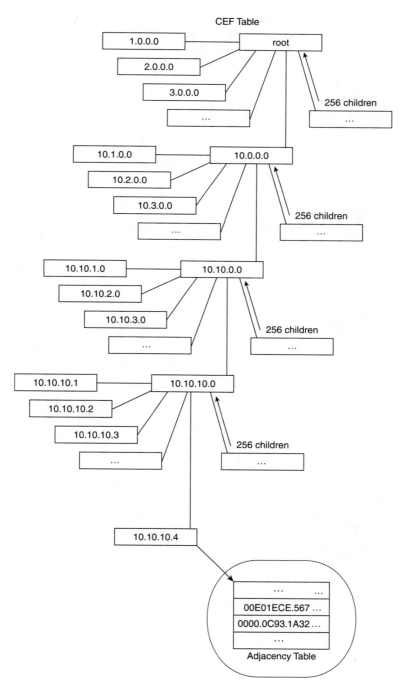

Adjacency Table

The adjacency table contains the MAC-layer packet-header data for directly connected next hops. The adjacency table is populated with data from the ARP table, the Frame Relay map table, and other tables of this type. The **show adjacency** command displays the adjacency table, as demonstrated in Example 2-7.

Example 2-7 *Displaying Adjacency Table Information*

```
router#show adjacency
Protocol Interface              Address
IP       POS0/0/0               point2point(15)
IP       Serial1/0/0            point2point(5)
IP       FastEthernet6/0/0      17.1.1.2(16)
IP       Ethernet4/0            10.105.1.1(9)
IP       Ethernet4/0            10.105.1.179(5)
Router#
```

There are several types of adjacency entries you might see in the **Address** column of **show adjacency**:

- **Cached adjacency**—A prebuilt MAC header for the next hop toward this destination.

- **Punt**—Packets destined to this address must be passed up to the next switching path to be switched.

- **Host-route**—This destination is a directly connected host.

- **Drop**—Packets destined to this address are dropped.

- **Incomplete**—The MAC-layer header for this destination is incomplete; typically, this means the ARP cache entry for this destination is incomplete or otherwise malformed.

- **Glean**—This is a directly attached destination, but there is no pre-built MAC-layer header; an ARP request needs to be sent so a MAC-layer header can be built.

The CEF Method and Its Advantages

Like fast switching, CEF switching utilizes cache entries to perform its switching operation entirely during a processor interrupt. A major difference between fast switching and CEF switching, however, is the point at which the cache entries are built. While fast switching requires the first packet to any given destination be process switched to build a cache entry, CEF does not. Instead, the CEF table is built directly from the routing table and the adjacency table is built directly from the ARP cache. These CEF structures are built before any packets are switched.

Because CEF pre-builds the cache before any packets are switched, every packet received for a reachable destination can be forwarded by the IOS during the receive interrupt. It is never necessary to process switch a packet to get a cache entry built. Pre-building the cache greatly improves the routing performance on routers with large routing tables. With normal fast switching, IOS can be overwhelmed with process-level traffic before the route cache entries are created. With CEF, this massive process-level load is eliminated, preventing the IOS from choking on the process-level switching bottleneck when network routes are flapping.

Splitting the reachability/interface data and the MAC-layer header data into two structures also provides other advantages: Because the tables used in switching packets are directly related to their information sources, the cache doesn't need an aging process anymore.

Entries in the CEF structures never age out. Any changes in the routing table or the ARP cache can be easily reflected in the CEF structures. Also, with CEF there is no longer any need to invalidate a large number of entries when the routing table or the ARP cache change.

Traffic Load Sharing with CEF

Traffic load sharing with CEF switching can be either per source/destination pair (the default) or per packet. Traffic sharing based on the source/destination pair resolves the problems described in the earlier fast switching example, where all the traffic destined to the server would take one link because the cache is built on a per-destination basis. How does it do this? Instead of pointing to an entry in the adjacency table, an entry in the CEF table can also point to a *load share* structure, as shown in Figure 2-11.

When the CEF switching method finds a load-share entry—rather than an adjacency table entry—as the result of a CEF table search, it uses the source and destination address to decide which of the entries to use from the load-share table. Each entry in the load-share table then points to an adjacency table entry that contains the MAC header and other information needed to forward the packet.

Figure 2-11 *The Load Share Table in CEF*

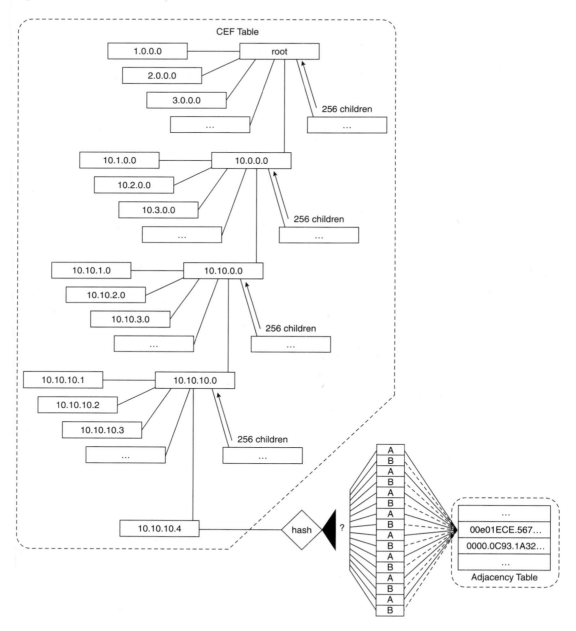

Order of Operations in the Switching Path

In what order do operations on a packet occur when a packet is being switched? The short list that follows might not include all the features available in IOS, but it can give you a start:

- Compression and decompression
- Encryption
- Inbound access list (packet filters)
- Unicast reverse path checking
- Input rate limiting
- Physical broadcast handling, such as helper addresses
- Decrement the TTL if it has not already been done
- Inspection subsystem (firewall features)
- Outside to inside Network Address Translation (NAT)
- Handle any router alert flags in the IP header
- Search for outbound interface in the routing table
- Handle any policy routing that affects this packet
- Handle Web Cache Redirect
- Inside to outside NAT
- Encryption
- Output access list (packet filters)
- Inspection subsystem final checks (firewall features)
- TCP intercept processing

Summary

Cisco routers switch packets through one of several paths; the characteristics of the switching path depend on whether a route cache is used, how the cache is accessed or built, and what context (process or interrupt) in which the switching actually takes place:

- Process switching doesn't cache any information, and switches packets in the context of a process.
- Fast switching caches reachability information and the MAC headers needed to forward packets in a radix tree and switches packets during interrupts.

- Optimum switching caches reachability and the MAC headers in a multiway tree (mtree), and switches packets during interrupts.

- CEF switching caches reachability information in an mtrie, and the MAC headers needed to forward packets within an adjacency table. CEF switches packets during interrupts.

Table 2-1 summarizes characteristics of various switching methods.

Table 2-1   *Switching Paths in IOS*

Switching Method	Type of Cache	Processing Characteristics
Process switching	None	Packet switching is done by a scheduled process.
Fast switching	Hash table or two-way radix tree and route cache	Packet is switched by the main processor during an interrupt.
Optimum switching	mtree and fast route cache	Packet is switched by the main processor during an interrupt.
Cisco Express Forwarding (CEF)	mtrie and adjacency table	Packet is switched by the main processor during an interrupt.

This chapter covers the following key topics:

- Hardware Architecture for Shared Memory Routers
- Packet Buffers for Shared Memory Routers
- Packet Switching on a Shared Memory Router

CHAPTER 3

Shared Memory Routers

In the previous two chapters, we covered IOS' basic architecture and switching methods in the abstract. To understand how IOS actually works, though, it's helpful to see how it operates on a real router. Because IOS is so closely coupled to the hardware on which it runs, each implementation has its own platform-specific features.

This chapter examines a very basic IOS implementation—the one for a group of routers known collectively as *shared memory* routers. Shared memory routers consist of several products, including the Cisco 1600, 2500, 4000, 4500, and 4700 series of routers. Although individually they all have their own unique features, together they have two major things in common: they all have a bare-bones architecture (just a CPU, main memory, and interfaces) and they all use the system buffers for packet buffering.

Hardware Architecture for Shared Memory Routers

Let's examine the hardware architecture on these shared memory platforms in some detail. We start with an overview of the generic shared memory architecture in Figure 3-1, and then mention some of the unique hardware features of platforms within this group.

You can see the overall architecture is fairly basic, consisting of just three major components: the processor (CPU), memory (DRAM), and interface controllers, with the processor and the interface controllers connected to the memory via data busses. Figure 3-1 also shows memory is divided into logical regions, which we'll examine later.

Figure 3-1 *Shared Memory Router Architecture*

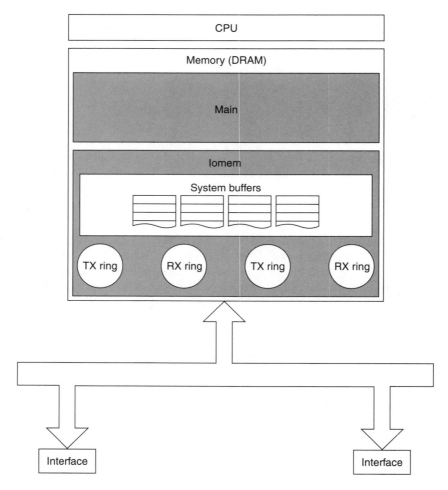

CPU

The processor in a shared memory router is truly the brains behind the entire show; it runs IOS and switches packets. The processor is responsible for executing all the switching methods supported on these platforms; there are no offload processors involved.

The type of processor used depends on the platform. For example, the Cisco 1600 and 2500 series use a Motorola 68000 series CPU while the 4500 and 4700 series use a MIPS RISC CPU. You can determine the specific type of processor by looking at the output of the **show**

version command. Example 3-1 shows the **show version** output from a Cisco 1600 router. Example 3-2 shows the **show version** output from a Cisco 4500 router.

Example 3-1   **show version** *Output from a Cisco 1600 Router*

```
router-1600>show version
Cisco Internetwork Operating System Software
....
cisco 1604 (68360) processor (revision C) with 17920K/512K bytes of memory.
Processor board ID 05385389, with hardware revision 00972006
....
```

Example 3-2   **show version** *Output from a Cisco 4500 Router*

```
router-4500#show version
Cisco Internetwork Operating System Software
....
cisco 4500 (R4K) processor (revision B) with 16384K/16384K bytes of memory.
Processor board ID 01657190
R4600 processor, Implementation 32, Revision 2.0
....
```

Memory

Shared memory platforms use dynamic random access memory (DRAM) to hold most of the data in the router. DRAM contains all the routing tables, the caches, the IOS data, the packet buffers, and, on many systems, the IOS code itself.

IOS divides the available DRAM into two logical memory classes: *Local* and *Iomem* (I/O memory). In most cases, Local memory is placed into the **main** region and I/O memory is placed into the **iomem** region, as illustrated by the **show region** command output in Example 3-3.

Example 3-3   *DRAM Memory Regions Revealed in* **show region** *Command Output*

```
Router-4500#show region
Region Manager:

        Start          End    Size(b)  Class  Media  Name
    0x30000000   0x30FFFFFF   16777216  Flash  R/O    flash
    0x38000000   0x383FFFFF    4194304  Flash  R/O    bootflash
    0x40000000   0x40FFFFFF   16777216  Iomem  R/W    iomem
    0x60000000   0x61FFFFFF   33554432  Local  R/W    main
    0x600088A0   0x607229BF    7446816  IText  R/O    main:text
    0x60726000   0x6096506F    2355312  IData  R/W    main:data
    0x60965070   0x609DB1CF     483680  IBss   R/W    main:bss
    0x609DB1D0   0x61FFFFFF   23219760  Local  R/W    main:mainheap
    0x80000000   0x81FFFFFF   33554432  Local  R/W    main:(main_k0)
    0x88000000   0x88FFFFFF   16777216  Iomem  R/W    iomem:(iomem_k0)
    0xA0000000   0xA1FFFFFF   33554432  Local  R/W    main:(main_k1)
    0xA8000000   0xA8FFFFFF   16777216  Iomem  R/W    iomem:(iomem_k1)
```

The sizes of these two regions also are reflected in the output of **show version,** as illustrated in Example 3-4.

Example 3-4   **show version** *Command Output Also Reveals Memory Region Sizes*

```
Cisco Internetwork Operating System Software
IOS (tm) 4500 Software (C4500-J-M), Version 11.1(24), RELEASE SOFTWARE (fc1)
....
cisco 4500 (R4K) processor (revision E) with 32768K/16384K bytes of memory.
Processor board ID 09337282
....
```

The number before the slash is the amount of Local memory present (32,768 Kb), and the number after the slash is the amount of I/O memory present (16,384 Kb). The total DRAM memory present is the sum of these two numbers (49,152 Kb). For the system in Example 3-3 and Example 3-4, the 32,768 Kb of Local memory is assigned to the region named **main** and the 16,384 Kb of I/O memory is assigned to the region named **iomem**.

On shared memory platforms, the **main** region is used for storing routing tables, caches, general IOS data structures, and often the IOS runtime code—but not for storing packet buffers. Packet buffers are stored in the **iomem** region, which often is called *shared memory* because it's shared between the processor and the media interfaces.

On many systems, the DRAM used for Local memory is physically separate from the DRAM used for I/O memory—usually two different banks. On those systems, IOS simply assigns all the available memory in a bank to the appropriate memory regions, one bank for **iomem** and one bank for **main**. For the Cisco 1600 and 2500, however, I/O memory and Local memory are both allocated from the same DRAM bank. The amount of I/O memory carved from the installed DRAM depends on the total memory installed:

- **1MB**—512 Kb of memory is used for I/O
- **2MB**—1 MB of memory is used for I/O
- **4MB and above**—2 MB of memory is used for I/O

Location of IOS Runtime Code on Shared Memory Systems

Some IOS shared memory platforms—in particular, the 1600 series and the 2500 series routers—can run IOS directly from Flash memory. If a system is running IOS from Flash, it doesn't use the **main** memory region for the IOS runtime code. Instead, it stores the runtime code in a region named **flash**, as demonstrated in Example 3-5.

Example 3-5 **show region** *Output for a Run-from-Flash System*

```
Router-2500#show region
Region Manager:

      Start         End     Size(b)  Class  Media  Name
   0x00000000  0x007FFFFF   8388608  Local  R/W    main
   0x00001000  0x0001922F     98864  IData  R/W    main:data
   0x00019230  0x000666B3    316548  IBss   R/W    main:bss
   0x000666B4  0x007FEFFF   7965004  Local  R/W    main:heap
   0x007FF000  0x007FFFFF      4096  Local  R/W    main:flhlog
   0x00800000  0x009FFFFF   2097152  Iomem  R/W    iomem
   0x03000000  0x03FFFFFF  16777216  Flash  R/O    flash
   0x0304033C  0x037A7D37   7764476  IText  R/O    flash:text
```

In Chapter 1, "Fundamental IOS Software Architecture," you saw that the *IText* class is where the IOS runtime code is stored. In Example 3-5, the IText memory is assigned to a subregion of **flash** called **flash:text**, indicating the system is running IOS from Flash.

You also can determine whether a router is running IOS from Flash or Local memory by checking the image's filename. The last one or two letters of the filename indicate whether the image is *relocatable* or *run-from-DRAM*. The run-from-DRAM images run in Local memory, while the relocatable images run from Flash memory.

The **show version** output in Example 3-6 is taken from a Cisco 2500, which runs IOS from Flash.

Example 3-6 *Flash-based IOS Image*

```
router-2500>show version
Cisco Internetwork Operating System Software
IOS (tm) 2500 Software (C2500-JS-L), Version 12.0(7.3)T,  MAINTENANCE INTERIM SE
Copyright (c) 1986-1999 by cisco Systems, Inc.
....
```

The last letter in the image name (**L**) means this image is relocatable, and therefore is running from Flash. On the other hand, if the image runs from Local memory (DRAM), the image name ends in either **M** or **MZ**, as you can see in the output of **show version** in Example 3-7.

Example 3-7 *DRAM-based IOS Image*

```
Router-4500>show version
Cisco Internetwork Operating System Software
IOS (tm) 4500 Software (C4500-P-M), Version 11.2(18)P,  RELEASE SOFTWARE (fc1)
Copyright (c) 1986-1999 by cisco Systems, Inc.
....
```

Memory Pools

IOS creates two memory pools to manage allocation and de-allocation of memory within the DRAM regions. These two pools are named *Processor* and *I/O*, as demonstrated in the **show memory** output in Example 3-8.

Example 3-8 **show memory** *Output Reveals Memory Pools*

```
router-2500#show memory
              Head    Total(b)   Used(b)    Free(b)  Lowest(b) Largest(b)
Processor     3BB08   16528632    878596   15650036  15564280   15630436
      I/O   4000000    2097152    473468    1623684   1603060    1623232
```

The **Processor** memory pool is created from memory in the **main:heap** subregion of Local memory and the **I/O** pool is created from memory in the **iomem** region of I/O memory. The size of the **I/O** pool (the number in the **Total** column in Example 3-8) correlates closely to the size of **iomem**. However, the size of the **Processor** pool is always less than the size of the **main** memory region. The **Processor** pool gets only a subset of the memory in the **main** region because the remainder must be reserved for the IOS data, the BSS segments, and, on many platforms, the IOS runtime image itself.

NOTE   Have you ever wondered why this collection of routers is called shared memory routers? All routers discussed in this book have shared memory, so why are these particular routers singled out? What's unique about these systems is not that they have shared memory, but that they have only one region of shared memory (I/O memory) and it's shared between a single main processor and all the interface controllers. In addition, that same memory is used for all packet switching—there's no data copied between regions to pass a packet from fast to process switching like there is on other platforms.

Interface Controllers

Interface controllers are responsible for transferring packets to and from the physical media. They have their own processors, called media controllers, but do not perform any switching or IOS processing operations. Interface controllers perform media control operations and move packets between I/O memory and the network media. Depending on the platform, interface controllers can be implemented as removable port modules or as components on the main system board.

Packet Buffers for Shared Memory Routers

You might recall from Chapter 1 that IOS maintains a set of packet buffers called *system buffers* that are used primarily for process switching packets. IOS on shared memory routers also uses system buffers, but in a distinct way—it uses the system buffers for *all* packet switching, not just process switching.

In addition to the standard public buffer pools, IOS on shared memory platforms also creates some private system buffer pools and special buffer structures for the interface controllers called *rings*.

Private Buffer Pools

Private buffer pools are used for packet switching just like the public pools, but are intended to prevent interface buffer starvation. All interfaces must compete for buffers from the public pools, increasing the probability for buffer contention (which degrades performance) and raising the possibility that a single interface can starve out others needing buffers from a single pool. With the addition of private pools, each interface is given a number of buffers dedicated for its use, so contention is minimized. Although most interfaces receive their own private pool of buffers, some lower speed interfaces, such as asynchronous interfaces, do not.

Unlike the dynamic public pools, the private pools are static and are allocated with a fixed number of buffers at IOS initialization. New buffers cannot be created on demand for these pools. If a buffer is needed and one is not available in the private pool, IOS *falls back* to the public buffer pool for the size that matches the interface's MTU.

The output of the **show buffers** command in Example 3-9 shows both the public and the private pools.

Example 3-9 **show buffers** *Command Output*

```
Router#show buffers
Buffer elements:
     500 in free list (500 max allowed)
     57288024 hits, 0 misses, 0 created

Public buffer pools:
Small buffers, 104 bytes (total 50, permanent 50):
     50 in free list (20 min, 150 max allowed)
     11256002 hits, 0 misses, 0 trims, 0 created
     0 failures (0 no memory)
Middle buffers, 600 bytes (total 25, permanent 25):
     24 in free list (10 min, 150 max allowed)
     3660412 hits, 12 misses, 36 trims, 36 created
     0 failures (0 no memory)
```

continues

Example 3-9 **show buffers** *Command Output (Continued)*

```
Big buffers, 1524 bytes (total 50, permanent 50):
     50 in free list (5 min, 150 max allowed)
     585512 hits, 14 misses, 12 trims, 12 created
     2 failures (0 no memory)
VeryBig buffers, 4520 bytes (total 10, permanent 10):
     10 in free list (0 min, 100 max allowed)
     0 hits, 0 misses, 0 trims, 0 created
     0 failures (0 no memory)
Large buffers, 5024 bytes (total 0, permanent 0):
     0 in free list (0 min, 10 max allowed)
     0 hits, 0 misses, 0 trims, 0 created
     0 failures (0 no memory)
Huge buffers, 18024 bytes (total 0, permanent 0):
     0 in free list (0 min, 4 max allowed)
     0 hits, 0 misses, 0 trims, 0 created
     0 failures (0 no memory)
Interface buffer pools:
Ethernet0 buffers, 1524 bytes (total 32, permanent 32):
     8 in free list (0 min, 32 max allowed)
     3398 hits, 3164 fallbacks
     8 max cache size, 7 in cache
Serial0 buffers, 1524 bytes (total 32, permanent 32):
     7 in free list (0 min, 32 max allowed)
     25 hits, 0 fallbacks
     8 max cache size, 8 in cache
Serial1 buffers, 1524 bytes (total 32, permanent 32):
     7 in free list (0 min, 32 max allowed)
     25 hits, 0 fallbacks
     8 max cache size, 8 in cache
```

Although most of these fields are explained in Chapter 1, some are unique to the interface buffer pools:

- **fallbacks**—The number of times the interface processor had to fall back to the public buffer pools to find a buffer in which to store a packet.

- **max cache size**—Some number of buffers in each private buffer pool are cached for faster access; this is the maximum number of buffers that can be cached.

- **in cache**—The number of cached private buffers.

Notice the private pools do not have a **creates** or a **trims** field; this is because these pools are static pools.

Receive Rings and Transmit Rings

In addition to public and private buffer pools, IOS also creates special buffer control structures, called rings, in I/O memory. IOS and interface controllers use these rings to control which buffers are used to receive and transmit packets to the media. Rings are actually a common control structure used by many types of media controllers to manage the memory for packets being received or waiting to be transmitted. The rings themselves consist of media controller–specific elements that point to individual packet buffers elsewhere in I/O memory. IOS creates these rings on behalf of the media controllers and then manages them jointly with the controllers.

Each interface has a pair of rings: a receive ring for receiving packets and a transmit ring for transmitting packets. These rings have fixed sizes determined by several factors. The size of the receive ring depends on the specific interface and is dictated by the media controller specification. The transmit ring size, however, is dependent on the media controller specification and the type of queuing configured on the interface.

Receive rings have a constant number of packet buffers allocated to them that equals the size of the ring. The receive ring's packet buffers initially are allocated from the interface's private buffer pool. During operation, they might be replaced with buffers from either the private pool or a public pool.

The number of buffers allocated to a transmit ring can vary from zero up to the maximum size of the transmit ring. Transmit ring packet buffers come from the receive ring of the originating interface for a switched packet or from a public pool if the packet was originated by IOS. They're de-allocated from the transmit ring and returned to their original pool after the payload data is transmitted.

The **show controller** command in Example 3-10 displays the sizes and the locations of the receive and the transmit rings. Although most interface types produce output similar to what's shown, the exact content of the output varies.

Example 3-10 **show controller** *Command Output Displays Receive and Transmit Ring Sizes and Locations*

```
isp-4700b#show controller ethernet
AM79970 unit 0 NIM slot 1, NIM type code 14, NIM version 1
Media Type is 10BaseT, Half Duplex, Link State is Down, Squelch is Normal
idb 0x60AE8324, ds 0x60AE9D10, eim_regs = 0x3C110000
IB at 0x40006E64: mode=0x0010, mcfilter 0000/0000/0100/0000
station address 0060.837c.7089  default station address 0060.837c.7089
buffer size 1524
RX ring with 32 entries at 0x400303D0
Rxhead = 0x400303D0 (0), Rxp = 0x60AE9D28 (0)
00 pak=0x60AF2468 ds=0xA80C745E status=0x80 max_size=1524 pak_size=0
01 pak=0x60AF2254 ds=0xA80C6DA2 status=0x80 max_size=1524 pak_size=0
02 pak=0x60AF2040 ds=0xA80C66E6 status=0x80 max_size=1524 pak_size=0
....
```

continues

Example 3-10 **show controller** *Command Output Displays Receive and Transmit Ring Sizes and Locations (Continued)*

```
TX ring with 32 entries at 0x40059BD0, tx_count = 0
tx_head = 0x40059BD0 (0), head_txp = 0x60AE9E3C (0)
tx_tail = 0x40059BD0 (0), tail_txp = 0x60AE9E3C (0)
00 pak=0x000000 ds=0xA8000000 status=0x03 status2=0x0000 pak_size=0
01 pak=0x000000 ds=0xA8000000 status=0x03 status2=0x0000 pak_size=0
02 pak=0x000000 ds=0xA8000000 status=0x03 status2=0x0000 pak_size=0
```

The following list describes some of the more interesting fields in the **show controller** output from Example 3-10:

- **RX ring with 32 entries at 0x400303D0**—The size of the receive ring is 32 and it begins at memory location 0x400303D0 in I/O memory.

- **00 pak=0x60AF2468 ds=0xA80C745E status=0x80 max_size=1524 pak_size=0**— This line is repeated for each ring entry in the receive ring. Each ring entry, called a *descriptor*, contains information about a corresponding packet buffer allocated to the receive ring. All the fields in the descriptor except for **pak** are device specific and vary from media controller to media controller. The **pak** field points to the memory address of the *header* for the packet linked to this descriptor. All IOS packet buffers have a corresponding header containing information about the contents of the buffer and a pointer to the actual location of the buffer itself. Although packet buffers on shared memory systems are located in I/O memory, their headers might reside in Local memory, as is the case here.

- **TX ring with 32 entries at 0x40059BD0, tx_count = 0**—Shows the transmit ring size and the number of packets waiting to be transmitted. In this case, the transmit ring size is 32 and there are no packets awaiting transmission on this interface.

- **00 pak=0x000000 ds=0xA8000000 status=0x03 status2=0x0000 pak_size=0**— This line is repeated for each entry in the transmit ring. Like the receive ring, each entry in the transmit ring is a descriptor containing information about a corresponding packet buffer on the ring. The **pak** field points to the header of a corresponding packet buffer waiting to be transmitted. The other fields are media controller specific. Unlike receive ring descriptors, transmit ring descriptors are linked only to a packet buffer when there is a packet waiting to transmit. After a packet buffer is transmitted, the buffer is unlinked from the transmit descriptor, returned to its original free pool, and its descriptor **pak** pointer reset to 0x000000.

Packet Switching on a Shared Memory Router

Now that we've looked at the general hardware architecture of the shared memory routers and how IOS divides their memory, let's look at how IOS actually switches packets. IOS on shared memory routers supports the following:

- Process switching
- CEF switching
- Fast switching

There are three stages in IOS packet switching:

1 Receiving the packet

2 Switching the packet

3 Transmitting the packet

Receiving the Packet

Figure 3-2 illustrates the steps of the packet receive stage.

Figure 3-2   *Receiving the Packet*

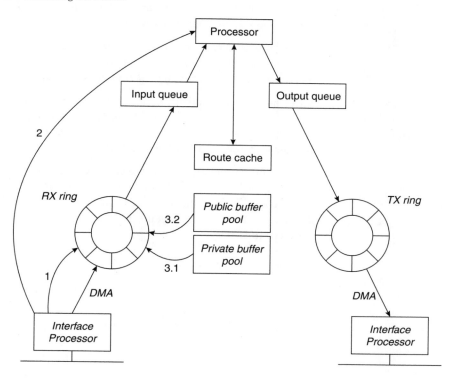

Step 1   The interface media controller detects a packet on the network media and copies it into a buffer pointed to by the first free element in the receive ring (that is, the next buffer the media controller owns). Media controllers use the DMA (direct memory access) method to copy packet data into memory.

Step 2   The media controller changes ownership of the packet buffer back to the processor and issues a receive interrupt to the processor. The media controller does not have to wait for a response from the CPU and continues to receive incoming packets into other buffers linked to the receive ring.

NOTE   Notice in Step 2 the media controller can continue to receive incoming packets into the receive ring. Therefore, it's possible for the media controller to fill the receive ring before the processor processes all the new buffers in the ring. This condition is called an *overrun*; when it occurs, all incoming packets are dropped until the processor catches up.

Step 3   The CPU responds to the receive interrupt, and then attempts to remove the newly-filled buffer from the receive ring and replenish the ring from the interface's private pool. Three outcomes are possible:

　　3.1   A free buffer is available in the interface's private pool to replenish the receive ring: The free buffer is linked to the receive ring and packet switching continues with Step 4.

　　3.2   A free buffer is not available in the interface's private pool, so the receive ring is replenished by *falling back* to the global pool that matches the interface's MTU. The *fallback* counter is incremented for the private pool.

　　3.3   If a free buffer is not available in the public pool as well, the incoming packet is dropped and the *ignore* counter is incremented. Further, the interface is *throttled*, and all incoming traffic is ignored on this interface for some short period of time.

Switching the Packet

Step 4 After the receive ring is replenished, the CPU begins actually switching the packet. This operation consists of locating information about where to send the packet (next hop) and the MAC header to rewrite onto the packet.

IOS attempts to switch the packet using the fastest method configured on the interface. On shared memory systems, it first tries CEF switching (if configured), then fast switching, and finally falls back to process switching if none of the others work. Figure 3-3 illustrates the steps of the packet switching stage and the list that follows describes the steps illustrated in the figure.

Figure 3-3   *Switching the Packet*

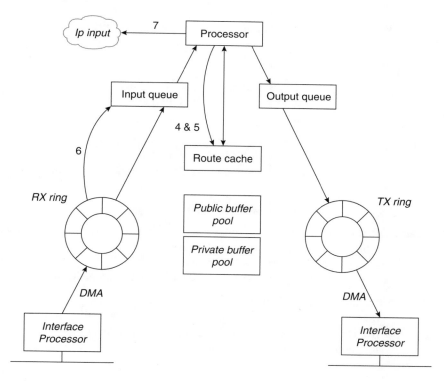

Step 5   While still in the receive interrupt context, IOS attempts to use the CEF table (first) or fast switching cache (second) to make a switching decision.

> **5.1**   **CEF switching**—If CEF switching is enabled on the interface, then CEF switching is attempted. Four different outcomes are possible:
>
> > **5.1.1**   *If there are valid CEF and adjacency table entries, IOS rewrites the MAC header on the packet and begins transmitting it in Step 8, the packet transmit stage.*
> >
> > **5.1.2**   *If the CEF adjacency entry for this destination points to a punt adjacency, IOS proceeds to try fast switching (see Step 5.2).*
> >
> > **5.1.3**   *If the CEF table entry for this packet points to a receive adjacency, the packet is queued for process switching.*
> >
> > **5.1.4**   *If there is no CEF entry for the destination, the packet is dropped.*
>
> **5.2**   **Fast switching**—If CEF is not enabled or the packet cannot be CEF switched, IOS attempts to fast switch the packet.
>
> > **5.2.1**   *If there is a valid fast cache entry for this destination, IOS rewrites the MAC header information and begins transmitting the packet (Step 8, packet transmit stage).*
> >
> > **5.2.2**   *If there is no valid fast cache entry, the packet is queued for process switching (Step 6).*

Step 6   **Process switching**—If both CEF switching and fast switching fail, IOS falls back to process switching. The packet is placed in the input queue of the appropriate process (an IP packet is placed in the queue for the IP Input process, for instance), and the receive interrupt is dismissed.

Step 7   Eventually, the packet switching process runs, switching the packet and rewriting the MAC header as needed. Note the packet still has not moved from the buffer it was originally copied into. After the packet is switched, IOS continues to the packet transmit stage, for process switching (Step 9).

Transmitting the Packet

Figure 3-4 illustrates the steps of packet transmit stage.

Figure 3-4   *Transmitting the Packet*

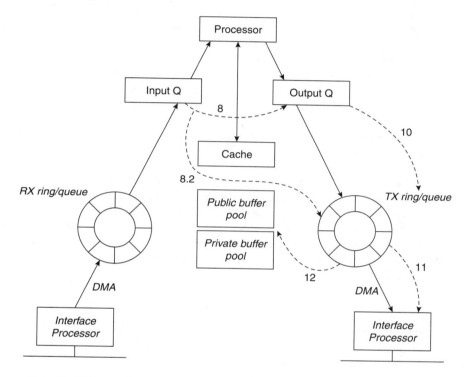

Step 8   If the packet was CEF switched or fast switched, then while still in receive interrupt context IOS checks to see if there are packets on the output queue of the outbound interface.

> **8.1**   If there are packets already on the output hold queue for the interface, IOS places the packet on the output hold queue instead of directly into the transmit ring to reduce the possibility of out-of-order packets, and then proceeds to Step 8.3.

> **8.2**   If the output hold queue is empty, IOS places the packet on the transmit ring of the output interface by linking the packet buffer to a transmit ring descriptor. The receive interrupt is dismissed and processing continues with Step 11. If there is no room on the transmit ring, the packet is placed on the output hold queue instead and the receive interrupt is dismissed.

8.3 If the output hold queue is full, the packet is dropped, the output **drop** counter is incremented, and the receive interrupt is dismissed.

NOTE   In Step 8 of the transmit stage, notice that IOS checks the output hold queue first before placing any CEF or fast switched packets on the transmit ring. This reduces the possibility of transmitting packets out of order. How can packets get out of order when they're being switched as they're received? Consider the following example.

Let's assume the first packet in a given conversation (flow) between two hosts arrives at the router. IOS attempts to fast switch the packet and finds there is no fast cache entry. So, the packet is handed off to the IP Input process for process switching.

So far, everything is fine. In the process of switching the packet, IP Input builds a cache entry for this flow of packets and places the first packet on the output queue of the outbound interface.

Now, let's assume that just at this moment a second packet arrives for the same flow. IOS fast switches the second packet (because the cache entry has now been built) and gets ready to transmit it. If IOS puts this second packet directly on the transmit ring, it is transmitted before the first packet, which is still waiting in the output queue. To prevent this situation from occurring, IOS always makes certain the output queue of the outbound interface is empty before placing any CEF-switched or fast-switched packets directly on the transmit ring.

Step 9   If the packet was process switched, the packet is placed on the output queue for the output interface. If the output queue is full, the packet is dropped and the *output drop* counter is incremented.

Step 10   IOS attempts to find a free descriptor in the output interface transmit ring. If a free descriptor exists, IOS removes the packet from the output hold queue and links the buffer to the transmit ring. If no free descriptor exists (that is, the ring is full), IOS leaves the packet in the output hold queue until the media controller transmits a packet from the ring and frees a descriptor.

Step 11   The outbound interface media controller polls its transmit ring periodically for packets that need to be transmitted. As soon as the media controller detects a packet, it copies the packet onto the network media and raises a transmit interrupt to the processor.

Step 12 IOS acknowledges the transmit interrupt, unlinks the packet buffer from the transmit ring, and returns the buffer to the pool of buffers from which it originally came. IOS then checks the output hold queue for the interface; if there are any packets waiting in the output hold queue, IOS removes the next one from the queue and links it to the transmit ring. Finally, the transmit interrupt is dismissed.

Summary

This chapter covered the IOS implementation on Cisco's shared memory architecture routers, including the 2500 series, of which there are more than 1 million in use today. You saw how IOS divides memory into regions and how it actually switches packets on these platforms.

This chapter covers the following key topics:

- AGS+ Hardware Architecture
- Packet Switching with the Cbus
- The Cisco 7000 Series Router

CHAPTER 4

Early Cbus Routers

Chapter 2, "Packet Switching Architecture," examined how changes in the IOS software implementation have been used to improve packet switching performance. Cisco also uses special hardware designs to improve switching performance. The first notable example of this was the introduction of the Cbus with the AGS+ router and its successor, the Cisco 7000 series router, in the early 1990s. Although these products are no longer sold or supported in current IOS versions, a large part of their design was adapted for the Cisco 7500 series routers that are widely deployed today. This chapter covers the AGS+ and 7000 routers because a sizeable part of the 7500-specific switching features actually had their origins in the IOS design for these early platforms.

AGS+ Hardware Architecture

The AGS+ router was an improved version of the original AGS router. The AGS (without the plus) was based on a Motorola 68000 series CPU (M68k) and used media interface cards interconnected by a relatively slow 155-Mbps data bus called the Multibus. Due to the speed limitations of this processor and the Multibus, packet switching performance was limited to the range of 7000 to 14,000 packets per second (pps) even with fast switching—pretty anemic by today's standards. In fact, under some conditions the Cisco 2500 series routers can outperform these switching speeds!

The Cisco AGS+ and 7000 routers were designed before the advent of high speed computer buses and economical RISC-based CPUs. So, when Cisco's engineers started looking for ways to boost switching performance, there weren't many off-the-shelf solutions from which to choose. The engineers decided to solve the problem by designing their own high-speed data bus and packet switching engine. Thus was born the *Cbus*.

The original Cbus (short for "Cisco bus") was a 32-bit bus operating at 16.67 MHz, giving a total bandwidth of 533 Mbps—a vast improvement over the Multibus. The bus was designed with 32 data lines, 24 address lines, and 8 command lines.

The Cbus switching engine was based on a microcoded 16-bit slice microprocessor with an 80-bit instruction word that allowed several operations to execute concurrently in a single cycle. Unlike general purpose processors such as the M68k, the Cbus processor had a small, customized instruction set designed specifically to support data switching operations. The processor was packaged on a special interface card containing memory for the processor's instructions (called *control store*), fast packet memory, and interfaces to both the Multibus and the Cbus. This card comprised the switching engine and was called the *Cbus Controller*.

These two new features, the Cbus and the Cbus Controller, were added to the original AGS architecture to create the AGS+ router. Figure 4-1 shows a diagram of the AGS+ architecture.

Figure 4-1   *AGS+ Architecture*

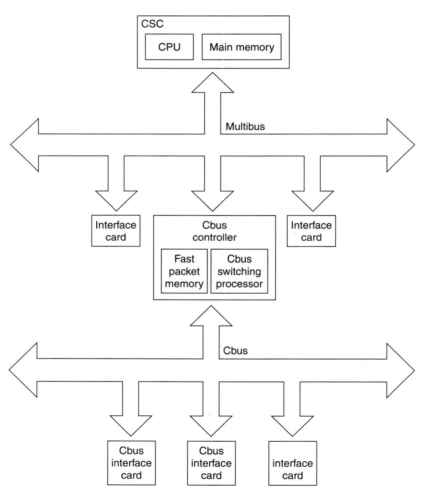

The following list describes each of the major components shown in Figure 4-1:

- **Processor (CPU)**—Runs IOS and performs process switching functions, and performs fast switching between Multibus interfaces. The processor also performs fast switching for packets that are received from Cbus interfaces but can't be autonomously switched.

- **Main Memory**—DRAM containing the running IOS image, its data, and system packet buffers.

- **Multibus**—Data bus interconnecting the processor with the Multibus interface cards. The Cbus controller card also has a connection to the Multibus.

- **Cbus Switching Processor**—Runs optimized non-IOS microcode to perform fast switching of packets between Cbus interfaces. This processor is on the Cbus controller card.

- **Fast Packet Memory**—High-speed memory on the Cbus controller card that is dual-ported between the Cbus switching processor and the Cbus interface cards. Used to store packets received from or transmitted to Cbus interfaces. This memory is referred to by the name *MEMD* in the Cbus architecture.

- **Cbus**—The Cisco proprietary data bus interconnecting the Cbus controller card with the Cbus interface cards.

NOTE   The Cbus processor, MEMD, and Cbus bus control circuitry were contained on the same card and collectively referred to as the CBUS controller or CBUSII card. The Cbus processor itself was often just referred to as "the processor on the CBUSII card." *Cbus Switching Processor* is used here to identify the processor and should not be confused with the *Switch Processor* on the C7000 router.

The AGS+ retained the Motorola 68000 series processor and the Multibus backplane used on the AGS. The Cbus enhancement was made by converting five of the interface card slots on the backplane to access the Cbus. This allowed Multibus interface cards to be used in the same chassis with the new Cbus interface cards.

After the hardware enhancements were added to the AGS+, how did IOS actually use them to increase switching performance? Let's examine how IOS put these enhancements to work.

Packet Switching with the Cbus

Recall the descriptions of fast switching and process switching from Chapter 2, "Packet Switching Architecture." In both of these methods, the receiving interface hardware copies the received packet into I/O memory and interrupts the *main* processor to begin switching the packet. Whether during the interrupt or in a background process, the main processor has to do all the work of actually switching the packet; the interface hardware just receives the packet and transmits it to the media. Also, packet switching is just one of the many tasks the main processor has to do, so not all of its capacity is available for packet switching.

The Cbus and the Cbus Controller provided another processing alternative on the AGS+. Instead of IOS performing all the switching on the main processor, much of the switching could be performed by the Cbus Controller without involving the main processor at all. The Cbus Controller was capable of performing fast switching autonomously on the switching processor as long as both the receiving and the transmitting interfaces were on Cbus cards. This capability provided a new method of switching appropriately called *autonomous switching*.

Autonomous Switching

Autonomous switching worked essentially like fast switching—except on a different processor. It was triggered by a packet receive interrupt (this time to the switching processor) and used a local cache to look up forwarding information, just like fast switching. In fact, autonomous switching used the same hash table structure for its fast cache that IOS used prior to release 10.2. IOS maintained both the main fast cache and the local switching processor (Cbus) cache during process switching in the same way. Each time an entry was added or invalidated in the main cache it also was added or invalidated in the Cbus cache.

Autonomous switching did differ from fast switching in a couple ways, though. Autonomous switching didn't support as many protocols as fast switching—only IP, IPX, and bridging—and it handled cache misses differently.

Recall that in fast switching, if a packet is received and there is no fast cache entry for it, the packet is queued for process switching. In autonomous switching, however, if there was no Cbus cache entry for a packet, the packet was sent to the main processor for possible *fast* switching. If the packet was destined to another Cbus interface, the main processor could fast switch the packet while it was still in the Cbus Controller. However, if the packet was destined to a Multibus interface, the whole packet had to be copied across the slow Multibus to a system buffer, and then process switched. Although the Cbus Controller had a Multibus interface, it couldn't use it to autonomously switch packets.

Cbus Fast Packet Memory

The Cbus Controller design introduced a new strategy for IOS packet buffering that is still in use today on the Cisco 7500 series. On the AGS+, process switching and fast switching used the system buffers for packets as described in Chapter 1, "Fundamental IOS Software Architecture." However, these system buffers held a distinct disadvantage for autonomous switching: They were located in main memory on the main processor card, which made them inaccessible to Cbus interface cards.

To provide packet buffers for the Cbus interfaces, Cisco designed the Cbus Controller with its own local dedicated packet buffer memory. The memory, referred to as *MEMD*, was a fixed 512 KB region that could be addressed by both the switching processor and the Cbus interface cards. Of the total 512 KB available, the first 8 KB (called *page zero*) was set aside for control structures, leaving the rest available to be carved into packet buffers.

MEMD

You might be wondering where the name MEMD came from. Contrary to popular belief, MEMD is not the name of a type of memory but is instead the name Cisco assigned to a class of memory used on its Cbus-based routers. MEMD is really just SRAM, but it's always used for packet buffering to and from Cbus interfaces.

The name MEMD was derived from the word *memory* (MEM) plus the alphabetic letter *D*, indicating it is the fourth in a series of Cbus memory classes. There were also other Cbus memory classes used on the AGS+. For example, *MEMA* referred to memory used to hold the autonomous cache and the global pointers used by the switching processor.

What's most interesting about MEMD is how it was logically organized. Like the system buffers, MEMD was divided into buffers of varying sizes to accommodate different sized packets. Unlike the system buffers, MEMD buffer sizes were determined by the actual MTU sizes of the Cbus interfaces present on the router—not by a predetermined set of sizes.

The buffers were divided into a maximum of four pools, and then they were allocated to the interfaces from those pools. Within each pool, all buffers were the same size. Due to the limited size of MEMD and its control structures in page zero, the maximum number of packet buffers that could be defined was limited to 470 regardless of the number of Cbus interfaces present.

The switching processor maintained two queues in MEMD's page zero for each Cbus interface: a *receive queue* and a *transmit queue*. These queues were similar in function to the input queues and the output queues maintained by IOS. When a Cbus interface detected an incoming packet, it allocated a MEMD buffer from the appropriate pool, copied the packet data into the buffer, and placed the buffer on its receive queue to await switching by the switching processor. If the packet was autonomously switched, the switching processor switched it and placed the modified packet on the transmit queue of the destination Cbus interface. If the packet was fast switched, the main processor switched it and directed the switching processor to place it on the appropriate Cbus transmit queue. For packets that had to be process switched, the switching processor copied the packet to the main processor memory over the Multibus and returned the MEMD buffer to its original pool.

The switching processor also maintained counters and limit values in MEMD for each of the receive queues and the transmit queues. Each receive queue had a *receive queue limit* (RQL) and each transmit queue had a *transmit queue limit* (TQL) to prevent a single interface from hoarding all the MEMD buffers.

The RQL value determined the maximum number of packet buffers that could be held on the receive queue at any time. When a receive queue contained the RQL number of buffers, it was considered full and any additional packets received were dropped until the number of buffers dropped below the RQL level. Similarly, the TQL value determined the maximum number of packet buffers that could be held on the transmit queue at any given time. Any additional packets switched to an interface while its transmit queue was full were dropped until its transmit queue depth dropped below the TQL value.

You can find a more detailed description of the MEMD counters and the buffer carving process in Chapter 6, "Cisco 7500 Routers."

The Cisco 7000 Series Router

The Cisco 7000 series router represented the next step in the evolution of the AGS and the Cbus architecture. Other than the mechanical structure and outward appearance, the 7000 wasn't drastically different from its predecessor, the AGS+. The biggest architectural difference was the elimination of the Multibus and Multibus interface cards—only Cbus interface cards were supported on the 7000.

Some of the changes were mostly superficial. On the 7000, the AGS+ processor card was replaced by the *Route Processor* (RP) card and the Cbus Controller was replaced by the 7000's *Switch Processor* (SP) card, but the RP and SP retained the same CPUs as their AGS+ counterparts. Although there was no Multibus, per se, on the 7000, the switching processor on the SP still connected to the main processor on the RP via a 155-Mbps Multibus-like interface. These similarities allowed the IOS software and switching processor microcode to work on the 7000 without requiring a large number of changes.

The 7000 did introduce a new hardware feature not present on the AGS+: *hot-swappable interface cards*. The 7000 routers allowed Cbus interface cards (called *interface processors* on the 7000) to be removed and re-inserted while IOS was operational with minimal operational disruption to other interface processors. When IOS detected that a card was being removed or inserted, it momentarily stalled operations on the Cbus while the insertion/removal was underway. When the insertion/removal completed, IOS resumed operation of the Cbus and continued switching packets where it left off.

This new feature necessitated a change in the operation of the switching processor microcode. Whereas the composition of interfaces was fixed on the AGS+ while IOS was in operation, on the 7000 that composition could change on the fly. The original switching processor microcode on the AGS+ was designed to carve a static MEMD buffer allocation at initialization time. On the 7000, however, the microcode had to be changed to re-carve the buffer allocation each time a card was inserted or removed. This allowed the SP to keep the most efficient use of packet memory resources even if the interface composition changed.

Summary

The architecture of the AGS+ and Cisco 7000 routers formed the foundation from which the later Cbus-based routers were built. Although Cisco's router architecture has now shifted toward newer designs, it's still useful to examine these early systems because much of the current IOS switching architecture is a relic of these early designs.

Chapter 5 moves on to one of the newer Cisco router architectures—Particle-Based Systems.

This chapter covers the following key topics:

- Buffer Management Using Particles
- The Cisco 7200 Series Routers
- Packet Switching on the Cisco 7200 Series Routers

Particle-Based Systems

All the packet buffering schemes discussed so far have one thing in common: they carve up pools of various-sized buffers, and then allocate one buffer per packet. These types of buffers often are called *contiguous* buffers because the entire contents of a packet reside in a single buffer in one contiguous area of memory. Buffers either are sized to accommodate the largest packet possible on an interface or they're sized according to a fixed schedule.

Although contiguous buffers are easy to manipulate, they don't always provide the most efficient use of memory. Contiguous buffering schemes can waste memory by oversizing buffers or by promoting buffer usage imbalances. Consider the Cbus MEMD scheme, for example. The MEMD scheme creates interface buffers to be at least as large as the MTU of the interface—the size of the largest packet that can appear. If the average packet received is much smaller than the MTU, then much of the packet buffer is wasted. For example, if an interface's MTU is 4 KB, but most of its packets (90 percent) are less than 1 KB, 75 percent of the interface's buffer memory is wasted 90 percent of the time!

In IOS Release 11.1CA, Cisco introduced a new buffering scheme called *particle buffering* designed to address the inefficiencies of contiguous buffers. Although not universally supported on all platforms, particle buffering is used on the Cisco 2600 series, the Cisco 3600 series, the Cisco 7500 VIP, the Cisco 7200 series, and the derivatives of the 7200, such as the Cisco 7100 and the Cisco 6400 NRP. This chapter covers particle buffering and examines how it's used for packet switching on one of the supported platforms, the Cisco 7200 series router.

Buffer Management Using Particles

Particle buffering uses a scatter-gather approach for packet buffer memory management. Instead of allocating one piece of contiguous memory for a buffer, particle buffering allocates dis-contiguous (scattered) pieces of memory, called *particles*, and then links them together (gathers) to form one logical packet buffer, called a *particle buffer*. With this scheme, a single packet can be spread across multiple physical buffers.

Particle buffers are built—that is, individual particles are linked together—as each packet is received on an interface, as you'll see when you study the Cisco 7200 router example. This method differs from that of contiguous buffers, which need no assembly before use. As a result, there are no pools of pre-built particle buffers like there are for contiguous buffers. After all, how would IOS know how many particles to add to each buffer? Instead, IOS maintains pools of particles and draws from those pools to build packet buffers as it receives packets. The particles are the basic building blocks and the pools provide the raw materials to build the packet buffers.

Within a given pool, all particles are the same size; so any free particle in the pool can be used to build a buffer without regard to the particle's size. This uniformity simplifies the particle management algorithms and helps contribute to efficient memory use. IOS particle size varies from platform to platform, but within a platform there is usually one primary size. There are exceptions—platforms can have pools with secondary particle sizes as you'll see later in this chapter—but there is usually a primary particle size. The size is chosen so it's large enough to contain the average packet while minimizing wasted memory, typically 512 bytes. This way, most packet buffers can be composed of just one particle.

To understand how the particle buffering scatter-gather approach works, consider the example illustrated in Figure 5-1. In this simple example, there is one particle pool in memory and all packet buffers are built from that pool.

Figure 5-1   *Particle Example*

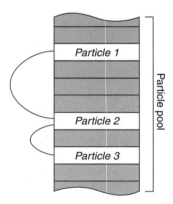

Assume that the pool's particle size is 512 bytes and three free particles, labeled P1, P2, and P3, exist in the pool. Now, let's trace what happens when IOS receives a 1200-byte packet.

Step 1   IOS gets the next free particle (P1 in this example) and begins copying the packet data into the particle. The first 512 bytes of the packet are copied.

Step 2   When the first particle is filled, IOS moves to the next free particle (P2 in this example), links it to P1, and continues copying packet data into this second particle. The next 512 bytes of the packet are copied.

Step 3 When the second particle is filled, 176 bytes of packet data still are left.
So, IOS moves to the next free particle (P3 in this example), links it to
P2, and copies the remaining 176 bytes into this third particle.

Upon completion, IOS has copied the entire 1200 bytes into three dis-contiguous pieces of
memory that are all logically part of a single packet buffer.

Particle buffers actually consist of more than just the memory that contains packet data.
Some amount of overhead is required (in the form of additional components) to maintain
data about the packet as well as to link the scattered memory pieces together. Figure 5-2
shows the components of a particle buffer and how each one is related.

Figure 5-2   *Particle Buffer Components*

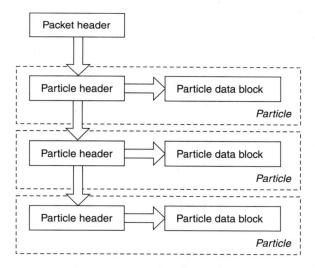

Each particle buffer consists of a *packet header* linked to one or more particles. A particle
consists of a *particle header* and an associated *particle data block*. The following list
examines each of these components in more detail:

- **Packet header**—The packet header is the same as the header for contiguous buffers.
  It contains information about the type and the size of the packet in the buffer as well
  as pointers to specific fields in the packet. The packet header also contains a link to
  the first particle.

- **Particle header**—The particle header is a control block containing a link to the
  particle data block and a link to the next particle in the buffer (if there is one). It also
  contains other information, such as the number of data bytes in the data block and the
  pool that owns the particle.

- **Particle data block**—The particle data block is the piece of memory containing the
  actual particle data—basically, this is just a buffer.

Particle Pools

IOS uses the same pool management strategy for particle pools as it does for contiguous packet buffers on shared memory systems. IOS creates a private static particle pool for each interface, and then creates a public dynamic pool, called the *normal pool*, that all interfaces and processes share. The private particle pools use the public pool as a *fall-back* in case they run out of particles.

IOS also creates another public particle pool on most systems, called the *fast switching pool*, containing small 128-byte particles. These particles are used when IOS needs to prepend data to a packet during fast switching—for example, to rewrite a larger media header onto a packet. To prepend the data, IOS must insert a new particle at the beginning of a particle buffer after it already has been linked together. Because the prepended data is usually small, it uses the particles from this special pool.

The partial output from the **show buffers** command in Example 5-1 shows a sample of the public and private particle pools IOS creates. The fast switching pool is labeled **F/S**.

Example 5-1 **show buffers** *Command Output Displays Public and Private Particle Pools*

```
Router-7200#show buffers
....
Public particle pools:
F/S buffers, 128 bytes (total 512, permanent 512):
     0 in free list (0 min, 512 max allowed)
     512 hits, 0 misses
     512 max cache size, 512 in cache
Normal buffers, 512 bytes (total 1024, permanent 1024):
     1024 in free list (512 min, 2048 max allowed)
     0 hits, 0 misses, 0 trims, 0 created
     0 failures (0 no memory)

Private particle pools:
FastEthernet0/0 buffers, 512 bytes (total 400, permanent 400):
     0 in free list (0 min, 400 max allowed)
     400 hits, 0 fallbacks
     400 max cache size, 271 in cache
Ethernet1/0 buffers, 512 bytes (total 128, permanent 128):
     0 in free list (0 min, 128 max allowed)
     128 hits, 0 fallbacks
     128 max cache size, 64 in cache
Ethernet1/1 buffers, 512 bytes (total 128, permanent 128):
     0 in free list (0 min, 128 max allowed)
     128 hits, 0 fallbacks
     128 max cache size, 64 in cache
...
```

Particle Coalescing

Although particle buffers do improve memory efficiency, they also tend to increase the complexity of the programs that manipulate their contents. For example, with particles, packet fields can be split arbitrarily across particle boundaries. Packet switching methods have to accommodate that possibility.

All fast switching methods, for most protocols, are equipped to handle particle buffers. However, this is not the case for process switching. Because process switching adds little benefit, only complexity, Cisco decided not to equip the process switching method for particle buffers. Process switching still requires a packet to reside in a contiguous buffer. As a result, particle-buffered packets queued to process switching must be transferred to a contiguous buffer through a process is called *coalescing*.

Coalescing essentially involves copying the contents of all the particles in a packet buffer, one by one, into an appropriately sized contiguous buffer. Depending on the platform, this task either can be performed by the main CPU or by a separate DMA engine. The coalescing process works as follows:

Step 1   IOS allocates an appropriately sized contiguous buffer from one of the system buffer pools. IOS must find a buffer large enough for the entire packet or the coalescing process fails.

Step 2   IOS copies the data from each packet buffer particle into the new contiguous buffer.

Step 3   IOS frees all the particles, returning them to their original pool.

Step 4   Finally, IOS unlinks the packet header from the freed particles and links it to the new contiguous buffer.

When the process is complete, the resulting packet looks the same as the original (same packet header) except it resides in a physically contiguous block of memory.

To understand how particle buffers are used in IOS, it's helpful to look at an implementation example. The following sections describe how particle buffers are used on the Cisco 7200 router series, the first platform to support particles.

The Cisco 7200 Series Routers

The 7200 router was the first Cisco router designed to use the now common, industry-standard PCI bus. The 7200 series has a modular architecture that uses replaceable media interfaces called *port adapters* and an interchangeable main processor called the *Network Processing Engine* (NPE).

The 7200 is available in several configurations based upon combinations of chassis models and available NPEs. The number of slots and the type of midplane installed distinguish the chassis models. At the time of this writing, two midplane designs are available for the 7200 series chassis:

- **Original midplane**—Contains two PCI buses running at 25 MHz. Each bus connects to half the slots in a chassis. This midplane supports all NPEs except the NPE-300.

- **VXR midplane**—Contains two dual-speed PCI buses capable of running at either 25 or 50 MHz. Each bus connects to half the slots in a chassis. In addition, the midplane contains a TDM (time division multiplexing) switch with two dedicated links, called *Multiservice Interchange Connections*, to each chassis slot. This midplane primarily is intended for use with the NPE-300, but it supports all NPEs.

The 7200 series chassis is available in two-slot, four-slot, and six-slot versions. The following list examines the 7200 series chassis configurations:

- **7202**—A two-slot chassis used in some niche applications. This router has the original 25-MHz midplane and supports only the NPE-150.

- **7204**—A four-slot chassis with the original midplane.

- **7206**—A six-slot chassis with the original midplane.

- **7204VXR**—A four-slot chassis with the VXR midplane.

- **7206VXR**—A six-slot chassis with the VXR midplane.

Several NPEs have been developed for the 7200 series router; all feature a MIPS-compatible CPU. Most are interchangeable, with a few exceptions. For example, the two-slot 7202 chassis supports only the NPE-150, and the NPE-300 is supported only in a chassis with the VXR midplane. Each NPE is distinguished by its CPU speed and the type of memory it contains:

- **NPE-100**—An early 7200 series NPE with a VR4700-100 100-MHz CPU and DRAM memory only (no SRAM).

- **NPE-150**—Contains a VR4700-150 CPU running at 150 MHz. Uses DRAM for main memory and both DRAM and SRAM for packet buffers.

- **NPE-175**—Contains an RM5270-200 CPU running at 200 MHz with a 2 Mb unified cache. Uses SDRAM for main memory and packet buffers.

- **NPE-200**—Contains a VR5000-200 CPU running at 200 MHz. Uses DRAM for main memory and both DRAM and SRAM for packet buffers.

- **NPE-225**—Contains an RM5271-262 CPU running at 262 MHz with a 2 Mb unified cache. Uses SDRAM for main memory and packet buffers.

- **NPE-300**—Contains an RM7000-300 CPU running at 300 MHz and two independent banks of SDRAM memory. This NPE has two separate PCI/memory bus controllers allowing concurrent access to SDRAM from two different port adapters, providing improved performance. The NPE-300 also operates the PCI busses at 50 MHz and requires the VXR midplane.

Hardware Architecture

The 7200 series hardware architecture varies from model to model and depends upon the combination of chassis and NPE, but it generally can be separated into two major designs: routers with the original midplane and an early NPE (NPE-100, NPE-150, NPE-200), and routers with the VXR midplane and an NPE-300. Figure 5-3 illustrates the components of a Cisco 7200 series router employing the original midplane design. This particular example illustrates a 7206 with an NPE-150.

Figure 5-3   *Cisco 7200 Architecture—Original Midplane*

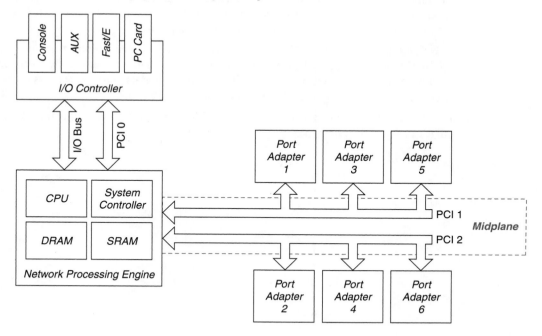

The following list explains the Cisco 7200 components as illustrated in Figure 5-3.

- **NPE**—Contains the main memory, the CPU, the PCI memory (SRAM, except on the NPE-100 which uses DRAM), and the control circuitry for the PCI busses. As noted previously, several types of NPEs are available—all are supported with the original midplane except the NPE-300.

- **PCI Bus**—There are three PCI data busses in a Cisco 7200: PCI 0, PCI 1, and PCI 2. PCI 1 and PCI 2 extend from the NPE to the midplane and interconnect the media interfaces (port adapters) to the CPU and the memory on the NPE. PCI 0 is separate and is used to connect the media interface and the PCMCIA on the I/O controller to the CPU and the memory on the NPE. Running at 25 MHz, PCI 0, PCI 1, and PCI 2 provide up to 800 Mbps in bandwidth each.

- **I/O bus**—Interconnects the non-PCI components on the I/O Controller (console port, AUX port, NVRAM, Boot ROM, and Boot FLASH) to the CPU on the NPE.

- **Port Adapters (PAs)**—These are modular interface controllers that contain circuitry to transmit and receive packets on the physical media. These are the same port adapters used on the VIP processors on a Cisco 7500 series router. Both platforms support most port adapters, but there are some exceptions.

- **I/O Controller**—Provides the console connection, the auxiliary connection, the NVRAM, the Boot ROM, the Boot FLASH, and a built-in interface controller—either an Ethernet or Fast Ethernet interface. The I/O Controller also provides access to the Flash memory cards in the PCMCIA card slot via PCI bus 0.

Figure 5-4 illustrates the components of the Cisco 7200VXR hardware architecture. This particular example illustrates a 7206VXR with an NPE-300.

Figure 5-4   *Cisco 7200VXR Architectural Components*

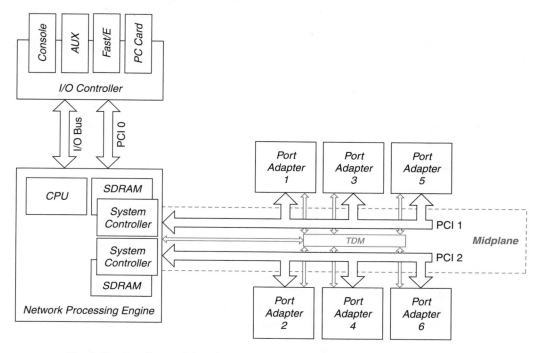

The following list explains the Cisco 7200VXR components as illustrated in Figure 5-4:

- **Network Processing Engine**—Contains the main memory, the CPU, the PCI memory, and the PCI bus control circuitry. The NPE-300 has two PCI bus controllers and two independent banks of SDRAM used for both main memory and packet memory.

- **PCI Bus**—Three PCI data busses exist in a Cisco 7200VXR: PCI 0, PCI 1, and PCI 2. PCI 1 and PCI 2 extend to the midplane and interconnect the media interfaces (port adapters) to the CPU and the memory on the NPE. PCI 0 is separate and is used to connect the media interface and the PCMCIA on the I/O Controller to the CPU and the memory on the NPE. PCI 0 runs at 25 MHz. PCI 1 and PCI 2 run at 50 MHz when a 50 MHz–capable NPE is installed (like the NPE-300 in this example); otherwise, they run at 25 MHz.

- **TDM switch**—The midplane contains a *time division multiplexing* (TDM) switch with two dedicated connections to each chassis slot. The TDM switch supports interconnection between port adapters that have TDM interfaces.

- **I/O bus**—Interconnects the non-PCI components on the I/O Controller (console port, AUX port, NVRAM, Boot ROM, and Boot FLASH) to the CPU on the NPE.

- **Port Adapters (PAs)**—These are the same port adapters used on the non-VXR 7200 routers. However, some PAs that require the TDM switch are supported only on the 7200VXR. The 7200VXR supports both legacy PAs with a 25-MHz internal PCI speed and 50 MHz PAs; any bus speed mismatch is resolved by the bus isolation between the midplane and the PAs.

- **I/O Controller**—Provides the console connection, the auxiliary connection, the NVRAM, the Boot ROM, the Boot FLASH, and a built-in interface controller—either an Ethernet or Fast Ethernet interface. The I/O Controller also provides access to the Flash memory cards in the PCMCIA card slot via PCI bus 0.

Memory

The 7200 series routers use DRAM, SDRAM, and SRAM memory on the NPE in various combinations depending on the NPE model. Three memory pools divide the available memory: the standard *processor* pool, the *I/O* pool, and the *PCI* pool (*I/O-2* on NPE300). Example 5-2 illustrates some **show memory** command output showing these three pools. The first is from an NPE-200 and the other is from an NPE-300.

Example 5-2   **show memory** *Command Output Displays Memory Pool Information for 7200 Series Routers*

```
router-NPE-200#show memory
               Head    Total(b)   Used(b)    Free(b)   Lowest(b)  Largest(b)
Processor   61BEBC60   96551840   7287388   89264452   88777932   88547216
      I/O    7800000    8388608    901616    7486992    7463324    7480508
      PCI   4B000000    4194304    993276    3201028    2227180    2702716

router-NPE-300#show memory
               Head    Total(b)    Used(b)    Free(b)   Lowest(b)  Largest(b)
Processor   612A02A0  106298720   7408336   98890384   98748252   98836460
      I/O   20000000   33554432   3604696   29949736   29925740   29949692
    I/O-2    7800000    8388608     35608    8353000    8353000    8352956
```

Figure 5-5 illustrates the memory pools shown in Example 5-2. Figure 5-5 also shows how the available memory is allocated to the pools on these two sample NPEs.

Figure 5-5   *Memory Types*

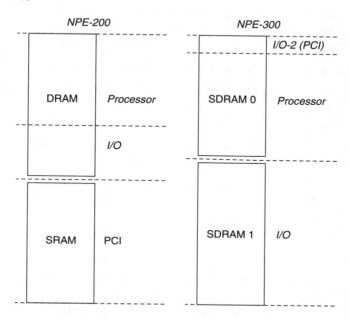

The following sections examine how IOS distributes available memory between the pools.

Processor Memory

The processor memory pool is used for storing the IOS code, general data structures (such as the routing table), and the system buffers. The entire memory pool is allocated from the DRAM region on the NPE-100, the NPE-150, and the NPE-200; the SDRAM region on the NPE-175 and the NPE-225; and SDRAM bank 0 on the NPE-300.

I/O Memory

The I/O memory pool is used for particle pools. The interface private particle pools are allocated from this memory as well as the public particle pool *normal*.

On NPE-100, NPE-150, and NPE-200 platforms, this memory pool is created in DRAM, so it's used primarily to allocate private particle pools for slower speed interfaces. The size of I/O memory is dependent on the total amount of DRAM memory available on the NPE. For example, on an NPE-150, the following set of conditions determine the I/O memory:

- An NPE-150 with 16 MB total DRAM gets 4 MB allocated to I/O memory.
- An NPE-150 with between 24 MB and 48 MB of DRAM gets 6 MB allocated to I/O memory.
- An NPE-150 with more than 48 MB of DRAM gets 8 MB allocated to I/O memory.

Other NPEs use different formulas for determining how much DRAM should be used for I/O memory, too many to list here.

On the NPE-300, the I/O memory pool is created in SDRAM bank 1 and is fixed at 32 MB. All private interface particle pools are created in I/O memory on this NPE, regardless of the media speed.

PCI Memory

The PCI memory pool is used for interface receive and transmit rings. It also is used to allocate private interface particle pools for high-speed interfaces in some cases. On NPE-175, NPE-225, and NPE-300 systems, this pool is created in SDRAM. On NPE-150 and NPE-200 systems, it is created entirely in SRAM.

PCI memory is generally a small pool. As you can see from Example 5-2, the NPE-200 has only 4 MB of PCI memory and the NPE-300 has approximately 8 MB, labeled I/O-2.

Packet Switching on the Cisco 7200 Series Routers

The Cisco 7200 supports process switching, fast switching, and Cisco Express Forwarding (CEF), but doesn't support any form of distributed switching. The main CPU in the NPE performs all the switching tasks.

Packet Receive Stage

Figure 5-6 illustrates what occurs when a packet is received.

Figure 5-6 *Receiving a Packet*

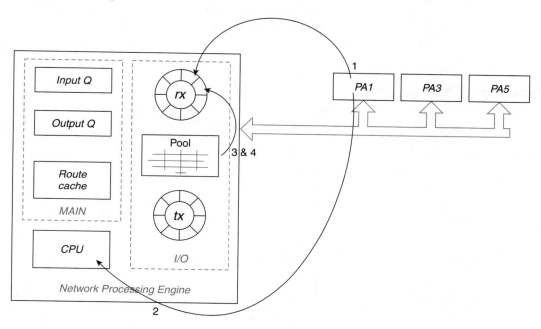

Step 1 The packet is copied from the media into a series of particles linked to the interface's receive ring. The particles can reside in either I/O memory or PCI memory depending on the platform and the interface's media speed.

Step 2 The interface raises a receive interrupt to the CPU.

Step 3 The IOS acknowledges the interrupt and begins attempting to allocate particles to replace the ones filled on the interface's receive ring. IOS checks the interface's private pool first, and then checks the public normal pool if none are in the private pool. If not enough particles exist to replenish the receive ring, the packet is dropped (the packet's particles on the receive ring are flushed) and the *no buffer* counter is incremented.

IOS also throttles the interface in this case. When an interface is throttled on the 7200, all received packets are ignored until the interface is unthrottled. IOS unthrottles the interface after the depleted particle pool is replenished with free particles.

Step 4   IOS links the packet's particles in the receive ring together, and then links them to a particle buffer header. It then replenishes the receive ring with the newly allocated particles by linking them to the ring in place of the packet's particles.

Packet Switching Stage

Now that the packet is in particles, IOS switches the packet. Figure 5-7 illustrates the process as described in the sequential list following the figure.

Figure 5-7   *Switching a Packet*

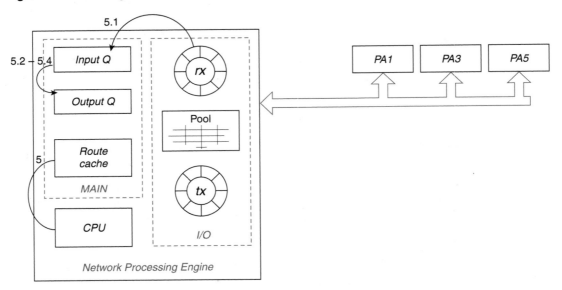

Step 5   The switching code first checks the route cache (fast or CEF) to see if it can fast switch the packet. If the packet can be switched during the interrupt, it skips to Step 6; otherwise, it continues to prepare the packet for process switching.

   5.1   The packet is coalesced into a contiguous buffer (system buffer). If no free system buffer exists to accept the packet, it's dropped and the **no buffer** counter is incremented, as indicated in the output of the **show interface** command:

```
Router#show interface
Ethernet2/1 is up, line protocol is up
....
  Output queue 0/40, 0 drops; input queue 0/75, 0 drops
   5 minute input rate 5000 bits/sec, 11 packets/sec
   5 minute output rate 0 bits/sec, 0 packets/sec
      1903171 packets input, 114715570 bytes, 1 no buffer
       Received 1901319 broadcasts, 0 runts, 0 giants, 1 throttles
....
```

If IOS can't allocate a system buffer to coalesce a particle buffer, it also throttles the interface and increments the **throttles** counter, as indicated in the preceding **show interface** command output example. All input traffic is ignored while an interface is throttled. The interface remains throttled until IOS has free system buffers available for the interface.

> **5.2** When the packet is coalesced, it is queued for process switching and the process that handles this type of packet is scheduled to run. The receive interrupt then is dismissed.
>
> **5.3** Let's assume this is an IP packet. When the IP Input process runs, it consults the routing table and discovers the outbound interface. It consults the tables associated with the outbound interface and locates the MAC header that needs to be placed on the packet (not shown in Figure 5-7).
>
> **5.4** After the packet has been switched successfully, it's copied into the output queue for the outbound interface.
>
> **5.5** From here, IOS proceeds to the transmit stage.

Step 6 The IOS switching code (fast or CEF) rewrites the MAC header in the packet for its destination (not shown in Figure 5-7). If the new MAC header is larger than the original header, IOS allocates a new particle from the F/S pool and inserts it at the beginning of the chain of particles to hold the larger header.

Packet Transmit Stage

Now you have a successfully switched packet, with its MAC header rewritten. Figure 5-8 picks up the story.

Figure 5-8   *Transmitting the Packet*

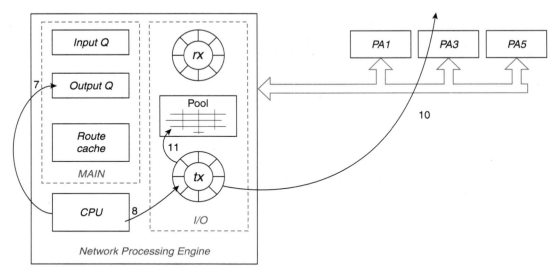

The packet transmit stage operates differently depending on whether IOS is fast switching the packet (fast or CEF) or process switching the packet. The following sections cover the packet transmit stage in the fast and process switching environments for Cisco 7200 series routers.

Packet Transmit Stage: Fast Switching and CEF

The following list describes the packet transmit stage in a fast switching environment:

Step 7   IOS first checks the interface's output queue. If the output queue is not empty or the interface's transmit ring is full, IOS queues the packet on the output queue and dismisses the receive interrupt. The packet eventually gets transmitted either when another process-switched packet arrives or when the interface issues a transmit interrupt. If the output queue is empty and the transmit ring has room, IOS continues to Step 8.

Step 8   IOS links each of the packet's particles to the interface's transmit ring and dismisses the receive interrupt.

Step 9   The interface media controller polls its transmit ring and detects a new packet to be transmitted.

Step 10 The interface media controller copies the packet from its transmit ring to the media and raises a transmit interrupt to the CPU.

Step 11 The IOS acknowledges the transmit interrupt and frees all the transmitted packet's particles from the transmit ring, returning them to their originating particle pool.

Step 12 If any packets are waiting on the interface's output queue (presumably because the transmit ring was full up until now), IOS removes the packets from the queue and links their particles or contiguous buffers to the transmit ring for the media controller to see (not shown in Figure 5-8).

Step 13 IOS dismisses the transmit interrupt.

Packet Transmit Stage: Process Switching

The following list describes the packet transmit stage in a process switching environment. Figure 5-8 does not illustrate these steps.

Step 14 IOS checks the size of the next packet on the output queue and compares it to the space left on the interface's transmit ring. If enough space exists on the transmit ring, IOS removes the packet from the output queue and links its contiguous buffer (or particles) to the transmit ring. Note, if multiple packets exist on the output queue, IOS attempts to drain the queue, putting all the packets on the interface's transmit ring.

Step 15 The interface's media controller polls its transmit ring and detects a new packet to be transmitted.

Step 16 The interface media controller copies the packet from its transmit ring to the media and raises a transmit interrupt to the CPU.

Step 17 The IOS acknowledges the transmit interrupt and frees the transmitted packet's contiguous buffer (or particles) from the transmit ring, returning them to their originating pool.

Summary

Particle buffering provides an efficient way to buffer packets of varying sizes with minimum memory waste. Since its introduction in Cisco IOS Release 11.1, particle buffering has become the de-facto Cisco IOS buffering scheme and now many new Cisco IOS-based platforms are being designed to use it.

This chapter covers the following key topics:

- Hardware Architecture of the Cisco 7500 Router
- Packet Switching on Cisco 7500 Router
- VIP Architecture
- Troubleshooting Tips for the Cisco 7500 Router

CHAPTER 6

Cisco 7500 Routers

The Cisco 7500 router platform was introduced in 1995 to address the ever-increasing demands of high performance routing driven by the explosion of the Internet and mission-critical enterprise applications. The 7500's architecture was derived from the earlier Cisco Advanced Gateway Server+ (AGS+) and Cisco 7000 architectures, but offers significant performance improvements over them. This chapter covers the hardware architecture of the 7500 series routers, the implementation-specific details of IOS switching on the 7500, and the architecture of *Versatile Interface Processors (VIPs)*.

Hardware Architecture of the Cisco 7500 Router

Figure 6-1 provides a high-level diagram of the 7500 router architecture. As you can see from this diagram, there are two components central to understanding the unique features of IOS on the 7500: the data bus and *Route Switch Processor (RSP)*.

Figure 6-1 *The 7500 Architecture*

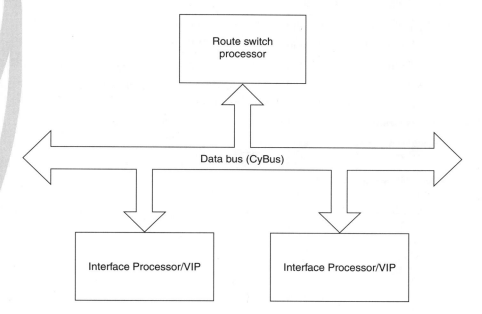

The Data Bus

The data bus in the 7500 router, like that of its predecessors (the AGS+ and 7000), is based on the proprietary Cbus architecture. The Cbus used in the 7500 is a faster version of the 7000's Cbus called the *CyBus* (the 7000's Cbus is often called the *CxBus*). Like the original Cbus, the CyBus is a 32-bit bus with 32 data lines, 8 command lines, 24 address lines, and other lines used for control operations such as bus access, acknowledging successful transactions, and error reporting.

Thirty-two lines of data might seem small in comparison to other modern buses, some of which use 128 or more data lines, but this number was chosen so older CxBus interface processors would still work when connected to a CyBus. Newer CyBus-enabled interface processors are capable of performing two transactions (two 4-byte reads) during each bus clock cycle (60 ns/16.67 MHz), while CxBus interface processors can perform only one transaction (one 4-byte read) in each clock cycle. As a result, the CyBus offers 1.066 Gbps (64 bits * 16.67 MHz) of bandwidth, effectively doubling the bandwidth offered by the 533-Mbps CxBus (32 bits * 16.67 MHz).

NOTE   When a combination of CyBus- and CxBus-capable interface processors are present on the CyBus, CyBus-capable interface processors can use the full 1.066-Gbps bandwidth. The CxBus-capable interface processors are still restricted to 533 Mbps.

There are four different router models within the 7500 family, as follows:

- **7505**—Single CyBus and five slots (one RSP slot)
- **7507**—Dual CyBus and seven slots (two RSP slots)
- **7513**—Dual CyBus and 13 slots (two RSP slots)
- **7576**—Two independent 7500 routers in the same chassis, each with dual CyBusses

A 7500's model number can be determined by executing **show environment all** on the router's console. Example 6-1 illustrates the output from a 7505 and 7507 router.

Example 6-1 **show environment all** *Command Output on 7505 and 7507 Routers*

```
7505#show environment all
Arbiter type 1, backplane type 7505 (id 1)
....
7507#show environment all
Arbiter type 1, backplane type 7507 (id 4)
....
```

Route Switch Processor

The Route Switch Processor, more commonly called the RSP, performs centralized routing and switching functions (what a surprise!). The RSP is often considered the heart of a 7500 series router because it makes switching decisions, runs routing protocols, and performs maintenance tasks.

The RSP is essentially equivalent to a combined Route Processor (RP) and Switch Processor (SP) from the Cisco 7000 router. Combining the RP and SP function on a single board eliminates the relatively slow Multibus (155 Mbps) needed on the 7000 and AGS+ to connect the RP and SP systems together. This is one of the reasons why an RSP outperforms an RP/SP so dramatically.

Table 6-1 shows the four different RSP types supported by Cisco 7500s.

Table 6-1   *Cisco 7500 Router RSP Types*

RSP	Characteristics
RSP1	MIPS R4600 or R4700 CPU; single CyBus interface; can be used only on a 7505; Max 128 MB DRAM; 2 MB MEMD
RSP2	MIPS R4600 or R4700 CPU; dual CyBus interface; can be used on a 7505, 7507, 7513, or 7576; Max 128 MB DRAM; 2 MB MEMD
RSP4	MIPS R5000 CPU; dual CyBus interface; can be used on 7507, 7513, or 7576; Max 256 MB DRAM; 2 MB MEMD
RSP8	MIPS R7000 CPU; dual CyBus interface; can be used on 7507, 7513, or 7576; Max 256 MB ECC DRAM; 8 MB MEMD

The type of RSP installed in a 7500 can be determined using **show version**, as demonstrated in Example 6-2.

Example 6-2   *Determining the RSP Type Used on a 7500 Router*

```
router#show version
cisco RSP2 (R4700) processor with 32768K/2072K bytes of memory.
R4700 CPU at 100Mhz, Implementation 33, Rev 1.0
....
```

Figure 6-2 illustrates a high level overview of the RSP.

Three of these components play a major role in how IOS—in particular, how IOS switching—operates on the 7500 router.

- CPU
- Fast packet memory (designated by MEMD)
- Main memory (designated by DRAM)

The following sections describe these components in more detail.

Figure 6-2 *A Route Switch Processor*

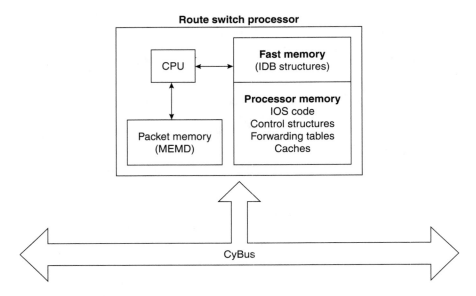

CPU

The RSP's CPU is the main processor on the 7500 router; it's responsible for running IOS and switching packets. Unlike the 7000 and AGS+, there's no separate packet switching microcode (SP microcode or Cbus controller microcode); with the exception of distributed switching, all switching decisions on the 7500 are performed in IOS running on the RSP CPU. RSPs use MIPS Reduced Instruction Set Computer (RISC) processors; the clock rate, the cache size, and the type of cache depend on the model.

Fast Packet Memory

RSP1s, RSP2s, and RSP4s have a fixed 2 MB bank of SRAM reserved for packet buffers; the RSP8 has 8MB of SDRAM reserved for packet buffers. This fast packet memory region is named *MEMD* just like the similar region in the Cisco 7000 and AGS+. The 7500's MEMD is connected to both the RSP CPU and the interface processors (via the CyBus); both have direct access to it as a shared resource.

Although MEMD is carved into pools of buffers using an algorithm similar to the one used on the Cisco 7000, some changes in the hardware allowed improvements to be made. For example, the 7500 can carve up to 3520 buffers, a vast improvement over the 7000's limit of 470. A complete description of the algorithm is beyond the scope of this book, but a simplified overview of the process follows:

Step 1   Interfaces on the router are classified into various groups based on MTU size. The range of MTU sizes accepted in each group is initially set to a variance of 256 bytes. If there are more MTU sizes than can be accommodated by four groups, the variance is doubled to 512 bytes. If there are still more than four groups, the variance is doubled again to 1024, and so on until at most four groups are defined.

Step 2   Each of the buffer pools from Step 1 gets 20 percent (360 KB) of MEMD, the remaining MEMD is then divided among the pools based on the aggregate bandwidth of all interfaces within a pool.

To illustrate the process, assume there are five interfaces on a router with MTUs of:

- 512 bytes
- 1024 bytes
- 1500 bytes
- 4096 bytes
- 16,000 bytes

IOS begins by defining five packet buffer pools:

- **poolA**—512 byte buffers, serves interfaces with MTU in the range $256 < MTU \leq 512$ bytes

- **poolB**—1024 byte buffers, serves interfaces with MTU in the range $768 < MTU \leq 1024$ bytes

- **poolC**—1500 byte buffers, serves interfaces with MTU in the range $1244 < MTU \leq 1500$ bytes

- **poolD**—4096 byte buffers, serves interfaces with MTU in the range $3840 < MTU \leq 4096$ bytes

- **poolE**—16,000 byte buffers, serves interfaces with MTU in the range $15,744 < MTU \leq 16,000$ bytes

Because there are more than four pools, the algorithm tries again using the 512 byte variance and comes up with new pool definitions:

- **poolA**—512 byte buffers, serves interfaces with MTU in the range $0 < \text{MTU} \leq 512$ bytes

- **poolB**—1500 byte buffers, serves interfaces with MTU in the range $988 < \text{MTU} \leq 1500$ bytes

- **poolC**—4096 byte buffers, serves interfaces with MTU in the range $3584 < \text{MTU} \leq 4096$ bytes

- **poolD**—16,000 byte buffers, serves interfaces with MTU in the range $15,488 < \text{MTU} \leq 16,000$ bytes

This time, all five interfaces can fit into four pools. Notice poolB now accommodates interfaces with the 1024- and 1500-byte MTUs.

It's rare there would be more than four MTU sizes on a given router, so this process generally doesn't iterate further than the first step. If there are less than four MTU sizes configured across the interfaces, IOS creates only the number of pools needed.

After the pool sizes have been decided, IOS divides MEMD into five parts, each representing 20 percent of the total memory available. One part is placed in each of the four pools, and the remaining part (20 percent) is divided among the pools based on the types and speeds of interfaces associated with each pool. There is some overhead associated with MEMD control structures—for example, some MEMD is reserved for communication between the CPU and the interface processors—so the entire 2 MB of MEMD is never available solely for packet buffers.

In the preceding example, we assumed the MEMD buffer sizes were equal to the MTU in each buffer pool for simplicity, but in practice, MEMD buffers are created slightly larger than the largest MTU accommodated by a pool. MEMD buffers must be large enough to hold the largest MTU and still have room for an encapsulation header to be added on. Beyond this, MEMD buffers must be an even multiple of 32 bytes so they align properly in the hardware memory cache for optimum performance. As a result, MEMD buffers receive a memory allocation based on the formula $size = mtu + e + n$, where mtu equals the largest MTU, e equals the largest encapsulation that can be added for the associated interface, and n is the number of filler bytes (0–31) required to make the result an even multiple of 32.

MEMD Buffer Carving and Unused Interfaces

The MEMD buffer carving algorithm does not take into account the state of an interface (that is, whether it is up or down) when deciding what size pools to create. Buffers are allocated to unused and administratively down interfaces just as if they were up and running full traffic. The rationale is those administratively down interfaces could still be turned on at a later time and require the use of MEMD resources, so they have to be taken into account. Because the presence of unused interfaces can result in thinner distribution of MEMD buffers overall, it's best to remove any unused interface processors, if possible, to make the maximum amount of MEMD available to the active interfaces.

MEMD resources are used most efficiently if all interfaces are configured for a common MTU size (typically 1500 bytes). That way, the MEMD carving algorithm creates only one buffer pool shared among all the interfaces.

The **show controller cbus** command output provides a snapshot of MEMD control structures and shows how it has been carved—invaluable information for troubleshooting. Example 6-3 shows a partial output from the command followed by descriptions of some interesting fields.

Example 6-3 **show controller cbus** *Command Output*

```
router#show controller cbus
 MEMD at 40000000, 2097152 bytes (unused 2976, recarves 4, lost 0)
 RawQ 48000100, ReturnQ 48000108, EventQ 48000110
 BufhdrQ 48000128 (2939 items), LovltrQ 48000140 (11 items, 2016 bytes)
 IpcbufQ 48000150 (16 items, 4096 bytes)
 IpcbufQ_classic 48000148 (8 items, 4096 bytes)
 3570 buffer headers (48002000 - 4800FF10)
 pool0: 9 buffers, 256 bytes, queue 48000130
 pool1: 278 buffers, 1536 bytes, queue 48000138
 pool2: 305 buffers, 4544 bytes, queue 48000158
 pool3: 4 buffers, 4576 bytes, queue 48000160
 slot1: EIP, hw 1.5, sw 20.06, ccb 5800FF30, cmdq 48000088, vps 4096
 software loaded from system
  Ethernet1/0, addr 00e0.8f6d.a820 (bia 00e0.8f6d.a820)
    gfreeq 48000138, lfreeq 48000168 (1536 bytes), throttled 015
    rxlo 4, rxhi 101, rxcurr 0, maxrxcurr 1
    txq 48000170, txacc 48000082 (value 49), txlimit 50
```

- **MEMD at 40000000, 2097152 bytes (unused 2976, recarves 4, lost 0)**—This line
  shows MEMD begins at address 0x40000000 in the CPU's memory and is 2 MB. The
  unused field reports the number of unused bytes—this is usually small (less than the
  largest MTU) and is nothing to worry about. The **recarves** field indicates the number
  of times the IOS MEMD carving algorithm has run. Several situations can cause a
  MEMD recarve, including the insertion or removal of a line card, changing the MTU
  on an interface, or a microcode reload. This field is set to 1 when the initial MEMD
  carve is run during IOS initialization.

- **RawQ 48000100, ReturnQ 48000108, EventQ 48000110**
  BufhdrQ 48000128 (2939 items), LovltrQ 48000140 (11 items, 2016 bytes)
  IpcbufQ 8000150 (16 items, 4096 bytes)
  IpcbufQ_classic 48000148 (8 items, 4096 bytes)—These lines show the memory
  addresses of various internal MEMD queue data structures. These data structures
  represent lists of MEMD buffers (actually, buffer headers, which are described in the
  following bullet), some of which are used in processing packets. Of particular interest
  is the one called *RawQ*. The RawQ, as described later in the section on packet
  switching, is used to queue all packets received by interface processors to the CPU on
  the RSP.

- **3570 buffer headers (48002000 - 4800FF10)**—This line shows the total number
  of addressable MEMD *buffer headers*. A buffer header is a control structure
  containing data about a MEMD buffer and a pointer to the actual location of the
  buffer (see Figure 6-3). Every MEMD buffer has its own unique buffer header.

Figure 6-3   *Buffer Headers*

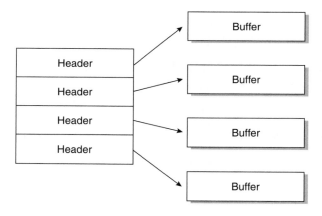

These buffer headers are a lot like labels on a soup can; they provide a quick snapshot of what's inside without having to open the can. The headers provide a convenient way for IOS to pass around descriptive information about MEMD packet buffers without having to send the buffers themselves. On the RSP there can be a total of 3570 buffer headers.

- **pool0: 9 buffers, 256 bytes, queue 48000130**
  pool1: 278 buffers, 1536 bytes, queue 48000138
  pool2: 305 buffers, 4544 bytes, queue 48000158
  pool3: 4 buffers, 4576 bytes, queue 48000160—These lines show how the available 2 MB of MEMD has been carved. The first buffer pool (**pool0**) and the last pool (**pool3** in this example) are reserved for interprocess communication between the interface processors and the RSP CPU, while the other two pools, **pool1** and **pool2**, are carved for packet buffers.

  Packets are stored in MEMD buffers based on the interface they are received on, not the size of the packet. For example, if a 64-byte packet is received on an interface with a 1500-byte MTU (1536-byte MEMD buffer size), it still is stored in a 1536-byte buffer—even if another pool exists with smaller buffers.

  If a packet arrives on an interface and there no available MEMD buffers in the interface's pool, the packet is dropped and the interface's **ignored** counter is incremented. This situation occurs even if there are buffers available in other pools. Setting all the interface MTUs to the same size results in all MEMD buffers being placed in one pool, which reduces the likelihood of a packet being dropped because the interface pool is empty.

- **slot1: EIP, hw 1.5, sw 20.06, ccb 5800FF30, cmdq 48000088, vps 4096**
  software loaded from system—This shows data about the interface processor in slot 1; each slot populated with an interface processor will have similar information displayed. An Ethernet interface processor (**EIP**) is in slot 1, its hardware version (**hw**) is 1.5, and the software version (**sw**) is 20.06. The **ccb** and **cmdq** are data structures used for communicating with the RSP.

- **Ethernet1/0, addr 00e0.8f6d.a820 (bia 00e0.8f6d.a820)**
  gfreeq 48000138, lfreeq 48000168 (1536 bytes), throttled 015
  rxlo 4, rxhi 101, rxcurr 0, maxrxcurr 1
  txq 48000170, txacc 48000082 (value 49), txlimit 50—These lines provide further information about each interface, including pointers to the locations of their various MEMD data structures:

— **gfreeq** is a pointer to the *global free queue*. The global free queue is a list of all the free MEMD buffers in a particular pool. All interfaces sharing the same MEMD buffer pool point to the same global free queue.

— **lfreeq** is a pointer to the interface's private *local free queue*. In addition to the global list of free MEMD buffers in each pool, individual interfaces can keep a local "stash" of free buffers obtained from the global pool. While all free buffers initially come from the global free queue, once an interface has used a buffer, it can keep the buffer for a short period of time. This helps prevent ignored packets when there are other busy interfaces competing for buffers in the global free pool. Unused free buffers on the local free queue are periodically returned to the global free queue for use by other interfaces.

— **rxhi** shows the maximum number of MEMD buffers a particular interface can hold at any time. This prevents one interface from holding all the free buffers in the global pool and starving other interfaces.

— **rxcurr** represents the number of buffers currently held by this interface (this counter may constantly be non-zero for a very busy interface).

— **maxrxcurr** represents the maximum number of buffers this interface has ever held since the last time MEMD was recarved—that is, it's a "high water" mark. This number should never be higher than the *rxhi* value.

— **rxlo** is always 4. This field indicates the smallest number of buffers this interface will hold in its local free queue when idle (assuming there was ever traffic on this interface).

— **txq** is a pointer to a list of buffers containing packets waiting to be transmitted out this interface. The list is called the *transmit queue* and this field is known as the *transmit queue pointer*.

— **txlimit** is the maximum number of buffers allowed on the interface's transmit queue at any time. The value in parentheses preceding this field shows the remaining number of buffers allowed on the transmit queue. In Example 6-3, the value in the parentheses is 49 and the txlimit is 50. This means that one packet is currently enqueued on the interface's transmit queue. A value of zero within the parentheses indicates no more packets can be placed on the transmit queue until some are removed.

Main Memory

Main memory on an RSP consists of up to 128 MB (256 MB on RSP4s and RSP8s) of upgradable DRAM. In general, RSP main memory contains the IOS code plus all the data structures IOS uses at runtime. Example 6-4 displays the output from **show memory summary** on a Cisco 7500 router.

Example 6-4   **show memory summary** *Command Output for 7500 Router*

```
router#show memory summary
            Head    Total(b)    Used(b)    Free(b)   Lowest(b)  Largest(b)
Processor  60AD9EE0  55730464    9405352   46325112   45891060   46251636
    Fast   60AB9EE0    131072      82168      48904      48904      48860
....
```

From this example, you can see IOS divides RSP main memory into two memory pools: *processor* and *fast.* The fast memory pool is used to store interface data structures called *interface descriptor blocks,* while the processor pool is used to store instructions, data, control structures, packet forwarding tables, system packet buffers, and the heap. Although it might appear limited, the small amount of memory in the fast memory pool is not a constraining factor; if the number of interface descriptor blocks exceeds the available fast pool, IOS simply begins using memory from the processor memory pool.

Processor memory on the 7500 platform also contains the system buffer pools, which are described in Chapter 1, "Fundamental IOS Software Architecture."

Packet Switching on the Cisco 7500 Router

IOS on the Cisco 7500 provides the most varied range of switching methods of all the platforms, including:

- Process switching
- Fast switching
- Optimum switching
- Cisco Express Forwarding (CEF)
- Distributed fast switching
- Distributed CEF (dCEF)
- NetFlow switching

Distributed Fast and Distributed CEF switching are made possible by the VIP interface processor, which is discussed later in this chapter. NetFlow switching is covered in Appendix A.

The following sections describe RSP-based switching. The description is divided into the three stages: receiving the packet, switching the packet, and transmitting the packet.

RSP Switching: Receiving the Packet

Figure 6-4 illustrates the steps of the RSP based packet receive stage; each step is described in the numbered sequence that follows.

Figure 6-4 *RSP Switching: Receiving the Packet*

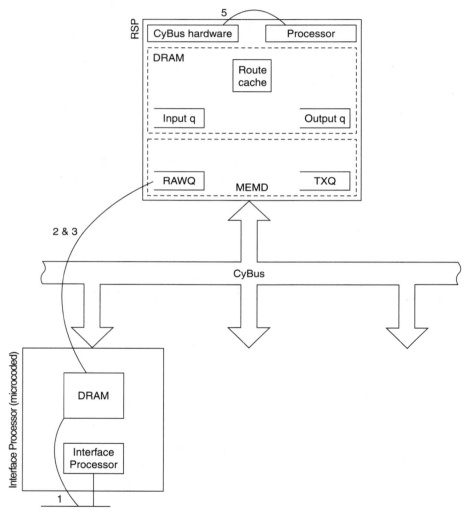

Step 1 An interface media controller detects an incoming packet and begins receiving the packet data into the interface processor's internal RAM. Microcode running on the interface processor (for example, an EIP) assembles the data into a contiguous packet in internal RAM.

Step 2 The interface processor microcode attempts to find a MEMD packet buffer for the incoming packet. First, the interface tries to obtain a MEMD buffer from its local free queue (lfreeQ). If there are no free buffers in the local free queue, the microcode attempts to obtain a MEMD buffer from the interface's assigned global free queue (gfreeQ). There are three possible outcomes:

    2.1 There might be no free MEMD buffers in the global pool, in which case the packet is dropped and the interface's **ignore** counter is incremented.

    2.2 Free buffers are available in the global pool, but the interface can't obtain any because it's already holding the maximum buffers allowed by its *rxhi* value (that is, rxcurr = rxhi). Again, in this case, the packet is dropped and the interface's **ignore** counter is incremented.

    2.3 The microcode successfully obtains a free buffer from the global free queue.

Step 3 After a free MEMD packet buffer is obtained, the microcode copies the packet data from its internal RAM across the CyBus to the MEMD buffer.

Step 4 The interface processor then enqueues the MEMD buffer header onto the Raw Queue (RawQ) for processing by the RSP.

Step 5 Special CyBus hardware detects a buffer has been placed in the RawQ and raises a network interrupt to the RSP CPU.

RSP Switching: Switching the Packet

Figure 6-5 illustrates packet switching on the RSP. The numbered list following describes each step.

Figure 6-5   *RSP Switching: Switching the Packet*

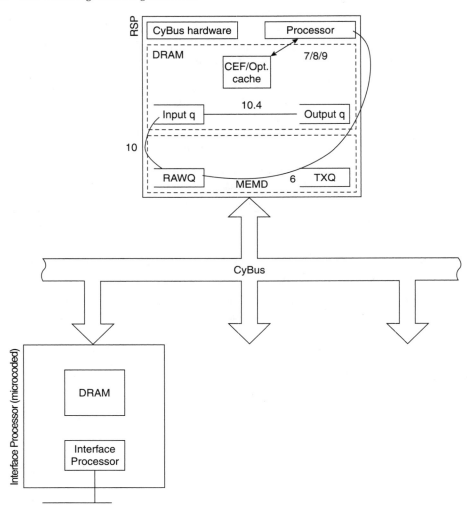

Step 6   The RSP CPU acknowledges the network interrupt. IOS begins processing the packet by removing the MEMD buffer header from the RawQ, locating the MEMD packet buffer, and inspecting the buffer's contents. Note the remainder of these steps assume IOS is processing only one packet during a network interrupt. In practice, IOS continues to process packets during an interrupt as long as there are buffer headers waiting on the RawQ. IOS now decides how the packet should be switched.

    6.1   If the contents are an IP packet and the inbound interface is configured for CEF switching, go to CEF switching.

    6.2   If the contents are an IP packet and the inbound interface is configured for optimum switching (on by default on most interfaces), then go to optimum switching. If the input interface is not configured for optimum switching, then go to fast switching.

    6.3   If the contents are an IP packet and the inbound interface is configured for NetFlow switching, then go to NetFlow switching.

    6.4   If the contents are not an IP packet, then go to fast switching by default.

Step 7   CEF switching. While still processing the network interrupt, the CPU looks through the CEF cache for the outbound interface and next hop.

    7.1   There is a valid entry in the CEF table for the destination. The packet is re-encapsulated in the same MEMD buffer, and processing continues in the transmit stage.

    7.2   The packet is destined to the router itself or is a control packet, such as a routing update. In this case, the packet is prepared for process switching (see "Process Switching" in Step 10).

    7.3   There is no matching CEF entry. In this case, the packet is dropped, the CEF drop counter is incremented, the CPU completes its interrupt processing, and the network interrupt is dismissed (this step is not illustrated in Figure 6-5).

    7.4   The CEF lookup leads to a punt adjacency. The packet is passed to fast switching. This situation occurs, for example, if the outbound interface encapsulation is not supported by CEF.

Step 8   Optimum switching. While still processing the network interrupt, the CPU looks through the optimum cache to determine which interface and next hop information to use in switching the packet.

> **8.1**   If the forwarding information is found in the optimum cache, the packet is re-encapsulated in the same MEMD buffer and processing continues in the transmit stage.
>
> **8.2**   If there is no entry in the optimum cache, the packet is passed to fast switching.

Step 9   Fast switching. While still processing the network interrupt, the CPU does a lookup of the destination IP address in the fast cache.

> **9.1**   If the cache lookup is successful, the packet is re-encapsulated in the same MEMD buffer and processing continues in the transmit stage.
>
> **9.2**   If the cache lookup is not successful or the packet is destined for the router itself, the packet is prepared for process switching (see Step 10).

Step 10 Process switching.

> **10.1** While still processing the network interrupt, the CPU looks for a free system buffer in which to copy the packet from the MEMD buffer. Process switched method packets must be copied into a system buffer in main memory because MEMD packet buffers are reserved for interrupt level packet processing only (to prevent MEMD buffer starvation).
>
> **10.1.1** *If IOS fails to get a system buffer, the **input drop** and the **no buffer** interface counters are incremented and the packet is dropped. The CPU finishes processing the interrupt and it's dismissed.*
>
> **10.1.2** *If a system buffer is available but the interface's input hold queue count is at its maximum, the interface is throttled, the **input drop** counter is incremented, and the packet is dropped. IOS finishes processing the interrupt and dismisses it. By default, interfaces are allowed to have 75 packets in input hold queues waiting to be processed.*
>
> **10.1.3** *If the CPU succeeds in obtaining a system buffer, the packet is copied from MEMD to the system buffer and the MEMD buffer is returned to the local free queue of the interface. The **input hold queue** count is incremented.*

10.2 The packet (now contained in a system buffer) is enqueued to a switching process based on its type. The CPU finishes processing the interrupt and dismisses it.

10.3 The packet is eventually switched by a background process; see Chapter 2, "Packet Switching Architecture," for more details.

10.4 After the packet has been switched, it's placed in the outbound interface's output hold queue. If the output hold queue is full (the default maximum is 40 packets), the packet is dropped and the outbound interface's **output drop** counter is incremented. If the packet is dropped, the inbound interface's **input hold queue** count will also be decremented at this point.

10.5 IOS attempts to obtain a MEMD packet buffer so the packet can be transmitted by the interface processor. IOS attempts to obtain the MEMD buffer from the outbound interface's global free list. If there are no available MEMD buffers, or the outbound interface's transmit queue is full, IOS leaves the packet on the output hold queue (in a system buffer) and tries again later to output the packet.

10.6 IOS copies the packet from the system buffer into the MEMD packet buffer. The system buffer is removed from the output hold queue, freed, and returned to the system buffer pool. The input hold queue count for the inbound interface is also decremented at this point. IOS then moves to the packet transmit stage.

RSP Switching: Transmitting the Packet

Figure 6-6 illustrates the steps of the packet transmit stage for packet switching. The numbered sequence that follows describes each step.

Figure 6-6 *RSP Switching: Transmitting the Packet*

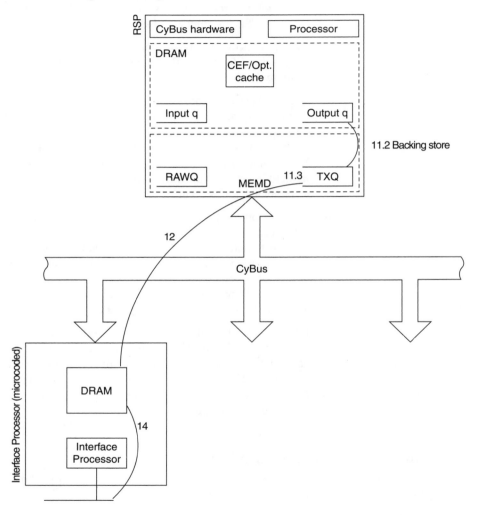

Step 11 IOS attempts to place the MEMD buffer header onto the transmit queue of the outbound interface.

> **11.1** If the outbound interface's transmit queue is full and the interface is not configured for *backing store*, the packet is dropped and the **output drop** counter is incremented.

11.2 If the outbound interface's transmit queue is full and the interface *is* configured for backing store, the packet is copied from the MEMD buffer to a system buffer and the system buffer is placed on the interface's output hold queue. The **output buffer's swapped out** counter is incremented. Note that if the outbound interface is configured for any type of fancy queueing (such as weighted fair queueing), backing store is enabled by default and cannot be disabled.

11.3 If the outbound interface's transmit queue is not full, the MEMD buffer header is placed on the queue and the value of the transmit accumulator (that is, the number of additional buffer headers that can be added to the queue) is decremented.

11.4 If IOS is still processing within a network interrupt, the CPU completes the interrupt processing and it is dismissed.

Step 12 The microcode on the outbound interface processor detects the buffer header in the transmit queue and copies the contents of the MEMD packet buffer across the CyBus into its internal RAM.

Step 13 The MEMD buffer header and buffer are freed and returned to the *inbound* interface's local free queue (lfreeq).

Step 14 The outbound interface media controller transmits the packet from the interface processor's internal RAM out to the media.

NOTE   Backing store is designed to prevent the router from dropping packets during bursts. Backing store causes packets that have already been switched to be copied to the outbound interface's output queue when the txQ for the interface is full—an extremely expensive operation. This feature should never be enabled on any interface with a bandwidth greater than 2 MBps because it can cause extreme stress on the router's CPU.

VIP Architecture

Cisco introduced the *Versatile Interface Processor* (VIP) to provide a scalable distributed architecture on top of an already proven platform. The VIP is based on a single motherboard and multiple port adapters that can have mixed media types (hence the name *versatile*).

VIP Components

VIPs are essentially routers mounted on Cisco 7500 interface processor cards. Each VIP has its own processor, packet memory, and main memory, and each runs its own copy of IOS. Figure 6-7 shows a high level architecture of the VIP.

Figure 6-7   *VIP Architecture*

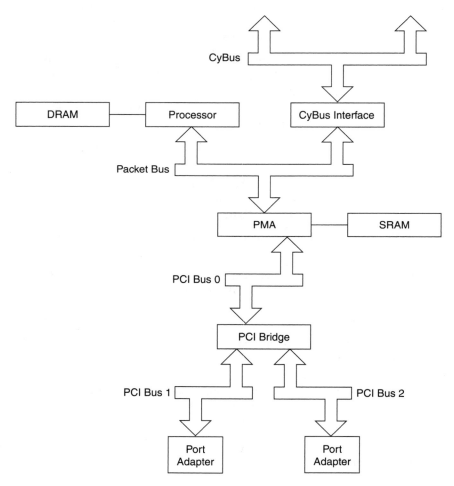

CyBus Interface

The VIP is a fully CyBus-capable interface processor, meaning it can perform two 4-byte reads in each bus clock cycle and exploit the full 1.066 Gbps bandwidth of the CyBus.

CPU

The local processor (a MIPS R4700, R5000, or R7000 CPU) on the VIP runs a special version of the IOS operating system. It's capable of performing packet switching, offloading this task from the main CPU on the RSP. The VIP IOS also supports local, advanced Layer 3 services, such as packet filtering, weighted fair queuing (WFQ), and weighted random early drop (WRED). This local packet switching and filtering capability forms the basis of the 7500's *distributed switching* architecture.

Main Memory

VIPs use upgradable dynamic RAM (DRAM) for their main memory regions. Like the main memory on the RSP, VIP main memory contains the IOS instructions, program data, switching control structures, and heap.

Packet Memory

VIPs have an upgradable bank of SRAM used for storing packet buffers and certain data structures used by the interfaces' media controllers. This bank of memory, called *packet memory*, is designed to provide high speed access to packet data, particularly for high speed interfaces.

VIP IOS divides the packet memory into pools of packet buffers used by the interfaces. Like IOS on the Cisco 7200, VIP IOS uses the particle buffer approach to provide packet buffers for interfaces.

VIPs have a fixed particle size, typically 256 bytes or 512 bytes, which applies to all interfaces on the board. The particular particle size used depends on the type of port adapters installed on the VIP. Executing the IOS command **show controller vip slot** *slot* **tech-support** displays the particle size.

Port Adapter

VIPs use the same port adapters as the Cisco 7200. Each VIP can accommodate up to two port adapters on its board, accepting either two single-wide port adapters or one double-wide port adapter. Note that VIP IOS does not support insertion or removal of the port adapters while the VIP is operating.

PCI Bus

VIPs use the CyBus to connect to the RSP, but within the VIP card PCI buses are used to connect the CPU to the port adapters, just like the 7200. A VIP has two PCI busses, bridged together, each 32 bits wide and operating at 25 Mhz, providing a theoretical bandwidth of 800 Mbps (25 MHz * 32 bits/cycle).

VIP Models

There are three VIP models available as of this writing: the VIP2-15, the VIP2-40, and the VIP2-50. The particular VIP model can be determined from the output of the **show diag** command. The VIP2-40 has an R4700 MIPS CPU, 2 MB of SRAM, and 32 MB of DRAM. The memory options on a VIP2-40 are static—they cannot be upgraded. A VIP2-50 has a R5000 MIPS CPU and can have up to 8 MB SRAM and 64 MB of DRAM.

Entering the **show diag** command on a VIP2-40 displays the output that appears in Example 6-5.

Example 6-5 **show diag** *Command Output for the VIP2-40 Model*

```
Router>show diag
Slot 2:
        Physical slot 2, ~physical slot 0xD, logical slot 2, CBus 0
        Microcode Status 0x4
        Master Enable, LED, WCS Loaded
        Board is analyzed
        Pending I/O Status: None
        EEPROM format version 1
        VIP2 controller, HW rev 2.04, board revision D0
        Serial number: 06745223   Part number: 73-1684-03
        Test history: 0x0E        RMA number: 16-96-31
        Flags: cisco 7000 board; 7500 compatible

        EEPROM contents (hex):
          0x20: 01 15 02 04 00 66 EC 87 49 06 94 03 0E 10 60 1F
          0x30: 68 00 00 00 00 00 00 00 00 00 00 00 00 00 00 00

        Slot database information:
        Flags: 0x4      Insertion time: 0x32B7F4 (3d04h ago)

        Controller Memory Size: 32 MBytes DRAM, 2048 KBytes SRAM
```

Entering the **show diag** command on a VIP2-50 displays output similar to Example 6-6.

Example 6-6 **show diag** *Command Output for the VIP2-50 Model*

```
Router>show diag
Slot 1:
        Physical slot 1, ~physical slot 0xE, logical slot 1, CBus 0
        Microcode Status 0x4
        Master Enable, LED, WCS Loaded
```

Example 6-6 **show diag** *Command Output for the VIP2-50 Model (Continued)*

```
Board is analyzed
Pending I/O Status: None
EEPROM format version 1
VIP2 R5K controller, HW rev 2.02, board revision A0
Serial number: 12345678  Part number: 73-2167-04
Test history: 0x00         RMA number: 00-00-00
Flags: cisco 7000 board; 7500 compatible

EEPROM contents (hex):
  0x20: 01 1E 02 02 00 93 63 AC 49 08 77 04 00 00 00 00
  0x30: 50 00 00 01 00 00 00 00 00 00 00 00 00 00 00 00

Slot database information:
Flags: 0x4       Insertion time: 0x14D4 (9w3d ago)

Controller Memory Size: 32 MBytes DRAM, 4096 KBytes SRAM
```

VIP Packet Operations: Distributed Switching

At their most basic level, VIPs perform the same functions other, less sophisticated, microcoded interface processors do; they assemble received packets from interface media for the RSP and transmit packets from the RSP out media interfaces. However, as mentioned previously, VIPs can also do something their microcoded predecessors cannot do. Because VIPs run IOS, they have built-in logic that allows them to make packet switching decisions—a very powerful feature. VIPs also contain hardware allowing them to use the CyBus to send data to other interface processors without involving the RSP CPU. These two capabilities make it possible for VIPs to operate like independent packet switching engines in the 7500 chassis and provide a means to distribute the packet switching work to multiple CPU's in the router. This concept is the basis of the IOS *distributed switching* feature.

To understand how distributed switching works, the following sections examine the three packet operation stages within the context of the VIP IOS—receiving the packet, switching the packet, and transmitting the packet.

Distributed Switching: Receiving the Packet

Figure 6-8 illustrates the steps of the packet receive and packet switching stages for distributed switching. Each step is described in the numbered list that follows.

Figure 6-8 *Distributed Switching: Receiving the Packet*

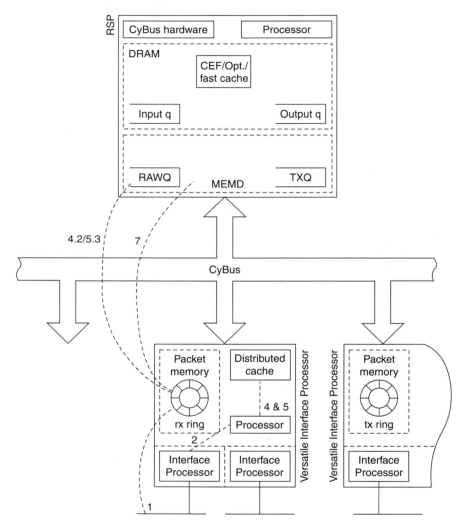

Step 1 An interface's media controller (on a port adapter) detects an incoming packet on the media. The media controller receives the packet into one or more free particle buffers held within its local receive area in packet memory (called a *receive ring*).

Step 2   The media controller raises a network interrupt to the VIP CPU. The VIP CPU acknowledges the interrupt and VIP IOS begins interrupt processing by calling on packet receive processing for the interrupting interface.

Step 3   Packet receive processing logic attempts to take the packet's particle buffers from the receive ring and replace them with empty particle buffers acquired from the global particle buffer pool (this step is not shown in Figure 6-8).

> **3.1**   If there aren't sufficient empty particle buffers in the global pool to replace the ones in the receive ring, the packet is dropped and the interface's **ignore** counter is incremented. The packet's particle buffers are left in the receive ring and are marked as free to be reused by a later packet.

> **3.2**   If the receive processing logic successfully replenishes the receive ring, it continues by inspecting the particle buffer's contents to determine the packet type.

> **3.2.1**   *If the received packet is an IP packet, then go to distributed switching (distributed optimum or distributed CEF).*

> **3.2.2**   *If the packet is not an IP packet, then distributed switching is not supported. The packet is passed to the RSP in MEMD via the CyBus using the same procedure as the microcoded interface processors. VIP IOS then finishes the interrupt processing and the VIP CPU dismisses the network interrupt.*

Distributed Switching: Switching the Packet

Figure 6-8 also shows the steps in the packet switching stage for distributed switching. All distributed switching decisions are made by the VIP CPU. The following steps describe the distributed packet switching stage.

Step 4   Distributed Optimum Switching. A full copy of the optimum switching cache from the RSP is kept in the VIP's main memory so switching decisions can be made by the VIP CPU. The RSP cache and the distributed cache are kept in sync by messages between the two CPUs. While still processing the network interrupt, VIP IOS looks for forwarding information in the local optimum cache.

4.1 If the information needed to switch the packet is found in the local optimum cache, the packet is encapsulated with the new MAC information and the packet is passed to the packet transmit stage.

4.2 If the information needed to switch the packet is not found in the local optimum cache, the packet is passed to the RSP in MEMD via the CyBus using the same procedure as the microcoded interface processors. VIP IOS then finishes the interrupt processing and the VIP CPU dismisses the network interrupt.

Step 5 Distributed CEF switching. A copy of the CEF table and the adjacency table from the RSP are kept in the VIP's local main memory so the VIP CPU can CEF switch incoming packets. Messages passed between the RSP CPU and the VIP CPU keep the master tables on the RSP and the slave tables on the VIP in sync. While still processing the network interrupt, the VIP IOS searches the CEF table for the information needed to switch the packet.

5.1 If the information needed to switch the packet is found in the local CEF table, the packet is re-encapsulated and is passed to the packet transmit stage.

5.2 If searching the local CEF table fails to produce the information needed to switch the packet, the packet is dropped. VIP IOS finishes interrupt processing and the VIP CPU dismisses the network interrupt.

5.3 If the results of the CEF search result in a punt or receive adjacency, the packet is passed to the RSP in MEMD via the CyBus using the same procedure as the microcoded interface processors. VIP IOS then finishes the interrupt processing and the VIP CPU dismisses the network interrupt.

Distributed Switching: Transmitting the Packet

Figure 6-9 illustrates the steps of the packet transmit stage for distributed switching. Each step is described in the numbered list that follows.

Figure 6-9 *Distributed Switching: Packet Transmit Stage*

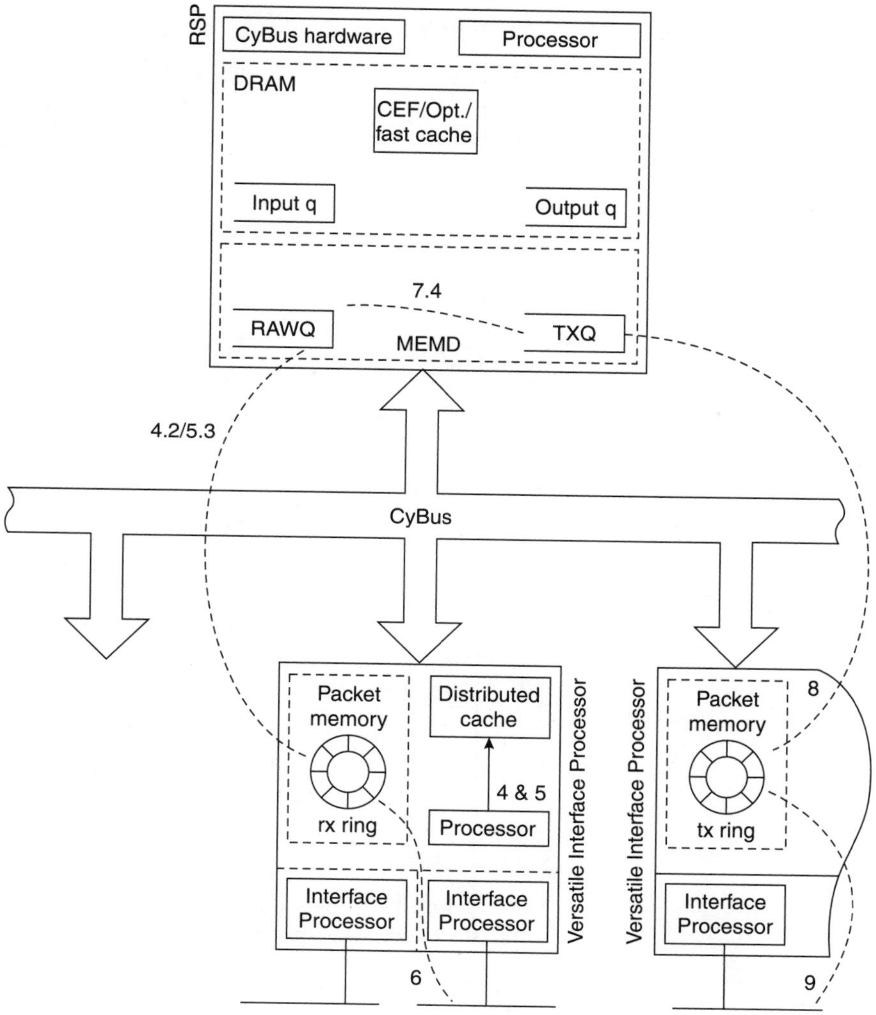

Step 6 If the packet is destined for an interface on the same VIP, it can be transmitted locally and never needs to cross the CyBus.

    6.1 The software running on the VIP places the packet's particle buffers in the local transmit area (called the *transmit ring*) for the outbound interface. VIP IOS finishes interrupt processing and the VIP CPU dismisses the network interrupt.

6.2 The outbound interface's media controller (on the port adapter) transmits the packet data from its transmit ring onto the media.

6.3 When the media controller completes transmitting the packet, it marks the packet's particle buffers as empty and notifies the VIP IOS (via another CPU interrupt) that the particles have been freed and might be returned to the global particle pool.

Step 7 If the packet is destined for an interface on some other interface processor, the VIP IOS transfers the packet to the other interface processor via MEMD across the CyBus.

7.1 VIP IOS attempts to obtain a free MEMD buffer, first from its local free queue and then from the global free queue.

7.2 If there are no MEMD buffers available, VIP IOS tries to hold the packet temporarily in packet memory rather than drop it (see the section, "VIP Receive Side Buffering"). Similarly, if the outbound interface's MEMD transmit queue is full, VIP IOS also tries to hold the packet temporarily in packet memory.

7.3 If VIP IOS succeeds in obtaining a MEMD buffer, it copies the packet data from the particle buffers into the MEMD buffer across the CyBus.

7.4 The MEMD buffer header for the packet is then placed directly on the outbound interface's transmit queue. The RSP's CPU is never interrupted during this process; it continues doing background processes, handling process switched traffic, maintaining the routing table, and so on.

7.5 VIP IOS finishes processing the interrupt and the VIP CPU dismisses the network interrupt.

Step 8 The outbound interface can be on a legacy interface processor or on another VIP. In either case, the outbound interface processor code detects a packet in the outbound transmit queue and copies the contents of the MEMD packet buffer across the CyBus into its internal memory.

Step 9 The outbound interface media controller transmits the packet from the interface processor's memory out to the media.

VIP Receive Side Buffering

Cisco 7500 interface processors, including the VIP, do not have the capability to directly access each other's internal memory. They only have access to their own internal memory and the RSP's MEMD memory. Because MEMD is the only common memory resource, every packet that passes from one interface processor to another over the CyBus must pass through an RSP MEMD packet buffer. MEMD, however, is a limited resource. So there is no guarantee a MEMD packet buffer will always be available when a VIP wants to transfer a packet to another interface processor.

In cases where the VIP is distributed switching a packet and no MEMD buffer is available, VIP IOS has the capability to buffer a received packet locally through a process called *receive side buffering*. Receive side buffering helps to reduce packet drops on the VIP by utilizing the packet memory on the VIP to temporarily hold packets that would otherwise be dropped due to lack of MEMD resources or a full transmit queue. It is particularly useful in situations where bursts of packets are received on a fast VIP interface and are destined for a slower interface on another interface processor.

With receive side buffering, VIP IOS creates an internal queue for every outbound interface requiring packet buffering. The size of each queue is derived from the configured bandwidth of the associated interface. At most, one second's worth of packets can be held on each queue.

You can display receive side buffering statistics by the IOS **show controller vip accumulator** command, as demonstrated in Example 6-7.

Example 6-7   **show controller vip accumulator** *Command Output*

```
Router#show controller vip 2 accumulator
Buffered RX packets by accumulator:
 Forward queue 0 : 573 in, 0 drops (0 paks, 0 bufs)
1 FastEthernet1/0:
2  MEMD txacc 0x0082: 4500 in, 300 drops (0 paks, 0/24414/24414 bufs) 100000kbps
3  No MEMD acc: 4500 in, 300 limit drops, 0 no buffer
4  No MEMD buf: 0 in, 0 limit drops, 0 no buffer
ATM2/0/0:
 local txacc 0x1A02: 0 in, 0 drops (0 paks, 0/37968/37968 bufs) 155520kbps
```

The set of lines numbered 1 through 4 constitutes the set of receive side buffering statistics for a particular outbound interface. These lines are repeated for each outbound interface.

In Example 6-7, line 2 indicates that a total of 4500 packets destined for FastEthernet1/0 were buffered in packet memory and 300 packets were dropped. There are currently 0 packets in the receive side buffer queue and a maximum of 24,414 packets will be buffered. This maximum number of buffers is the number of buffers needed to buffer one second's worth of traffic destined out the transmit interface. This can be expressed by the formula:

Max buffers = (Transmit interface bandwidth in bps/8) / particle size

In this example, bandwidth is 100 MB and the particle size is 512 bytes.

Line 3 indicates that all the packets counted as buffered in line 2 (4500 total) were buffered due to a transmit queue full condition (**No MEMD acc**). The 300 dropped packets occurred for the same reason. Note that if you see a non-zero **no buffer** drops counter on this line, it means there was insufficient packet memory resources to perform receive side buffering. This could indicate a shortage of packet memory (SRAM) on the VIP. Line 4 indicates there were no packets buffered due to lack of available MEMD packet buffers (**No MEMD buf**).

Troubleshooting Tips for the Cisco 7500 Router

This section provides information on how to troubleshoot common problems involving IOS on the Cisco 7500 platform. Some of these common scenarios include high CPU utilization, input drops, ignores, and output drops.

High CPU Utilization

Example 6-8 shows a portion of the output from the IOS **show process cpu** command on a router that is experiencing high CPU utilization.

Example 6-8 **show process cpu** *Command Output Revealing High CPU Utilization*

```
Router#show process cpu
CPU utilization for five seconds: 90%/80%; one minute: 60%; five minutes: 40% PID
Runtime(ms)  Invoked   uSecs    5Sec    1Min   5Min TTY Process
      1         1356   2991560       0   0.00%  0.00%  0.00%   0 BGP Router
      2       100804      7374   13670   0.00%  0.02%  0.00%   0 Check heaps
      3            0         1       0   0.00%  0.00%  0.00%   0 Pool Manager
      4            0         2       0   0.00%  0.00%  0.00%   0 Timers
      5         6044     41511000    0.00%  0.00%  0.00%   0 OIR Handler
      6            0         1       0   0.00%  0.00%  0.00%   0 IPC Zone Manager
      7            0         1       0   0.00%  0.00%  0.00%   0 IPC Realm Manager
      6         7700     36331     211      8%  0.00%  0.00%   0 IP Input
```

Example 6-8 shows that for the last 5 seconds, the average CPU utilization was 90 percent of the total CPU capacity and 80 percent of the total CPU capacity (88.8 percent of the CPU busy time) was spent processing interrupts. Furthermore, the rolling averages for 1 minute and 5 minutes are 60 percent utilization and 40 percent utilization, respectively. Because the largest utilization percentage is contributed by interrupt processing and the long-term utilization indicators are more moderate, it's quite possible that this router is just receiving large bursts of packets to switch.

It is also worth noting, however, that on 7500 routers and others that use the MIPS CPU's, interrupt processing CPU utilization can also run higher than normal due to an error called an *alignment error*. Alignment errors occur when the program running on the CPU attempts to access a memory value at an address that violates the memory alignment requirements of the CPU. On MIPS CPUs, 16-bit values must begin at a memory address divisible by 2, 32-bit values must begin at a memory address divisible by 4, and so on. If IOS attempts to access data at an address that violates these restrictions, the CPU generates an *exception* (basically an error) and calls a special IOS function that retrieves the data in segments that don't violate the restrictions. This exception function adds many more instructions and more CPU time to an otherwise simple operation of accessing a data item. For this reason, alignment errors can have a significant negative impact on performance by consuming extra CPU cycles. All IOS alignment errors are logged and can be inspected by issuing the IOS **show align** CLI command.

Consistently high CPU utilization by processes should be investigated to find out which process or processes are consuming the CPU. From the **show process cpu** output, it's easy to find out which processes are the biggest CPU users. Process names are fairly intuitive. For example, the IP Input process is responsible for processing all IP packets at process-level. If you see high CPU by IP Input, this likely means many of the IP packets coming into the router are taking the process switched path. A useful command to determine if the IP packets coming into the router are indeed being process switched is the **show interface stat** command, as demonstrated in Example 6-9.

Example 6-9   **show interface stat** *Command Output to Determine Packet Switching Path*

```
Router#sh int stat
POS8/1/0
            Switching path    Pkts In     Chars In    Pkts Out   Chars Out
                 Processor          2         4498       15586    23285531
               Route cache          0            0           0           0
         Distributed cache      60448     57737596       30772     1357152
                     Total      60450     57742094       46358    24642683
```

The following list highlights the columns in the output from Example 6-9 that you should monitor to determine packet traffic on a given router interface:

- **Pkts In**—The number of packets that came in the interface and the switching path they took. Example 6-9 shows that a total of 60,450 packets arrived into the interface POS8/1/0, two of those packets went to process-level, 0 took the fast/optimum/CEF path, and 60,448 packets that came in were distribute switched.

- **Chars In**—The number of bytes that arrived into the interface. Chars In/Pkts In can give an estimate of the average packet size of the packets that come into the interface.

- **Pkts Out**—The number of packets transmitted on this interface and the switching path they took. The packets transmitted out an interface might have arrived from many interfaces. Example 6-9 shows that a total of 15,586 packets that were transmitted out POS8/1/0 were process-switched and 30,772 packets took the distribute switched path.

The majority of packets received on any interface should be switched by the fastest switching method supported on the interface. Control packets (for example, routing updates or keepalives) and packets destined to the router are accounted as *process switched* inbound. When interpreting the output of the **show interface stat** command, remember packets received in an interface typically are transmitted out another interface and packets transmitted out an interface came in on another interface. Therefore, look at the **show interface stat** command for all interfaces to get an estimate of the overall traffic flow.

The following are some common reasons for high CPU (this list is by no means comprehensive):

- **Configuration**—Make sure all interfaces are configured for the fastest switching mode available.

- **Broadcast Storm**—All broadcast packets are sent to the process level for switching, so a broadcast storm can strain a router's CPU. A broadcast storm can occur due to a layer 2 issue (for example, Spanning Tree) or misconfigured hosts.

- **Denial of Service attack**—This is a very broad category. The *ping attack* is a common one where a malicious user can send a high stream of ping packets destined to the router. Make sure access lists are configured to prevent this. Committed access rate (CAR) is a rate-limiting feature that can also be used. Refer to the Cisco IOS documentation for more information on how to configure CAR.

- **Routing loop**—A routing loop can cause IP packets to terminate on the router because their TTL expires while looping. A constantly increasing *bad hop count* counter in the output of **show ip traffic** reflects this condition.

Input Drops

On the 75*xx* platform, the *input drop* counter in the **show interface** output is only incremented when packets destined to the process switched path are dropped. Some input drops are to be expected. However, the ratio of input drops to the total packets input is the important statistic. Although it is difficult to say when to start worrying about input drops, degrading network performance is usually a sign that it's time to begin looking at the number of input drops.

The default input hold queue size is 75. However, increasing it to a higher number might not be the solution. The root cause of why packets are going to process switching must be investigated. Some of the same reasons listed for high CPU utilization could also be responsible for input drops. If the *no buffer* counter in the **show interface** output is also incrementing along with input drops, it's an indication of buffer starvation—not enough buffers are available to accommodate the packets. The IOS **show buffers** command can be a useful tool to determine which buffer pool is being exhausted.

Ignores

An increasing *ignore* counter in the **show interface** output is indicative of a MEMD buffer shortage. Network traffic bursts can also contribute to ignores. Like input drops, the ratio of ignores to the total packet input count is the important metric, not the number of ignores alone.

Packets received on a high-speed interface and transmitted on a slow interface can also contribute to ignored packets. With this scenario, MEMD buffers from the input interface's pool can be tied up for long periods of time waiting on the transmit queue of the slow interface. This condition deprives other interfaces of buffers that use the same pool. One possible solution is to configure all the interfaces on the router for the same MTU size. With a common MTU size, there is one large MEMD buffer pool that all interfaces can draw upon, potentially providing more buffers. Configuring VIP-based interfaces for distributed switching, which allows receive side buffering, can also help alleviate ignores.

Output Drops

The *output drop* counter in the **show interface** output can be incremented for the following reasons:

- **Process switching**—A packet cannot be enqueued on the output hold queue because the hold queue is full.

- **Fast switching**—A packet cannot be enqueued on the interface's transmit queue because the transmit queue is full. The instantaneous value of an interface's transmit queue can be seen in the output of the **show controller cbus** command. A consistently low value indicates that the transmit queue is congested.

Increasing the output hold-queue limit won't help reduce output drops if the majority of packets are being dropped by fast switching. Like other drop counters, some output drops are to be expected. The absolute number of drops is not as important as the ratio of output drops to total packets output.

Summary

This chapter discusses the hardware architecture of the Cisco 7500 series routers. The 7500 router architecture has a 1-Gbps data bus known as the CyBus. The central CPU on the RSP supports fast, optimum, and process switching methods. The VIP architecture distributes the packet switching operations to the VIP CPU scaling the 7500 architecture.

This chapter covers the following key topics:

- Hardware architecture of the Cisco 12000 series routers
- Packet switching paths on the Cisco 12000 series routers

CHAPTER 7

The Cisco Gigabit Switch Router: 12000

When businesses began seeing the value of the Internet in the early 1990s, an explosion in growth began that eventually took its toll on the Internet's backbone routers—mostly Cisco 7500s. The traffic explosion was paralleled by an increasing demand for reliability, as people began using the World Wide Web and e-mail as ways of doing business.

To meet these traffic and reliability demands, Cisco developed the Gigabit Switch Router (GSR)—the Cisco 12000 series.

Hardware Architecture

The GSR is available in three configurations:

- **12008**—8-slot chassis with a 40-Gbps switch fabric.
- **12012**—12-slot chassis with a 60-Gbps switch fabric.
- **12016**—16-slot chassis with an 80-Gbps switch fabric that can be upgraded to 320 Gbps.

Figure 7-1 shows a high level overview of the Cisco 12000.

The following lists the most important components of the Cisco 12000 architecture:

- Switching Fabric
- Maintenance Bus (MBUS)
- Route Processor
- Line Cards

Figure 7-1 *Cisco 1200 Architecture*

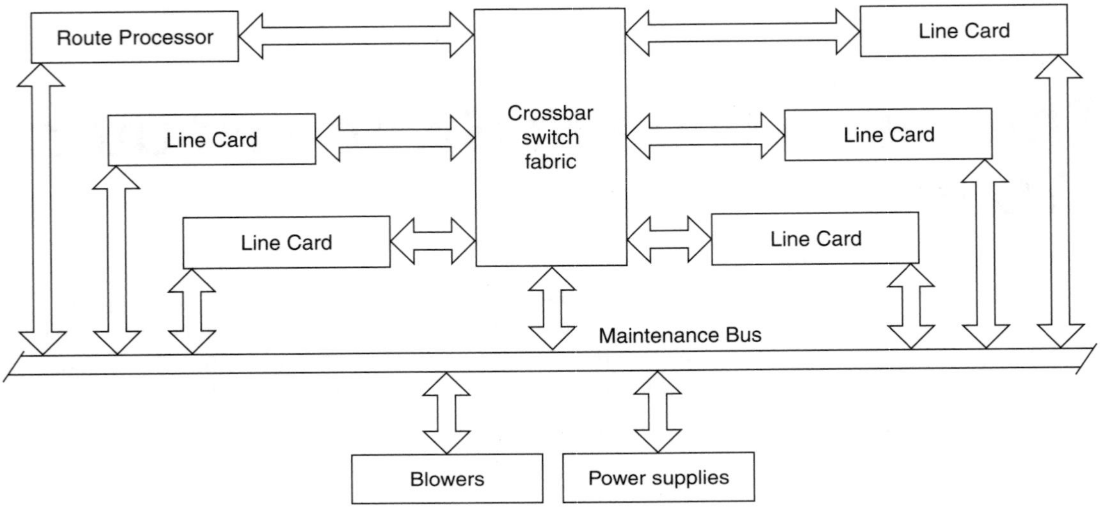

Switching Fabric

All the Cisco router platforms discussed in this book so far are based on a shared bus architecture. The following items limit bus-based systems:

- **Arbitration Overhead**—Each time a Line Card (LC) wants to transmit onto a shared bus, it must enter into an arbitration phase that determines when it can transmit.

- **Single Card Transmission**—Only one LC can transmit onto the bus at any given time. No matter how many cards are in the system, only one card can transmit, and only one can receive, at any time.

The speed of a bus can be increased, within practical limits, by increasing the amount of data that can be transmitted at once (the *width* of the bus) and by increasing the speed at which the bus operates.

Shared memory architectures can be much faster. As you increase the speed of a shared memory system, you run into two scalability limits:

- Excessive overhead required to ensure no two processes write to the same shared memory location at the same time

- Physical limitations of memory speed

The Cisco 12000 eliminates both problems by using a crossbar switching fabric as its backplane. A crossbar is essentially 2N busses (where *N* is the number of LCs connected to the switching fabric), connected by N*N *crosspoints*. Figure 7-2 illustrates the basic concept. If one of the crosspoints is on, the two LCs connected through that crosspoint are connected and can communicate with one another.

Figure 7-2   *Crossbar Switching Fabric*

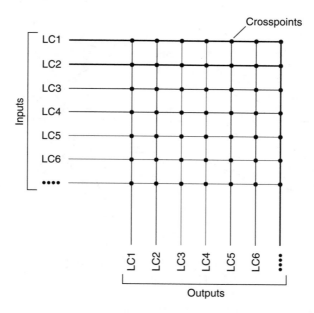

Although this crossbar switching fabric allows multiple LCs to transmit and receive data simultaneously, it's still possible (in fact, probable) that two cards might want to transmit data to a single outbound card at the same time. To resolve such conflicts, a scheduler is responsible for selecting which LCs transmit and which LCs receive during any given fabric cycle.

NOTE   The Cisco 12000 scheduler algorithm is based on a design from Stanford University. You can find a detailed description of switch fabric architectures in the paper, "Fast Switched Backplane for a Gigabit Switched Router," by Nick McKeown of Stanford University. You can find this paper on CCO at www.cisco.com/warp/public/cc/cisco/mkt/core/12000/tech/fasts_wp.pdf.

Physically, the Cisco 12000's switching fabric consists of up to five switch fabric cards. Two types of switch fabric cards exist in the system: the Clock Scheduler card (CSC) and the Switch Fabric Card (SFC). The CSC is a superset of the SFC.

Figure 7-3   *Cisco 12000 Switching Fabric*

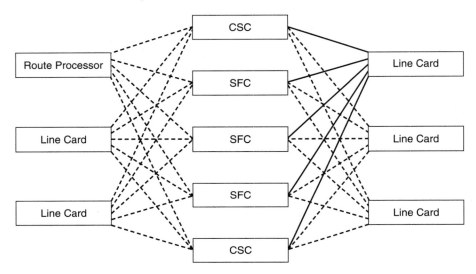

The CSC and SFC both contain crossbar ASICs, which provide 1.25 Gb/s full duplex bandwidth per slot. The CSC also contains a scheduler ASIC, which grants Line Cards access to the fabric, and a clock, which provides a reference clock for all other cards in the system. Each system must have at least one working CSC; if two are installed, the second CSC provides clock and scheduler redundancy.

The output of the command, **show controller fia**, displays the active CSC, as demonstrated in Example 7-1.

Example 7-1   **show controller fia** *Displays the Active CSC*

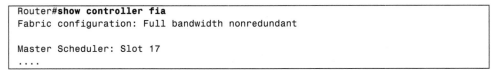

```
Router#show controller fia
Fabric configuration: Full bandwidth nonredundant

Master Scheduler: Slot 17
....
```

Example 7-1 shows that the active CSC is in slot 17. The following section explains the meaning of fabric configuration (full bandwidth as shown in Example 7-1). This example also shows that there is only one CSC in the system because the fabric configuration is *nonredundant*.

Switch Fabric Bandwidth

The GSR switch fabric can run in two modes:

- Full bandwidth
- Quarter bandwidth

To figure out the bandwidth provided by the switching fabric in any given configuration, you have to keep in mind that each switching card provides 1.25-Gbps full-duplex bandwidth *per slot*. In full bandwidth mode, there are five fabric cards—two CSCs and three SFCs. Recall that the second CSC is in standby mode and provides clock and scheduler redundancy; therefore, only four of the switching cards are actually used to pass data across the fabric, so you would multiply 4 by 1.25 Gbps per switching card, and then multiply this result by the number of Line Cards installed (the maximum number depends on the platform).

Table 7-1 documents the calculations to determine the total switch fabric bandwidth supported on each GSR configuration in full bandwidth mode.

Table 7-1   *Determining Total Switch Fabric Bandwidth by GSR Configuration in Full Bandwidth Mode*

GSR Configuration	Calculation	Total Switch Fabric Bandwidth Supported
12008	1.25 Gbps * 4 switching cards * 8 slots	40 Gbps
12012	1.25 Gbps * 4 switching cards * 12 slots	60 Gbps
12016	1.25 Gbps * 4 switching cards * 16 slots	80 Gbps

Note that in Figure 7-3, each Line Card connects to each switching card. In this configuration, traffic originating at a Line Card is segmented into equal size packets (64 bytes), divided into four 16-byte slices, and transmitted in parallel across the four connections to the switch cards. The fifth, redundant data path carries a CRC for the four slices to make possible error detection and some error recovery. If one of the four connections fails, the redundant data path is activated automatically with little or no loss of data. The unit of transfer across the switching fabric is always equal-size packets, also referred to as *Cisco cells*. This is covered in more detail in a later section in this chapter.

A *quarter bandwidth* configuration supports 1.25-Gbps full-duplex bandwidth per slot. Table 7-2 documents the calculations to determine the total switching fabric bandwidth for each configuration in quarter bandwidth mode.

Table 7-2   *Determining Total Switch Fabric Bandwidth by GSR Configuration in Quarter Bandwidth Mode*

GSR Configuration	Calculation	Total Switch Fabric Bandwidth Supported
12008	1.25 Gbps * 8 slots	10 Gbps
12012	1.25 Gbps * 12 slots	15 Gbps
12016	1.25 Gbps * 16 slots	20 Gbps

In the quarter bandwidth fabric configuration, traffic originating at a Line Card is segmented into equal-size cells, and then is sent on the only available connection to the active CSC.

NOTE   It's strongly recommended that you configure Cisco 12000s in full-bandwidth mode with redundancy. In fact, if the system has a high speed interface installed, such as a Gigabyte Ethernet, Fast Ethernet, DPT, OC-48/STM-16, or 4xOC12, full bandwidth mode is *mandatory*. Also note that the switching fabric offers bandwidth in only two modes— quarter or full—there is no half or three-quarter fabric bandwidth mode. Also, Cisco does not sell the quarter bandwidth mode.

The output of **show controller fia** (shown earlier in Example 7-1) displays the switch fabric mode in the system. In this example, the switch fabric is non-redundant, which means there is only one CSC in the system.

NOTE   The 12016 can be upgraded to an enhanced switch fabric based on a 64 x 64 crossbar that can provide up to 5-Gbps full-duplex bandwidth per switch fabric card per slot. The enhanced switch fabric in a full bandwidth mode provides 20 Gbps (5 Gbps * 4) bandwidth per slot, which is needed to support an OC-192 Line Card. The enhanced switch fabric is not available as of this writing.

Head of Line Blocking

Head of Line Blocking (HoLB) can severely reduce the throughput of a crossbar switch. Figure 7-4 illustrates HoLB.

Figure 7-4   *Head of Line Blocking*

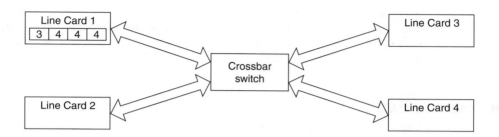

Figure 7-4 shows four different Line Cards connected via a crossbar switch; the packets are labeled according to the LC for which they are destined. The one packet destined to LC 3 cannot be transmitted until the three packets destined to LC 4 are switched through the crossbar switch. This phenomenon, where packets or cells can be held up by packets or cells ahead of them that are destined for a different output, is called Head of Line Blocking.

The GSR solves the HoLB problem by using *virtual output queues*, as shown in Figure 7-5.

Figure 7-5   *Virtual Output Queues*

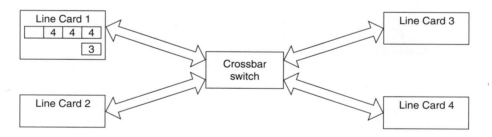

Packets or cells destined to each Line Card are placed in a separate queue called the *virtual output queue*, which eliminates the HoLB problem. These queues are FIFO by default but Modified Deficit Round Robin (MDRR) and Weighted Random Early Detection (WRED) both can be used on these queues to provide quality of service across the Cisco 12000's switching fabric; these QoS mechanisms are covered in more detail in Chapter 8, "Quality of Service."

Cisco Cells

The unit of transfer across the crossbar switch fabric is always fixed size packets, also referred to as Cisco cells, which are easier to schedule than variable size packets. Packets are broken into cells before being placed on the fabric, and are reassembled by the outbound LC before they are transmitted. Cisco cells are 64 bytes long, with an 8-byte header, a 48-byte payload, and an 8-byte CRC.

Maintenance Bus

The Maintenance Bus (MBUS) is a 1-Mbps serial bus that connects the Route Processor, the Line Cards, the switch fabric cards, the power supplies, and the fans. The MBUS, as the name suggests, is used for maintenance of the system. When the router boots, the Route Processor uses the MBUS to discover other cards in the system; to boot the Line Cards; and to gather revision numbers, environmental information, and general maintenance information. Data traffic never traverses the MBUS—data traffic always goes across the switching fabric and the MBUS is purely for managing components within the box.

Gigabit Route Processor

The Gigabit Route Processor, more commonly called the GRP, is the brain of the system. The GRP runs routing protocols, computes the forwarding table, builds the CEF and adjacency tables, and distributes them to all the Line Cards in the system via the switch fabric. Figure 7-6 shows the important components on the GRP, as described in the following list:

Figure 7-6   *Route Processor*

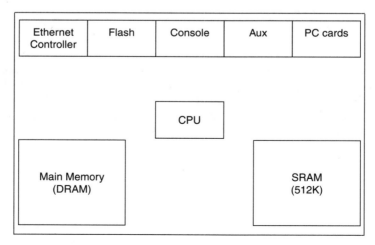

- **CPU**—The CPU on the GRP is the same R5000 processor used on the Cisco 7500's RSP4. The CPU is responsible primarily for running routing protocols and for maintaining a master copy of the CEF table for download to the Line Cards, which do the packet switching.

- **Main Memory (DRAM)**—Up to 256 MB used for storing IOS code and all data structures.

- **CSAR SRAM**—512 KB; this memory is used for reassembling cells arriving from the switching fabric into packets.

- **Ethernet Controller**—Designed for out-of-band management; traffic should not be switched between this port and ports on the LCs.

Line Card

Most packet switching occurs on Line Cards (LCs) in a Cisco GSR. The Line Card architecture can be broken into three sections:

- **Physical layer interface module (PLIM)**—The PLIM is the media-specific hardware module (ATM, POS, Fast Ethernet) that terminates the physical connection.

- **Switch Fabric Interface**—The Switch Fabric Interface prepares packets for transmission across the switching fabric to the destination LC.

- **Packet forwarding engine**—The packet forwarding engine switches packets. As of this writing, three types of packet forwarding engines exist; namely, engines 0, 1, and 2. Line Cards available as of this writing are classified by the packet forwarding engine type described in Table 7-3. Engine 0 was the first packet switching engine on the early GSR LCs, engine 1 LCs have some enhancements to improve packet switching performance, and engine 2 LCs further enhance packet forwarding performance and enable QoS features in hardware.

Table 7-3   *Classification of GSR Line Cards by Engine*

GSR Line Card	Engine 0	Engine 1	Engine 2
OC-12 PoS	X		
4xOC-3 PoS	X		
Channelized OC-12 to DS-3	X		
OC-12 ATM	X		
6- and 12-Port DS-3	X		
Time to Market (TTM) OC-48 PoS		X	
TTM 4 x OC-12 PoS		X	
1 x Gigabit (GE)		X	

continues

Table 7-3   *Classification of GSR Line Cards by Engine (Continued)*

GSR Line Card	Engine 0	Engine 1	Engine 2
8 x Fast Ethernet (FE)		X	
1 x OC-12 DPT		X	
Enhanced OC-48 PoS			X
Enhanced 4 x OC-12 PoS			X

The first two sections of the LC architecture are self-explanatory. The packet forwarding engine is the heart of the LC, and discussed in detail in the following section.

Packet Forwarding Engines

Three types of packet forwarding engines are available (engines 0, 1, and 2) as of this writing and a detailed description of each follows. Figure 7-7 illustrates the key components of the engine 0 and the engine 1 Line Cards.

Elements common to all engines include main memory and packet memory (receive and transmit), as described in the following sections.

Main Memory

Up to 265 MB of DRAM is used for storing the LCs IOS code and associated data structures, such as the CEF and Adjacency tables.

Figure 7-7 *Engine 0 and Engine 1 Packet Forwarding Engine*

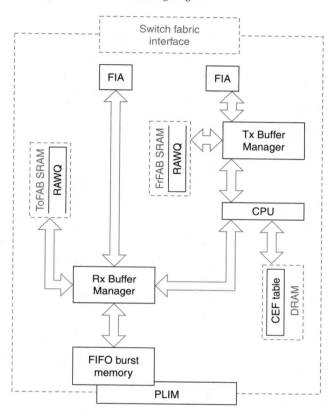

Packet Memory

Each LC can have up to 256 MB of SRAM (128 MB on engine 0 LCs), equally divided into receive and transmit packet memory. The output of **show diag** displays the amount of receive and transmit packet memory on the LC, as demonstrated in Example 7-2.

Example 7-2 **show diag** *Displays the Amount of Receive and Transmit Packet Memory*

```
Router#show diag 1
SLOT 1  (RP/LC 1 ): 4 Port Packet Over SONET OC-3c/STM-1 Multi Mode
....
FrFab SDRAM size: 67108864 bytes
ToFab SDRAM size: 67108864 bytes
....
```

The following list describes what Example 7-2 reveals about transmit and receive packet memory:

- **FrFab SDRAM**—Transmit packet memory.
- **ToFab SDRAM**—Receive packet memory.

Receive Packet Memory   Receive packet memory is carved into pools of packet buffers. To see how the receive memory is carved, **attach** to a Line Card and execute **show controller tofab queue**, as demonstrated in Example 7-3.

Example 7-3   **show controller tofab queue** *Displays How Receive Packet Memory Is Carved into Packet Buffer Pools*

```
LC-Slot1#show controller tofab queue
Carve information for ToFab buffers
SDRAM size: 67108864 bytes, address: 30000000, carve base: 30019100
67006208 bytes carve size, 0 SDRAM bank(s), 0 bytes SDRAM pagesize, 3 carve(s)
max buffer data size 4544 bytes, min buffer data size 80 bytes
65534/65534 buffers specified/carved
66789056/66789056 bytes sum buffer sizes specified/carved

        Qnum    Head    Tail        #Qelem  LenThresh
        ....    ....    ....        ......  .........

4 non-IPC free queues:
26174/26174 (buffers specified/carved), 39.93%, 80 byte data size
1       101     26274           26174   65535
19630/19630 (buffers specified/carved), 29.95%, 608 byte data size
2       26275   45904           19630   65535
13087/13087 (buffers specified/carved), 19.96%, 1568 byte data size
3       45905   58991           13087   65535
6543/6543 (buffers specified/carved), 9.98%, 4544 byte data size
4       58992   65534           6543    65535
IPC Queue:
100/100 (buffers specified/carved), 0.15%, 4112 byte data size
30      7       6               100     65535
Raw Queue:
31      0       0               0       65535
ToFab Queues:
Dest
Slot
        0       0       0               0       65535
        1       0       0               0       65535
        2       0       0               0       65535
        3       0       0               0       65535
        4       0       0               0       65535
        5       0       0               0       65535
        6       0       0               0       65535
        7       0       0               0       65535
        8       0       0               0       65535
        9       0       0               0       65535
        10      0       0               0       65535
        11      0       10              0       65535
```

Example 7-3   **show controller tofab queue** *Displays How Receive Packet Memory Is Carved into Packet Buffer Pools (Continued)*

12	0	0	0	65535
13	0	0	0	65535
14	0	0	0	65535
15	0	0	0	65535
Multicast	0	0	0	65535

The following list describes some of the key fields in Example 7-3:

- **SDRAM size: 67108864 bytes, address: 30000000, carve base: 30019100**—The size of receive packet memory and the address location where it begins.

- **max buffer data size 4544 bytes, min buffer data size 80 bytes**—The maximum and minimum buffer sizes.

- **65534/65534 buffers specified/carved**—Buffers specified by IOS to be carved and the number of buffers actually carved.

- **4 non-IPC free queues**—The non-IPC buffer pools are the packet buffer pools. Packets arriving into the Line Card would be allocated a buffer from one of these buffer pools depending on the size of the packet. The example output shows four packet buffer pools of sizes 80, 608, 1568, and 4544 bytes. For each pool, more detail is given:

  — **26174/26174 (buffers specified/carved), 39.93%, 80 byte data**—39.93 percent of the receive packet memory has been carved into 26,174 80-byte buffers.

  — **Qnum**—The queue number.

  — **#Qelem**—Number of buffers in this queue.

- **IPC Queue**—Reserved for inter-process communication, such as messages from the RP to the Line Cards.

- **Raw Queue**—When an incoming packet has been assigned a buffer from a non-IPC free queue, it's enqueued on the raw queue. The raw queue is a FIFO processed by the LC CPU during interrupts.

- **ToFab Queues**—Virtual output queues; one per destination slot plus one for multicast traffic. The highlighted portion of Example 7-3, taken from a 12012, shows 15 virtual output queues. The 12012 was designed originally as a 15-slot chassis; queues 13 through 15 are not used.

After the ingress Line Card CPU makes a packet switching decision, the packet is enqueued on the virtual output queue corresponding to the slot where the packet is destined. The number in the fourth column is the number of packets currently enqueued on a virtual output queue.

Transmit Packet Memory   Transmit packet memory is carved into pools as well; attaching to an LC and executing **show controller frfab queue** displays a snapshot of the transmit packet memory. The only field that is different from the output in Example 7-3 is the **Interface Queues** column—the fourth column in the following code.

```
0         0         0              0         65535
1         0         0              0         65535
2         0         0              0         65535
3         0         0              0         65535
```

One interface queue exists for each interface on the LC; packets destined out a specific interface are enqueued onto its interface queue. Now that you have looked at elements common to all engine LCs, take a look at engine-specific details.

Engine 0 Line Card

Each engine 0 LC has two Buffer Manager ASICs (BMAs), represented as Rx and Tx Buffer manager in Figure 7-7, which manage packet buffers and segment and reassemble packets for transmission across the switching fabric, as shown in Figure 7-7. The receive BMA is responsible for receiving packets from the PLIM, segmentation of packets into fixed size cells, and presenting them to the Fabric Interface ASIC (FIA) for transmission across the switch fabric. The transmit BMA, with help from the FIA, performs the re-assembly of the cells arriving from the switch fabric into packets, and hands packets to the PLIM for transmission from the box.

The primary responsibility of the CPU on an engine 0 LC is to switch packets.

Engine 1 Line Card

Elements common to engine 0 and engine 1 LCs, namely CPU, main memory, and packet memory, have the same function on the engine 1 LC as on the engine 0 LC. Packet switching performance of engine 1 LC is improved from an engine 0 LC by a new buffer manager ASIC and an improved switching engine.

Engine 2 Line Card

Figure 7-8 illustrates the key components of the engine 2 LC. Main memory and packet memory on this LC have the same function as the engine 0 and engine 1 LCs.

Figure 7-8   *Engine 2 Packet Forwarding Engine*

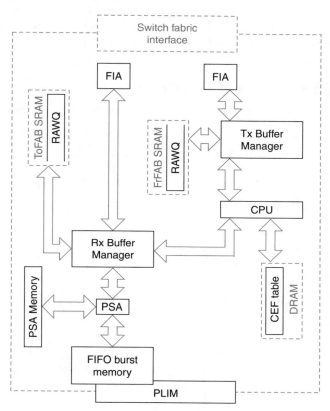

Engine 2 introduces a new packet switching ASIC (PSA) that greatly improves packet switching performance. A local copy of the global CEF table is stored in the PSA memory (up to 128 MB), which is used for CEF lookup for packet switching. All packet switching on an engine 2 LC is done in hardware by the PSA and the CPU on the LC is never interrupted for any packet forwarding decision. The introduction of new and optimized receive and transmit buffer management ASICs, referred to as Receive Buffer Manager (RBM) and Transmit Buffer Manager (TBM), also is key for hardware-based support for Class of Service (CoS) features on this LC.

Packet Switching

Now that you've looked at the various components that make up a Cisco 12000, take a look at how they are used to actually switch packets. Most packets switched through a

Cisco 12000 are switched by the Line Cards using dCEF; only control packets, such as those used for routing protocols, are punted to the GRP for processing. The packet switching path on the GSR depends on the type of forwarding engine on the LC. Let's look at the switching path with each of the forwarding engines.

Packet Switching: Engine 0 and Engine 1

Figure 7-9 illustrates the steps in the switching packets arriving into an engine 0 or engine 1 LC.

Figure 7-9   *Engine 0 and Engine 1 Switching Path*

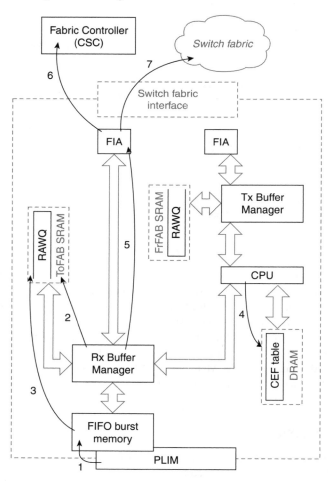

The switching path for engine 0 and engine 1 LCs is essentially the same, although engine 1 LCs have an enhanced switching engine and buffer manager for increased performance. The switching path is as follows:

Step 1   The interface processor (PLIM) detects a packet on the network media and begins copying it into a FIFO memory called *burst memory* on the LC. The amount of burst memory each interface has depends on the type of LC; typical LCs have 128 KB to 1 MB of burst memory.

Step 2   The interface processor requests a packet buffer from the receive BMA; the pool from which the buffer is requested depends on the length of the packet.

If there aren't any free buffers in the requested buffer pool, the packet is dropped and the interface's *ignore* counter is incremented. For example, if a 64-byte packet arrives into an interface, the BMA tries to allocate an 80-byte packet buffer. If no free buffers exist in the 80-byte pool, buffers are not allocated from the next available pool.

Step 3   When a free buffer is allocated by the BMA, the packet is copied into the buffer and is enqueued on the raw queue (RawQ) for processing by the CPU and an interrupt is sent to the LC CPU.

Step 4   The LC's CPU processes each packet in the RawQ as it is received (the RawQ is a FIFO), consulting the local dCEF table in DRAM to make a switching decision.

>   **4.1**   If this is a unicast IP packet with a valid destination address in the CEF table, the packet header is rewritten with the new encapsulation information obtained from the CEF adjacency table. The switched packet is enqueued on the virtual output queue corresponding to the destination slot.

>   **4.2**   If the destination address is not in the CEF table, the packet is dropped.

>   **4.3**   If the packet is a control packet (a routing update, for example), the packet is enqueued on the virtual output queue of the GRP and processed by the GRP.

Step 5   The Receive BMA fragments the packet into 64-byte Cisco cells, and hands off these to the FIA for transmission to the outbound LC.

At the end of Step 5, the packet that arrived into an engine 0 LC has been switched and is ready to be transported across the switch fabric as cells. Go to Step 6 described in the section, "Packet Switching: Switching Cells across Fabric."

Packet Switching: Engine 2 LC

Figure 7-10 illustrates the packet switching path when the packets arrive into an engine 2 LC, as described in the following list.

Figure 7-10 *Engine 2 Packet Switching Path*

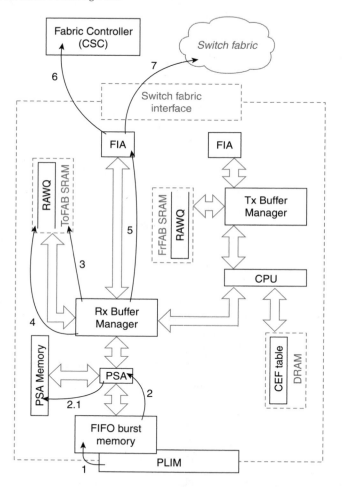

Step 1   The interface processor (PLIM) detects a packet on the network media and begins copying it into a FIFO memory called *burst memory* on the LC. The amount of burst memory each interface has depends on the type of LC; typical LCs have 128 KB to 1 MB of burst memory.

Step 2   The first 64 bytes of the packet, called the *header*, is passed through the Packet Switching ASIC (PSA).

    2.1   The PSA switches the packet by consulting the local CEF table in the PSA memory. If the packet cannot be switched by the PSA, go to Step 4; otherwise, go to Step 3.

Step 3   The Receive Buffer Manager (RBM) accepts the header from the PSA and copies it into a free buffer from the packet memory based on the length of the packet in the buffer header. If the packet is larger than 64 bytes, the *tail* of the packet also is copied into the same free buffer in packet memory and is queued on the outgoing LC virtual output queue. Go to Step 5.

Step 4   The packet arrives at this step if it cannot be switched by the PSA. These packets are placed on the RawQ and the switching path is essentially the same as engine 1 and engine 0 LC from this point (Step 4 in the case of engine 0). Note that packets that are switched by the PSA are never placed in the RawQ and no interrupt is sent to the CPU.

Step 5   The Fabric Interface Module (FIM) is responsible for segmenting the packets into Cisco cells and sending the cells to the Fabric Interface ASIC (FIA) for transmission to the outbound LC.

Packet Switching: Switching Cells across Fabric

You arrive at this stage after the packet switching engine switches the packets and the packets are segmented into Cisco cells and are waiting to be transmitted across the switch fabric. The steps for this stage are as follows:

Step 6   The FIA sends a grant request to the CSC, which schedules each cell's transfer across the switch fabric.

Step 7   When the scheduler grants access to the switch fabric, the cells are transferred to the destination slot. Note that the cells might not be transmitted all at once—other cells within other packets might be interleaved.

Packet Switching: Transmitting Packets

Figure 7-11 shows the cells containing the packet on the outbound Line Card.

Figure 7-11 *GSR Packet Switching: Transmit Stage*

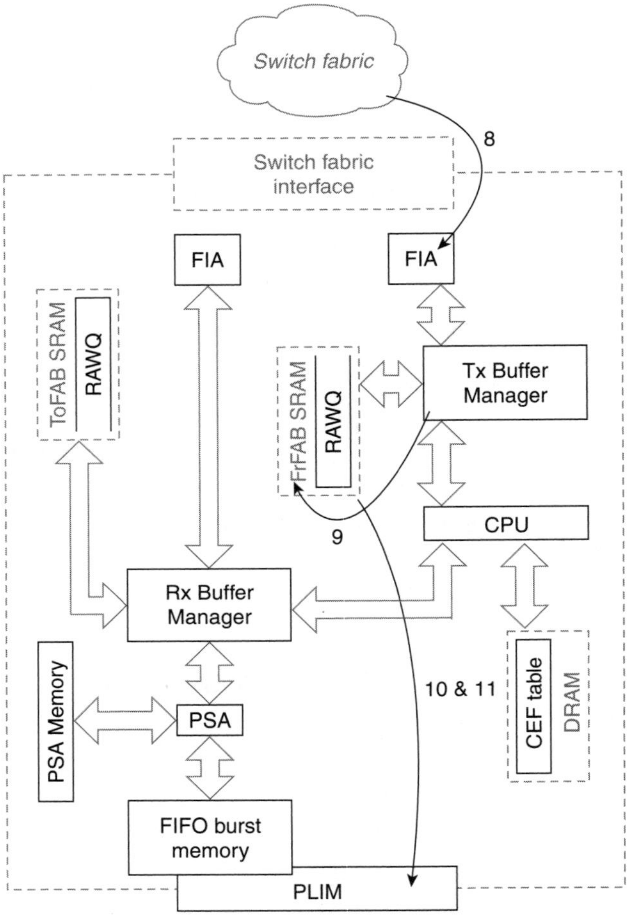

Step 8 The cells switched across the fabric arrive into the destination Line Card via the FIA.

Step 9 The transmit Buffer Manager allocates a buffer from the transmit packet memory and reassembles the packet in this buffer.

Step 10 When the packet is rebuilt, the transmit BMA enqueues the packet onto the destination interface's transmit queue on the LC. If the interface transmit queue is full (the packet cannot be enqueued), the packet is dropped and the *output drop* counter is incremented.

NOTE   In the transmit direction, the only time packets will be placed in the RAWQ is if the LC CPU needs to do any processing before transmission. Examples include IP fragmentation, multicast, and output CAR.

Step 11 The interface processor detects a packet waiting to be transmitted, dequeues the buffer from the transmit memory, copies it into internal FIFO memory, and transmits the packet on the media.

Summary

This chapter examined the most important architectural elements of the 12000, which are radically different from any of the shared memory or bus-based Cisco architectures. By using a crossbar switching fabric, the Cisco 12000 provides very large amounts of bandwidth and scalability. Further, the 12000 uses virtual output queues to eliminate Head of Line Blocking within the switching fabric.

Most switching on a Cisco 12000 is distributed to the Line Cards; in some cases, a dedicated ASIC actually switches packets. DCEF is the only switching mode available.

This chapter covers the following key topics:

- QoS Overview
- Priority Queuing
- Custom Queuing
- Weighted Fair Queuing
- Modified Deficit Round Robin
- Weighted Random Early Detection
- Selective Packet Discard
- Other QoS Features

CHAPTER 8

Quality of Service

The growing availability of data networks has fueled tremendous momentum toward placing all traffic—voice, video, and data—onto the infrastructure that provides data service alone today. Among the obstacles network engineers face when trying to combine voice, video, and data onto one network is that different types of traffic require different levels of service from the network. For example,

- Video requires high bandwidth and a consistent transit delay. This delay doesn't necessarily have to be small unless the session is interactive, but it does have to be consistent to prevent choppiness and other visual artifacts.

- Interactive voice traffic requires much less bandwidth than video traffic, but it requires a very short transit delay through the network. Excessive delay on a voice session introduces audio artifacts, such as echo, which are difficult to eliminate.

- Interactive terminal sessions, such as Telnet, require low delay. Inconsistent delay usually isn't noticeable, but consistently long delays can be very noticeable and quite annoying to users.

- File transfers benefit from high bandwidth, but are the most forgiving of all the types of network traffic, tolerating moderate to large and inconsistent delays. Delay affects the total transfer time for a file and becomes more noticeable as the file size increases.

How can a single infrastructure provide all of these types of service? The answer is in using various Quality of Service (QoS) mechanisms to condition traffic streams based on the types of service they require.

Although a complete discussion of QoS methods and protocols is beyond the scope of this book, we explore how IOS implements key QoS mechanisms.

QoS Overview

Consider a basic network of two computers connected by a single link. In a perfect world, these computers could send and receive as much data as they want without worrying about transit delay; the only thing bounding the number of file transfers, voice calls, and video sessions between them is the processing power of the systems themselves. They have a dedicated link with infinite bandwidth!

Real networks consist of shared links with limited bandwidth and some (measurable) amount of delay. Networks able to handle the full output rate of every connected node are rarely economical; instead, network designers attempt to balance costs with the average and peak rates of traffic they expect. Devices within the network, such as routers, employ various buffering and queuing mechanisms to handle temporary bursts above the average.

In previous chapters, we looked at the basic packet queuing mechanisms used in IOS, which is first-in, first-out (FIFO) in most cases. As long as there's sufficient link bandwidth and switching capacity, FIFO can meet all the service requirements for all traffic types.

To see why FIFO isn't always enough, though, take a look at the simple network shown in Figure 8-1.

Figure 8-1 *QoS in a Simple Network*

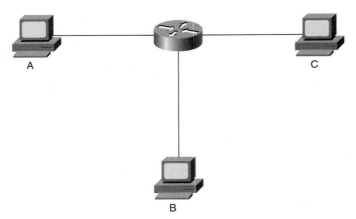

Let's assume all the links illustrated are 10 Mbps, and the router can switch at 50 Mbps. If the three hosts transmit an average of 700 Kb/s with an occasional burst of 5 Mbps, FIFO queuing on the router performs fine; the router's interfaces can always keep their transmit queues drained.

Increasing the maximum burst from 5 Mbps to 10 Mbps, however, quickly shows FIFO's weakness queuing. Switching capacity is not a problem—the router can handle up to five Ethernet interfaces going full speed. But if two of the hosts, A and B, try to send at 10 Mbps toward C at the same time, the total data arrival rate at the router (20 Mbps) exceeds the capacity of the output interface (10 Mbps).

Some number of the packets toward C need to buffered and queued on the transmit queue of the outbound interface—and anytime queues begin to grow, it's probable that packets waiting in those queues must wait longer than their acceptable delay.

The problem becomes even more pronounced if a significant difference in link speeds exists along a path. For example, if the link to C in Figure 8-1 is replaced with a T1 (1.544 Mbps), it only takes a burst from one host to overrun the router's interface to C. In fact, the T1 barely keeps up with the average transmission rates of A and B.

Two common QoS strategies are used to meet the service requirements of the traffic: *congestion management* and *congestion avoidance*. Congestion management assumes packets wait in queues, and attempts to minimize the effects of queuing by dequeuing packets in an order that satisfies their service levels. Congestion avoidance attempts to limit queuing itself by signaling traffic sources to slow down their transmission rates.

Congestion Management

Congestion management methods are distinguished by how they classify packets and the order in which they dequeue packets. Two general classes of congestion management exist in IOS: *platform independent* and *platform dependant*. Platform-independent methods are available on most Cisco routers, and run on the main processor, such as the RSP in a Cisco 7500. Platform-dependant methods are implemented on intelligent interface processors, and are only available on selected platforms.

Currently, two platform-dependant congestion management methods exist: Distributed Weighted Fair Queuing (DWFQ) and Modified Deficit Round Robin (MDRR). DWFQ is implemented on Cisco 7500 VIP cards, and MDRR is implemented on Cisco 12000 line cards.

Platform-independent congestion management techniques implemented in IOS include:

- Priority Queuing (PQ)
- Custom Queuing (CQ)
- Weighted Fair Queuing (WFQ)
    - Flow-Based WFQ
    - Class-Based WFQ

All these congestion management techniques, with the exception of MDRR, are applied between an interface's output hold and transmit queues.

NOTE   IOS platform-independent congestion management techniques occur between an interface's output hold and transmit queues (or transmit rings). The interface transmit queue is a first-in, first-out (FIFO) queue; when a packet is placed in the interface transmit queue, it is scheduled for transmission on the physical wire. Thus, for any type of fancy queuing (congestion management techniques) to take place, packets must pass through the output queue rather than be placed directly on the interface's transmit queue.

How does IOS decide when a packet should be placed on an interface's output queue rather than directly on its transmit queue?

- If a packet has been process switched (or it's generated by IOS itself), it's always placed on the output hold queue rather than on the interface transmit queue.

- If the interface transmit queue is full, any packets queued to the interface are placed on the output hold queue.

- Beyond this, if any packets are on an interface's transmit queue, all packets destined out that interface are placed on the output hold queue as well.

So, if the interface becomes congested, its transmit ring fills up and packets are placed on its output hold queue instead, triggering congestion management.

How many packets does it take for an interface's transmit queue to fill up? It depends on the platform and the type of interface. When any type of congestion management is configured on an interface, the transmit queue size is decreased to improve the odds of the congestion management taking effect.

Throughout this chapter, we assume congested interfaces for all examples given.

Congestion Avoidance

The objective of congestion avoidance algorithms is to prevent congestion from happening in the first place. Two general classes of congestion avoidance exist in IOS: platform independent and platform dependent. Platform-independent methods are implemented on a platform's main processor, such as the RSP on the Cisco 7500, whereas platform-dependent methods are implemented on intelligent interface processors on selected platforms. We discuss the Weighted Random Early Detection (WRED) implementation in this chapter.

Priority Queuing

Priority queuing is a platform-independent congestion management method that, as its name implies, provides some packets absolute priority over other packets. The simplest analogy is a grocery store with two checkout lines being serviced by one clerk.

Customers holding a special customer club card can enter one line, and the remaining customers can enter the second line. The clerk cannot check out any customers in the second line until he serves all the preferred customers (the ones holding the club cards in the first line).

This is exactly how routers implement priority queuing. Packets are classified based on a configurable policy and are placed in a queue. The IOS implementation has a total of four queues: high, medium, normal, and low.

The high queue must be empty before the medium queue can be serviced, the medium queue must be empty before the normal queue can be serviced, and the normal queue must be empty before the low queue can be serviced.

This method has one drawback—and it's easy to see if we go back to the grocery store example for a moment. If you're forced to enter the non–club card line, you could wait quite some time before the clerk finally gets around to checking you out. In fact, you might *never* get checked out if enough people continue to arrive in the club card line. You could starve standing there!

It's no different with priority queuing. Lower priority queues actually can starve—never being allowed to send any traffic. Because of this, priority queuing should be implemented with care. A packet classification policy should be chosen so it doesn't place packets in the high priority queue at a very high rate.

Configuring and Monitoring Priority Queuing

Example 8-1 demonstrates how to configure priority queuing.

Example 8-1   *Configuring Priority Queuing*

```
access-list 110 permit ip host 10.1.1.1 any
access-list 120 permit ip host 172.16.28.1 any
access-list 130 permit ip any any
!
priority-list 1 protocol ip high list 110
priority-list 1 protocol ip medium list 120
priority-list 1 protocol ip normal list 130
!
interface Serial0
 priority-group 1
```

For example, say a router has the following packets to transmit on Serial 0:

Packet 1—Sourced from 172.18.40.8, destined to 192.168.40.8
Packet 2—Sourced from 10.1.1.1, destined to 192.168.40.8
Packet 3—Sourced from 172.18.40.8, destined to 192.168.10.1
Packet 4—Sourced from 10.1.1.1, destined to 192.168.10.1
Packet 5—Sourced from 172.16.28.1, destined to 192.168.10.1
Packet 6—Sourced from 172.18.40.8, destined to 192.168.20.56

These packets first are enqueued into the high, medium, and normal queues based on the access lists referenced in the **priority-list** commands, with the results as shown in Figure 8-2.

Figure 8-2   *Packets Enqueued Based on the* **priority-list** *Command*

High			Packet 4	Packet 2
Medium				Packet 5
Normal		Packet 6	Packet 3	Packet 1

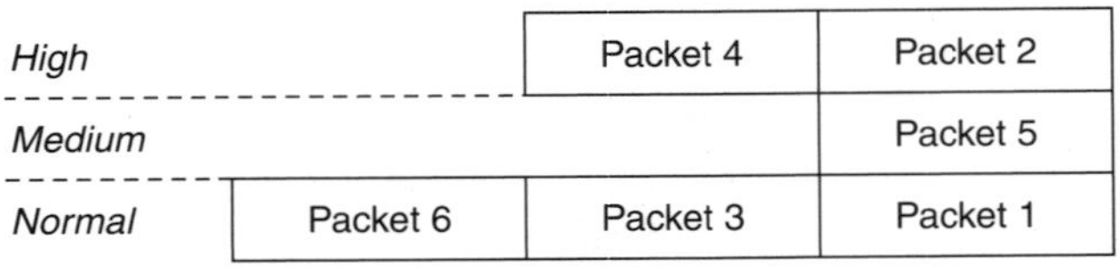

After the packets are placed into the correct queues, IOS services the high queue until no packets remain—packets 2 and 4 in this case. IOS then transmits the packets in the medium queue—packet 5 here. Finally, when the high and medium queues are empty, the packets remaining in the normal queue are transmitted.

Of course, while these packets are being transmitted, other packets continue to arrive and are placed into their appropriate queues. If enough packets enter the high and medium queues that the IOS never actually transmits anything out of the normal queue, the normal queue starves. Any applications or hosts that use the normal queue to pass traffic simply fail to function.

You can examine the priority queuing configuration using the **show queueing priority** command, as demonstrated in Example 8-2.

Example 8-2   **show queuing priority** *Displays Priority Queuing Status*

```
router#show queueing priority
Current priority queue configuration:

List   Queue  Args
1      high   protocol ip        list 110
1      medium protocol ip        list 120
1      normal protocol ip        list 130
```

The output of the **show queueing priority** command summarizes the current priority queuing configuration. It doesn't provide any information about the number of packets that were placed into or dropped from any given queue. To determine the number of packets that were passed through or dropped from each queue, examine the output of the **show interface** command as demonstrated in Example 8-3.

Example 8-3 **show interface** *Displays Packet Traffic through a Queue*

```
router#show interface serial 0
Serial0 is up, line protocol is up
....
  Queueing strategy: priority-list 1
  Output queue (queue priority: size/max/drops):
     high: 0/20/0, medium: 0/40/0, normal: 0/60/0, low: 0/80/0
```

From the output in Example 8-3, you can see the type of queuing enabled (in the **Queueing strategy** area), the specific priority group that is assigned to this interface, the number of packets currently in each of the queues, and the number of packets dropped from each queue.

The maximum size of each queue can be configured using the IOS **priority-list** *list-number* **queue-limit** configuration command.

Custom Queuing

Custom queuing is a platform-independent congestion management mechanism very similar to priority queuing. Custom queuing provides fairness in servicing the queues, unlike priority queuing, which can potentially starve non–high priority queues. Going back to the grocery store line example, let's say the clerk can now service only up to a certain number of customers from the club card line before returning to the customers in the non–club card line, and vice-versa. The clerk now alternates between the two lines, checking out the number of people allowed in one line before switching to the other line.

Custom queuing allows 16 configurable queues, each with a count specifying how many bytes of data should be delivered from the queue before IOS moves to the next one. In other words, the 16 queues are serviced in a round-robin fashion, and a configured number of bytes are serviced from each queue before moving to the next queue.

NOTE

There are actually 17 queues in IOS custom queuing but the user cannot classify packets into queue 0. Queue 0 is a special queue reserved for control traffic, such as interface keepalives and routing updates.

Let's use the configuration in Example 8-4 and work through a short example.

Example 8-4 *Custom Queuing Example*

```
access-list 110 permit ip host 10.1.1.1 any
access-list 120 permit ip host 172.16.28.1 any
!
queue-list 1 protocol ip 1 list 110
queue-list 1 protocol ip 2 list 120
queue-list 1 default 3
!
queue-list 1 queue 1 byte-count 1000
queue-list 1 queue 2 byte-count 1000
queue-list 1 queue 3 byte-count 2000
!
interface Serial 0
 custom-queue-list 1
```

Assume IOS receives the following packets for switching:

Packet 1—Sourced from 172.18.40.8, length 100 bytes
Packet 2—Sourced from 10.1.1.1, length 500 bytes
Packet 3—Sourced from 172.18.40.8, length 100 bytes
Packet 4—Sourced from 10.1.1.1, length 1000 bytes
Packet 5—Sourced from 172.16.28.1, length 200 bytes
Packet 6—Sourced from 172.18.40.8, length 100 bytes
Packet 7—Sourced from 10.1.1.1, length 100 bytes

After IOS receives and classifies these seven packets, the queues look like Figure 8-3.

Figure 8-3 *Initial Packet Distribution for Custom Queuing Example*

Queue 1	Packet 7/100	Packet 4/1000	Packet 2/500
Queue 2			Packet 5/200
Queue 3	Packet 6/100	Packet 3/100	Packet 1/100

IOS begins with queue 1; the first packet on the queue is removed and transmitted. This would be packet 2, which is 500 bytes long. The size of packet 2 is subtracted from the allowed byte count for this queue, 1000, leaving a remainder of 500. Because the remainder is greater than 0, the next packet, packet 4, is removed from queue 1 and is transmitted.

After transmitting packet 4, queue 1 has less than 0 bytes in its allowed byte count. So, IOS moves on to service queue 2. Figure 8-4 shows the queues after this first stage of processing.

Figure 8-4   *Packet Distribution after Queue 1 Is Serviced the First Time*

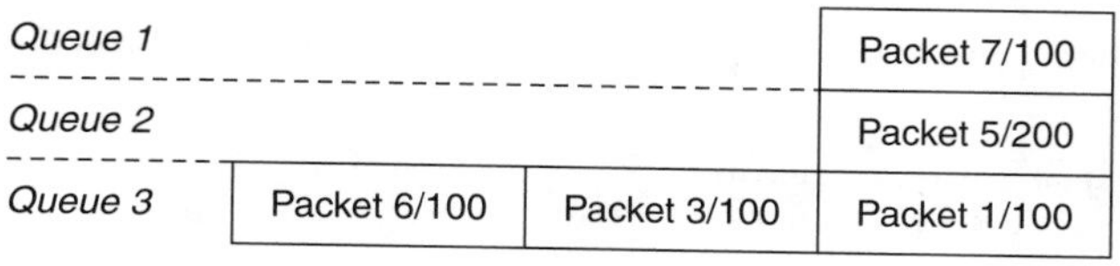

Queue 1			Packet 7/100
Queue 2			Packet 5/200
Queue 3	Packet 6/100	Packet 3/100	Packet 1/100

Next, packet 5 is transmitted from queue 2 and its length subtracted from the total bytes allowed for this queue, 1000, leaving 800 bytes. Another packet could be transmitted from this queue, but no packets remain to transmit. Figure 8-5 illustrates the queues after this second stage of processing.

Figure 8-5   *Packet Distribution after Queue 2 Is Serviced*

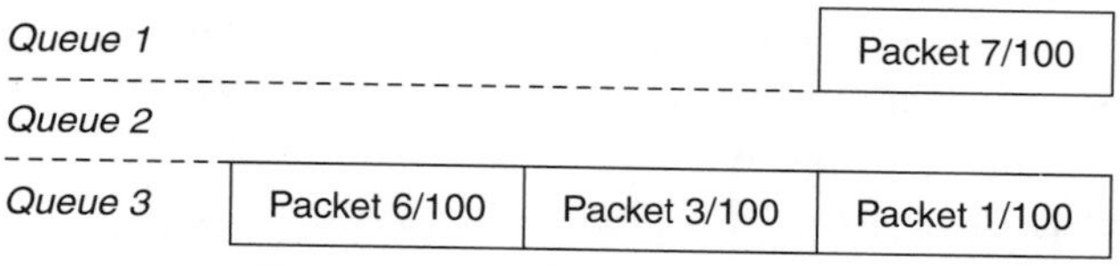

Queue 1			Packet 7/100
Queue 2			
Queue 3	Packet 6/100	Packet 3/100	Packet 1/100

Finally, we come to the last queue, queue 3. Packet 1 is transmitted and its length, 100 bytes, is subtracted from the total byte count of 2000 allowed for this queue. The remaining two packets, 3 and 6, also are transmitted. Finally, the router returns to queue 1 and transmits the final packet.

As you can see, custom queuing doesn't allow any queue to starve; it always services every queue at some point. If a queue fills up faster than it can be serviced, packets tail drop when the number of packets in the queue exceeds the maximum depth of the queue. Thus, custom queuing in effect provides a minimum bandwidth allocation for each configured type of traffic during periods of congestion, but doesn't guarantee delivery above that minimum bandwidth. Packets are delivered above that minimum bandwidth if the other queues are not congested. In this example, Queue 1 is guaranteed to be able to transmit at least 1000 bytes out of every cycle of about 4000 bytes. The end result of this is that Queue 1 is guaranteed to be able to utilize at least 25 percent of the interface bandwidth during periods of congestion.

NOTE   A queue can completely transmit its last packet of that cycle if there is at least 1 byte left in its byte count.

The **show queueing custom** command provides information on which queues are configured and how they are configured, as demonstrated in Example 8-5.

Example 8-5 **show queueing custom** *Displays Information about Which Queues Are Configured and How They Are Configured*

```
router#show queueing custom
Current custom queue configuration:

List   Queue   Args
1      3       default
1      1       protocol ip      list 110
1      2       protocol ip      list 120
1      1       byte-count 1000
1      2       byte-count 1000
1      3       byte-count 2000
```

Again, this output doesn't provide any information on how many packets are waiting in each queue or how many packets were dropped from any queue. For this information, you need to look at **show interface** as shown in Example 8-6.

Example 8-6 **show interface** *Displays Packet Traffic through a Queue*

```
router#show interface serial 0
Serial0 is up, line protocol is up
....
Queueing strategy: custom-list 1
  Output queues: (queue #: size/max/drops)
     0: 0/20/0 1: 0/20/0 2: 0/20/0 3: 0/20/0 4: 0/20/0
     5: 0/20/0 6: 0/20/0 7: 0/20/0 8: 0/20/0 9: 0/20/0
     10: 0/20/0 11: 0/20/0 12: 0/20/0 13: 0/20/0 14: 0/20/0
     15: 0/20/0 16: 0/20/0
....
```

From the output in Example 8-6, you can see the type of queuing listed (under **Queueing strategy**), the current number of packets in each queue, the maximum number of packets allowed in each queue, and the number of packets dropped out of each queue.

Weighted Fair Queuing

There are two implementations of Weighted Fair Queuing (WFQ) in IOS:

* Platform-independent WFQ

* Distributed Weighted Fair Queuing (DWFQ)

All Cisco platforms covered in this book, except Cisco 12000, support platform-independent WFQ. DWFQ is available only on VIP interfaces on 7500 series routers when dCEF switching is enabled.

Platform-Independent WFQ

IOS has two implementations of platform-independent WFQ:

- Flow-Based WFQ
- Class-Based CBWFQ

Flow-Based WFQ

Flow-Based WFQ is similar to custom queuing in its effect on traffic streams, but rather than defining a static policy to sort the packets into the individual queues, the streams are sorted automatically. Flow-Based WFQ is a legacy congestion management feature in IOS and has been available since IOS version 11.0; we refer to the legacy Flow-Based WFQ in the rest of this chapter as WFQ.

In WFQ, IP packets are classified into flows using

- ToS bits in the IP header
- IP protocol type
- Source IP address
- Source TCP or UDP socket
- Destination IP address
- Destination TCP or UDP socket

By default, WFQ classifies the traffic streams into 256 different flows; you can change this default using the **dynamic-queues** option of the **fair-queue** configuration command. If more flows exist than queues configured, multiple flows are placed in each queue.

NOTE   WFQ is enabled by default on all serial interfaces with bandwidths (clock rates) less than 2 Mbps. On the Cisco 7500, any special queuing (priority queuing [PQ], custom queuing [CQ], or WFQ) can cause each packet to be copied from an MEMD buffer to a DRAM buffer for processing. Copying data between MEMD and DRAM is very expensive in terms of processing cycles. As a result, use of platform-independent WFQ should be limited to low speed interfaces on the Cisco 7500.

As packets are sorted into queues, they are given weights that are used, in turn, to calculate a sequence number. The sequence number determines the order in which packets are dequeued and transmitted.

These weights are calculated using the following formula:

Weight = 4096 / (IP Precedence + 1)

As an example, assume three streams of packets arrive into a WFQ system:

- A1, A2—500 bytes each with precedence 0
- B1, B2—400 bytes each with precedence 0
- C1—40 bytes with precedence 3

When the first packet, A1, arrives, it's classified and enqueued into subqueue A. WFQ computes a sequence number for A1 using the following formula:

Sequence Number = Current Sequence Number + (weight * length)

Where current sequence number is either

- The same as the sequence number of the packet last enqueued for transmission, if the subqueue is empty.
- The sequence number of the last packet on the subqueue, if the subqueue is not empty.

The current sequence number when A1 arrives is 0 because it's the first packet to arrive into subqueue A. Its weight is 4096 (based on the ToS setting in the packet header) and its length is 500 bytes. Therefore, the sequence number of A1 is calculated as follows:

0 + (4096 * 500) = 2048000

A2 arrives next and WFQ code classifies A2 also into subqueue A. A2 is assigned the sequence number of 4096000 (A1's sequence number + 4096 * 500). A1 is scheduled to be transmitted next. Figure 8-6 shows the queues at this point.

Figure 8-6   *WFQ State after the First Pass*

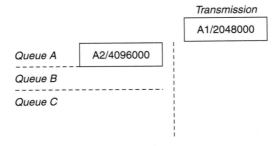

B1 and B2 arrive next and WFQ classifies them into subqueue B and computes sequence numbers for them as described in the paragraphs that follow.

Subqueue B is empty when B1 arrives into subqueue B, so B1's sequence number is computed using the sequence number of the last packet enqueued for transmission (A1):

$$2048000 + (4096 * 400) = 3686400$$

B2's sequence number is computed similar to A2's:

$$3686400 + (4096 * 400) = 5324800$$

At this point, A1 finishes transmission. WFQ sorts the subqueues based on the sequence numbers of the packets at the head of the queues. B1 has the smallest sequence number and is enqueued for transmission. Note that B1 is enqueued for transmission *before* A2, even though it arrived later. Figure 8-7 shows the queues at this point.

Figure 8-7   *WFQ State*

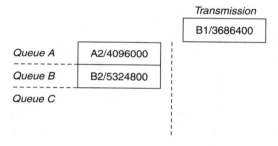

C1 arrives next and is placed into subqueue C. Because subqueue C is empty, C1's sequence number is based on the sequence number of the last packet enqueued for transmission, which was B1.

$$3686400 + (1024 * 40) = 3727360$$

B1 is transmitted at this point and all the queues are resorted again. C1 now has the lowest sequence number, as shown in Figure 8-8, so it's enqueued for transmission.

Figure 8-8   *WFQ State after the Second Pass*

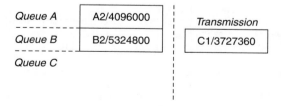

Note that C1 is transmitted *before* A2 or B2, even though it arrived after these two packets.

So what is the purpose behind all this weighting and sorting? The answer is to provide a fair amount of bandwidth for each flow based on its type of service (ToS). Because packet lengths are taken into account when assigning sequence numbers, flows with shorter than average packet lengths can send more packets than flows with longer than average packet lengths. For example, a flow that normally sends 500 byte packets can transmit three times as many packets than a flow that normally sends 1500 byte packets.

The classic example of how this is useful is Telnet traffic and FTP traffic. Telnet traffic uses small packets and the users are affected (and annoyed) by delays. FTP traffic uses large packets and is more tolerant of delays. WFQ automatically gives Telnet packets an earlier transmission time than an FTP packet that arrived slightly before it.

If the flows are weighted based on a type of service, flows with a greater type of service setting receive a greater amount of bandwidth.

Configuring and Monitoring WFQ

To enable WFQ on an interface, configure **fair-queue** at the interface level:

```
Router(config-if)# fair-queue [congestive-discard-threshold [dynamic-queues
[reservable-queues]]]
```

The *congestive-discard-threshold* (the default is 64) is the number of messages or packets allowed in each queue. When this threshold is reached, any packets that normally are placed into the queue are dropped.

dynamic-queues (the default is 256) are the WFQ subqueues into which packets are classified.

If a flow has a reservation through RSVP, its traffic is placed into a *reservable-queue.* The **show queueing** *interface-number* command can monitor the status of WFQ on an interface, as demonstrated in Example 8-7.

Example 8-7   **show queueing** *Monitors WFQ Status on a Router Interface*

```
Router#show queueing serial0
Input queue: 0/75/0 (size/max/drops); Total output drops: 0
Queueing strategy: weighted fair
Output queue: 3/1000/64/0 (size/max total/threshold/drops)
   Conversations  1/3/256 (active/max active/threshold)
   Reserved Conversations 0/1 (allocated/max allocated)

(depth/weight/discards/tail drops/interleaves) 2/4096/0/0/0
Conversation 1023, linktype: ip, length: 1504
source: 10.1.1.1, destination: 10.1.5.2, id: 0xC4FE, ttl:120,
ToS: 0 prot: 6, source port 1520, destination port 4563
```

The following list explains the relevant fields from the output of the **show queueing serial0**. The shaded portion of Example 8-7 highlights the statistics for a single flow or conversation; a conversation queue is the same as a subqueue discussed in the example previously.

- **Output queue: 3/1000/64/0 (size/max total/threshold/drops)**
  - — **size** is the instantaneous value of the packets in the queuing system.
  - — **max total** is the per interface limit on the total number of buffers that WFQ can consume.
  - — **threshold** is the congestive discard threshold described earlier. This is the maximum number of packets allowed in the sub-queue; this is a soft limit—more than **threshold** number of packets actually can be placed in a conversation queue. The **max total** number protects the WFQ system from consuming lots of memory and dropping packets when the max total is reached.
  - — **drops** is the number of packets dropped by WFQ either for a sub-queue exceeding the **threshold** or the total number of packets in the queues exceeding the **max total**.

- **Conversations 1/3/256 (active/max active/threshold)**
  - — **active** indicates the number of flows or conversations active at this instant. The example shows 1 active conversation.
  - — **max active** is the total number of conversations ever.
  - — **threshold** is the maximum number of configured conversation or flow queues. If more conversations exist than queues configured, multiple conversations are placed in a queue.

- **(depth/weight/discards/tail drops/interleaves) 2/4096/0/0/0**
  - — **depth** is the number of packets placed into this conversation queue.
  - — **weight** indicates the weight of each packet in the queue.
  - — **discards** is the number of packets dropped due to congestive discard threshold exceeded.
  - — **tail drops** is the number of packets dropped when the max-total was exceeded.
  - — **interleaves** occur when link layer fragmentation and interleaving is configured. This allows smaller packets to be interleaved between the fragments of larger packets.

Class-Based WFQ

Flow-Based WFQ, as discussed in the previous section, automatically classifies flows—you don't have any control over the classification mechanism. Class-Based WFQ (CBWFQ) was developed to provide a WFQing mechanism that allows flows to be sorted along user-designated policies. CBWFQ, like Flow-Based WFQ, is a platform-independent feature that is available on all router platforms covered in this book except the Cisco 12000. Distributed CBWFQ (DCBWFQ) also is available on VIP cards on 7500 series routers. This section deals only with platform-independent CBWFQ; DCBWFQ is covered in the section, "Distributed Weighted Fair Queuing."

NOTE As of this writing, CBWFQ is a relatively new feature; please check the IOS Release Notes for information specific to CBWFQ.

CBWFQ allows you to classify traffic into (up to) 64 classes based on such criteria as the protocol, the access control lists, and the input interface. Each class is allocated a percentage of the bandwidth available on the outbound link. By default, packets that overflow any of the traffic class queues are tail dropped, but Weighted Random Early Detection (WRED), a random drop algorithm discussed later in this chapter, can be configured instead to manage these drops within each queue.

A default class also can be configured; if no default class is configured, packets that are not otherwise classified into a user-defined class are sorted by flow and are given best-effort treatment.

NOTE CBWFQ allows you to configure the bandwidth allocated per class. If a class called "voice" is allocated 200 kbps of bandwidth but has no traffic, the 200 kbps is distributed among all the other classes in proportion to the bandwidth configured for the other classes.

Modular CLI for CBWFQ Configuration

CBWFQ configuration uses a new modular command-line interface (CLI), which is being standardized across all the IOS QoS features and platforms. The modular CLI provides a clean separation between the specification of a classification policy and the specification of other policies that act based on the results of the applied classification. The modular CLI has three constructs:

- **Class-map**—Classifies packets into classes.
- **Policy-map**—Describes the policy for each class.
- **Service-policy**—Applies the policies defined to an interface.

Example 8-8 provides a sample CBWFQ configuration.

Example 8-8 *Sample CBWFQ Configuration*

```
class-map class1
 match access-group 101
!
policy-map policy1
 class class1
 bandwidth 100
 queue-limit 20
 class class-default
 bandwidth 200
 random-detect
!
interface serial0
 service-policy output policy1
!
access-list 101 permit ip any any precedence critical
```

class-map defines a user-defined class called class1. Traffic is classified into the class1 queue by **access-list 101**.

policy-map applies policies to the configured classes. In this example, class1 is allocated 100 kbps of bandwidth (when the interface is congested). Bandwidth also can be allocated as a percentage using the **percent** option in the **bandwidth** command, as shown in Example 8-9.

Example 8-9 *Configuring Bandwidth as a Percentage*

```
Router#configure terminal
Enter configuration commands, one per line.  End with CNTL/Z.
Router(config)#policy-map policy1
Router(config-pmap)#class class1
Router#bandwidth percent ?
  <1-100>  Percentage
Router#
```

The **queue-limit** command determines the maximum number of packets that can be queued on the class queue (the default and the maximum is 64). A **policy-map** can apply policy for many classes (up to 64). Note that each **policy-map** command in Example 8-9 is associated with a previously defined class, tying a set of policies to a defined class.

The **class-default** option of the **class** command defines the policy applied to packets that don't fall into any other configured classes. WRED can be configured per class using the **random-detect** command under the class.

After specifying how the packets should be classified, and actions to take on the packets in each class, use the **service-policy** command to apply the policies to the traffic passing through an interface. An additional keyword (**input/output**) must be specified to indicate whether the policies apply to packets coming in (or going out of) the interface. CBWFQ can be applied only on packets outbound or an interface.

Monitoring CBWFQ

The **show policy** *policy-map* command can be used to display the configuration of all the classes in a policy map. Example 8-10 shows the output of this command:

Example 8-10 *CBWFQ:* **show policy** *Output*

```
ubrI19-2#show policy policy1
  Policy Map policy1
   class   class1

     Class class1
        Bandwidth 100 (kbps) Max Thresh 20 (packets)
   class   class-default

     Class class-default
        Bandwidth 200 (kbps)
        exponential weight 9
   class    min-threshold    max-threshold    mark-probability
            - - - - - - - - - - - - - - - - - - - - - - - - - - - - - - - - - - - - - - -

        0          -                -                1/10
        1          -                -                1/10
        2          -                -                1/10
        3          -                -                1/10
        4          -                -                1/10
        5          -                -                1/10
        6          -                -                1/10
        7          -                -                1/10
      rsvp         -                -                1/10
```

The random early detection (RED) parameters under **class-default** are explained in the section "Weighted Random Early Detection," later in this chapter.

The output of **show policy** *interface* is the key to determining how CBWFQ is functioning on the interface. Example 8-11 displays the output of this command:

Example 8-11 *Output of* **show policy** interface *to Monitor CBWFQ*

```
ubrI19-2#show policy int
  Serial0
   service-policy output: policy1
     class-map: class1 (match-all)
       0 packets, 0 bytes
       5 minute offered rate 0 bps, drop rate 0 bps
       match: access-group 101
       Output Queue: Conversation 265
         Bandwidth 100 (kbps) Packets Matched 0 Max Threshold 20 (packets)
         (discards/tail drops) 0/0
```

Example 8-11 *Output of* **show policy** *interface to Monitor CBWFQ (Continued)*

```
class-map: class-default (match-any)
  0 packets, 0 bytes
  5 minute offered rate 0 bps, drop rate 0 bps
  match: any
    0 packets, 0 bytes
    5 minute rate 0 bps
  Output Queue: Conversation 266
    Bandwidth 200 (kbps) Packets Matched 326
  random-detect:
  mean queue depth: 0
  drops: class  random    tail     min-th   max-th   mark-prob
           0      0         0        20       40       1/10
           1      0         0        22       40       1/10
```

The following list explains the relevant output from Example 8-11:

- **Bandwidth 100 (kbps) Packets Matched 0 Max Threshold 20 (packets)**

  — **Packets Matched** is the number of packets that matched this class policy.

  — **Max Threshold** is the same as the congestive discard threshold in the WFQ section; it's a soft limit on the number of packets that can be placed in the class queue.

- **(discards/tail drops) 0/0**

  — **discards** is the number of packets dropped when Max Threshold is reached.

  — **tail drops** is the number of packets dropped when max-total is reached; the default of max-total is 1000 and cannot be changed currently.

  — The RED parameters are explained in the section "Weighted Random Early Detection," later in the chapter.

Low Latency Queuing

The Low Latency Queuing (LLQ) feature combines strict priority queuing with Class-Based Weighted Fair Queuing (CBWFQ). Strict priority queuing allows delay-sensitive data, such as voice traffic, to be dequeued and sent first (before packets in other queues are dequeued). This feature can reduce jitter for voice traffic. To enqueue a class of traffic to the strict priority queue, you configure the **priority** command for the class after you specify the named class within a policy map (classes to which the priority command is applied are considered priority classes).

Within a policy map, you can give one or more classes priority status. When multiple classes within a single policy map are configured as priority classes, all the traffic from these classes is enqueued to the same, single, strict priority queue. Example 8-12 shows class1 from Example 8-11 now configured as a priority queue.

Example 8-12 *Configuring a Priority Queue in CBWFQ for LLQ*

```
policy-map policy1
  class class1
    priority 100
  class class-default
    bandwidth 200
    random-detect
```

Distributed Weighted Fair Queuing

Distributed Weighted Fair Queuing (DWFQ) is implemented on the VIP on the Cisco 7500. Platform-independent queuing mechanisms (PQ, CQ, or WFQ) do not scale to high-speed interfaces (greater than 2 Mbps) on the 7500 platform. The main reason for this performance limitation is that packets copied back and forth between MEMD and DRAM becomes a CPU-intensive operation when interface congestion occurs and any fancy queuing mechanism is configured.

DWFQ is designed for distributed switching on VIPs and greatly improves WFQ performance.

- All packet processing is performed on the VIP's processor, which frees the RSP's processor up for other tasks (such as running routing protocols).

- Packets aren't copied to and from various types of memory within the router; all queuing takes place within SRAM on the VIPs themselves.

- The algorithm used for DWFQ has been optimized for the VIP processor's environment and interface speeds.

As a result, DWFQ can be enabled on such high speed interfaces as the OC-3 (155 Mbps) interface on a VIP2-50. DWFQ is capable of classifying packets in four different ways:

- Flow-Based
- ToS-Based
- QoS Group–Based
- CBWFQ

Flow-Based DWFQ

Flow-Based DWFQ classifies the traffic destined out an interface based on the following:

- ToS bits in the IP header
- IP protocol type
- Source IP address

- Source TCP or UDP socket
- Destination IP address
- Destination TCP or UDP socket

Traffic is classified into 512 flows; each flow is serviced round-robin from the calendar queue (see the "DWFQ Implementation" section later in the chapter for more details). Each of the 512 flows shares an equal amount of bandwidth.

With distributed Cisco Express Forwarding (dCEF) enabled on the interface, configuring **fair-queue** on a VIP interface enables Flow-Based DWFQ. To configure DWFQ on an interface, use the command **fair-queue** on an interface for which dCEF is configured already:

```
Router(config-if)#fair-queue
```

ToS-Based DWFQ

ToS-Based DWFQ, also known as Class-Based DWFQ, classifies packets based on the lower two bits of the precedence field in the IP header, so there are four possible queues. The weight of each queue determines the amount of bandwidth the traffic placed in this queue receives if the outbound link is fully congested.

The following command enables ToS DWFQ:

```
Router(config-if)#fair-queue tos
```

Class 3, 2, 1, and 0 get default weights of 40, 30, 20, and 10, respectively. The default weights can be changed using

```
Router(config-if)#fair-queue tos 0 weight 20
```

The aggregate weight of all classes cannot exceed 100.

QoS Group–Based DWFQ

Another variant of ToS-Based (or Class-Based) DWFQ is based on QoS groups instead of the ToS bits in the IP header. QoS groups are created by local policies applied through Committed Access Rate (CAR) and can be propagated through Border Gateway Protocol (BGP) Policy Propagation. These concepts are beyond the scope of this book.

Distributed CBWFQ

Distributed ToS-based and QoS group–based WFQ are two forms of *CBWFQ*. The platform independent form of CBWFQ using the same modular CLI can also be configured on a VIP interface, including the Low Latency queuing feature.

DWFQ Implementation

DWFQ does not perform list sorting and re-ordering of packets like the platform-independent WFQ algorithm does. Instead, the DWFQ scheduling algorithm uses calendar queues to achieve similar behavior with much greater efficiency. This is the primary reason DWFQ can be enabled on an OC-3 (155-Mbps) interface with a VIP2-50.

The difference between the platform-independent WFQ and DWFQ is in the details of how the sorted queue is managed (that is, the difference is in the implementation details, not in the fundamentals of the algorithm). WFQ maintains a sorted, linked list where newly arriving packets are inserted into the sorted list based on the timestamp assigned to the packet. In DWFQ, a calendar queue is used to impose the sorted ordering. The calendar queue is more efficient in terms of CPU utilization.

Monitoring DWFQ

The primary command used to monitor the state of DWFQ is **show interface fair**, as demonstrated in Example 8-13.

Example 8-13 show interface fair *Monitors DWFQ State*

```
router#show interface fair
 FastEthernet11/1/0 queue size 0
        packets output 44404, wfq drops 1, nobuffer drops 0
 WFQ: aggregate queue limit 6746, individual queue limit 3373
       max available buffers 6746

       Class 0: weight 10 limit 3373 qsize 0 packets output 44404 drops 1
       Class 1: weight 20 limit 3373 qsize 0 packets output 0 drops 0
       Class 2: weight 30 limit 3373 qsize 0 packets output 0 drops 0
       Class 3: weight 40 limit 3373 qsize 0 packets output 0 drops 0
```

The following list explains the relevant fields in the output of the **show interface fair**:

- **Packets output**—Total number of packets transmitted out this interface.

- **wfq drops**—Packets dropped by DWFQ; an aggregate of the drops in each class. The drops could be due to three reasons:

  — The aggregate queue limit was exceeded.

  — The individual queue limit was exceeded (this is not enforced until two-thirds of the aggregate queue limit is reached).

  — There were **no buffers** available.

- **nobuffer drops**—Indicates the VIP is running out of SRAM and cannot enqueue packets to the DWFQ system. The total numbers of buffers available to DWFQ is indicated by **max available buffers**.

- **aggregate queue limit**—The maximum number of packets that can be enqueued to the DWFQ system. By default, this is equal to the **max available buffers**, but it can be tuned.

- **max available buffers**—This is the amount of SRAM carved for use by DWFQ. It is computed as a function of the bandwidth of the interface and the maximum available SRAM.

  — If there is sufficient SRAM available, then the aggregate queue limit assigned to an interface is equal to the number of buffers needed to hold half a second worth of traffic, assuming each packet is 250 bytes.

  — If there isn't enough memory to create a half a second worth of buffers, memory is allocated based on a complex algorithm.

- **individual queue limit**—The number of packets that are allowed in each class queue; half the aggregate limit by default. This is a soft limit, and is not enforced until two-thirds of the aggregate queue limit is reached. By default, the sum of the individual queue limits of each class exceeds the aggregate queue limit; this is intentional oversubscription and can be tuned.

Note	If many large packets belonging to a particular class (class1) arrive in a burst followed by a few packets of a second class (class2), it is possible for all the buffers to be consumed by the class1 packets, causing the class2 packets to be dropped due to **no buffers**. Possible workarounds are to add SRAM on the VIP or to tune down the aggregate limit and the individual limits so buffers are not exhausted. If you want to fully protect every class, then the sum of the individual limits must be less than the aggregate limit. In other words, you can't allow any oversubscription of the buffers if you want to guarantee one class won't starve another class.

- **qsize**—Instantaneous depth of the class queue.

Modified Deficit Round Robin

Unlike other Cisco platforms, the 12000 series of routers doesn't support priority queuing, custom queuing, or weighted fair queuing. Instead, they implement Modified Deficit Round Robin (MDRR) for congestion management. MDRR can be configured on inbound interfaces for packets outbound to the switching fabric, and outbound interfaces for packets awaiting transmission.

MDRR classifies packets into queues based on the precedence bits in the IP header. These queues are serviced round-robin, with a queue being allowed to transmit a number of bytes each time it's serviced (the *quantum*). A deficit counter tracks how many bytes a queue has transmitted in each round.

When the queues first are configured, their deficit counters are set to be equal with their quantum. As packets are transmitted from a queue, their lengths are subtracted from the deficit counter; when the deficit counter reaches 0 (or less than 0), the scheduler moves on to the next queue. In each new round, each non-empty queue's deficit counter is incremented by its quantum value.

Beyond these ToS-based queues, MDRR has a special queue that can be serviced in one of two modes:

- Strict priority mode
- Alternate mode

In strict priority mode, the special queue can be serviced whenever it is not empty. Strict priority mode provides low latency and delay for those packets in the special queue, but if enough packets are queued into the special queue, the remainder of the queues can starve.

In alternate mode, the scheduler alternates between the special queue and the rest of the ToS-based queues.

The quantum associated with each queue is configurable by configuring its weight. The number of bytes a queue can transmit during each round is:

Bytes dequeued = MTU + (configured weight − 1) * 512

Let's work through an example; assume we have three queues:

- **Queue 0**—Has a quantum of 1500 bytes; it's the low latency queue, configured to operate in alternate mode.
- **Queue 1**—Has a quantum of 3000 bytes.
- **Queue 2**—Has a quantum of 1500 bytes.

Figure 8-9 illustrates the initial state of the queues along with some packets that have been received and queued.

Figure 8-9   *MDRR Initial State*

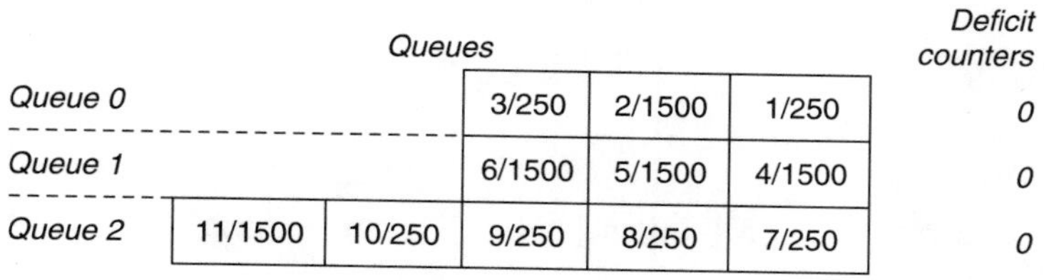

Queues							Deficit counters
Queue 0				3/250	2/1500	1/250	0
Queue 1				6/1500	5/1500	4/1500	0
Queue 2	11/1500	10/250	9/250	8/250	7/250		0

Queue 0 is serviced first; its quantum is added to its deficit counter. Packet 1, which is 250 bytes, is transmitted, and its size is subtracted from the deficit counter. Because queue 0's deficit counter is still greater than 0 (1500 – 250 = 1250), packet 2 is transmitted as well, and its length subtracted from the deficit counter. Queue 0's deficit counter is now –250, so queue 1 is serviced next; Figure 8-10 shows this state.

Figure 8-10   *MDRR State*

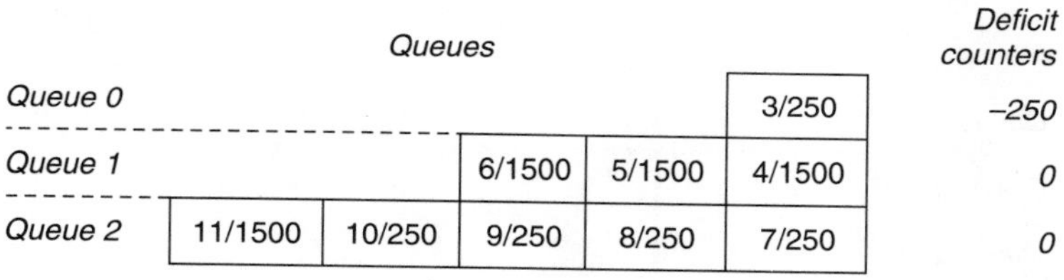

Queues							Deficit counters
Queue 0						3/250	–250
Queue 1				6/1500	5/1500	4/1500	0
Queue 2	11/1500	10/250	9/250	8/250	7/250		0

Queue 1's deficit counter is set to 3000 (0 + 3000 = 3000), and packets 4 and 5 are transmitted. With each packet transmitted, subtract the size of the packet from the deficit counter, so queue 1's deficit counter is reduced to 0. Figure 8-11 illustrates this state.

Figure 8-11   *MDRR State*

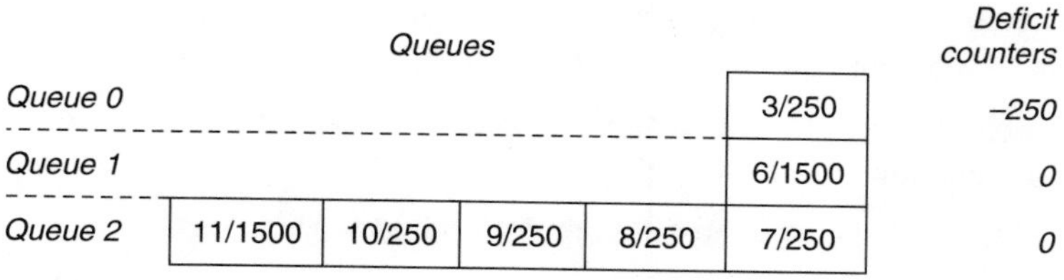

Queues						Deficit counters
Queue 0					3/250	–250
Queue 1					6/1500	0
Queue 2	11/1500	10/250	9/250	8/250	7/250	0

Because we are in alternate priority mode, we must return and service queue 0. Again, we add the quantum to the current deficit counter, and set queue 0's deficit counter to the result (–250 + 1500 = 1250). Packet 3 is now transmitted, because the deficit counter is greater than 0, and queue 0 is now empty. When a queue is emptied, its deficit counter is set to 0, as shown in Figure 8-12.

Figure 8-12 *MDRR State*

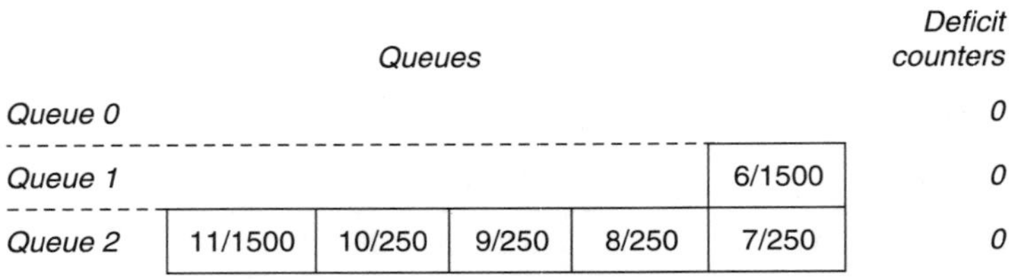

	Queues					Deficit counters
Queue 0						0
Queue 1					6/1500	0
Queue 2	11/1500	10/250	9/250	8/250	7/250	0

Queue 2 is serviced next; its deficit counter is set to 1500 (0 + 1500 = 1500). Packets 7 through 10 are transmitted, leaving the deficit counter at 500 (1500 – (4 * 250) = 500). Because the deficit counter is still greater than 0, packet 11 is transmitted also.

When packet 11 is transmitted, queue 2 is empty, and its deficit counter is set to 0, as shown in Figure 8-13.

Figure 8-13 *MDRR State*

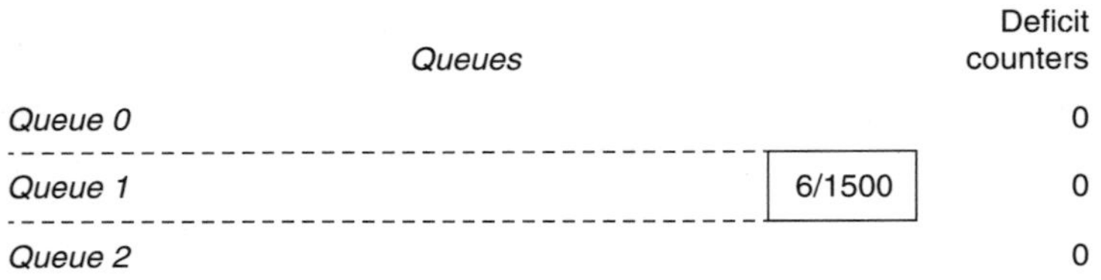

	Queues		Deficit counters
Queue 0			0
Queue 1		6/1500	0
Queue 2			0

Queue 0 is serviced again next (because we are in alternate priority mode). Because it's empty, we service queue 1 next, transmitting packet 6.

Configuration of MDRR

The command **cos-queue-group** places you in a subconfiguration mode, allowing you to create a CoS template, such as one of the following:

- **precedence**—Used to map the IP precedence to DRR queues and to configure the special low latency queue.

- **queue**—Sets the relative weight for each queue.

- **tx-cos**—Used to map cos-queue-group parameters on the transmit interface.

When using MDRR for inbound congestion management, cos-queue-groups are mapped to destination line card slots. The **slot-table-cos** and **rx-cos-slot** commands map the parameters defined in cos-queue-group to each of the destination slots.

Assume, for instance, that you have an OC-12 card in slot 2 of a 12000, and an OC-3 card in slot 3. You want to map precedence 7 traffic into the low-latency (special) queue, and service it in strict priority mode. You could use the configuration in Example 8-14.

Example 8-14 *MDRR Configuration on GSR*

```
Interface pos2/1
Description OC12 Interface
!
Interface 3/1
Description OC-3 Interface
tx-cos frfab
!
rx-cos_slot 2 table-a
!
slot-table-cos table-a
destination-slot 3 tofab
!
cos-queue-group frfab
precedence 7 queue low-latency
queue low-latency strict-priority 10
!
cos-queue-group tofab
precedence 7 queue low-latency
queue low-latency strict-priority 10
!
end
```

Weighted Random Early Detection

Random early detection (RED) is a congestion avoidance algorithm that is most useful when a majority of the traffic is adaptive, such as TCP. TCP uses packet drops as implicit signals of network congestion, reducing the rate at which traffic is sent (or *backing off*) when a packet is missed.

When a majority of the traffic on a congested link consists of TCP streams from various senders, FIFO queuing tail drops when the queue fills, causing all the TCP senders to back off at the same time. Over a period of time (*t*), the TCP senders ramp up the sending rate, and when the link gets congested again, the TCP senders all back off at the same time. This oscillating behavior is called *global synchronization*, as charted in Figure 8-14.

Figure 8-14 *Synchronized TCP Streams*

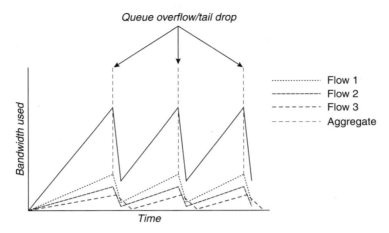

Various congestion management techniques, such as RED, are aimed at preventing this synchronization from occurring. The idea behind RED is quite simple: packets are randomly dropped *before* a queue is full, rather than waiting until it's actually full. If packet drops are spaced out over time, any TCP sessions passing traffic through the queue react to packet loss at different times and they don't synchronize.

RED defines a minimum threshold (min), a maximum threshold (max), and an average queue size (avg). RED computes the average queue size based on the following formula:

$$\text{Avg} = (\text{old\_avg} * (1 - 1/2^{exponential\text{-}weight\text{-}constant})) + (\text{current\_queue\_size} * 1/2^{exponential\text{-}weight\text{-}constant})$$

Note that RED computes an average queue size and not an instantaneous queue size—the average queue size depends on the previous average queue size. Therefore, RED is not biased towards bursty traffic. In other words, RED allows bursts. It typically is not recommended to change the exponential-weight constant.

NOTE   You can find a detailed description of RED in the *Random Early Detection for Congestion Avoidance* paper by Sally Floyd and Van Jacobson (*IEEE/ACM Transaction on Networking*, v. 1, n. 4, August 1993).

RED drops packets based on a probability, which is computed based on the following formulas:

If *avg* < *min*, no packets are dropped.
If *min* < *avg* < *max*, packets are dropped with increased probability as avg increases.
If *avg* > *max*, all packets are dropped.

Going a step further, Weighted Random Early Detection (WRED) weights the drop probability for each packet based on the precedence bits in the IP header, which allows for different classes of service. As with WFQ, there are two WRED implementations available on Cisco routers:

- Platform-independent WRED

- Distributed WRED (dWRED)

Platform-independent WRED is available on all platforms except the Cisco 12000 series of routers; dWRED is available only on Cisco 7500 series routers using VIP processors with dCEF.

Configuration and Monitoring of WRED

WRED is configured with a single command on the interface:

```
Router(config-if)#random-detect
```

To monitor WRED, use **show interface random**, as demonstrated in Example 8-15. The example is the output of dWRED configured on a VIP interface on a 7500.

Example 8-15 show interface random *Monitors WRED*

```
Router#show interface random
 POS8/1/0 queue size 0
       packets output 151051, wred drops 1, nobuffer drops 0
 WRED: queue average 0, weight 1/512, max available buffers 23523

     Precedence 0: 5880 min threshold, 11761 max threshold, 1/10 mark weight
       151043 packets output, drops: 0 random, 0 threshold
     Precedence 1: 6615 min threshold, 11761 max threshold, 1/10 mark weight
       (no traffic)
     Precedence 2: 7350 min threshold, 11761 max threshold, 1/10 mark weight
       (no traffic)
     Precedence 3: 8085 min threshold, 11761 max threshold, 1/10 mark weight
       (no traffic)
     Precedence 4: 8820 min threshold, 11761 max threshold, 1/10 mark weight
       (no traffic)
     Precedence 5: 9555 min threshold, 11761 max threshold, 1/10 mark weight
       (no traffic)
     Precedence 6: 10290 min threshold, 11761 max threshold, 1/10 mark weight
       (no traffic)
     Precedence 7: 11025 min threshold, 11761 max threshold, 1/10 mark weight
       (no traffic)
```

The following list explains the relevant fields from the output of **show interface random**:

- **packets output**—Total number of packets transmitted on this interface.
- **wred drops**—Packets dropped by WRED.
- **no buffer drops**—Indicates the number of packets dropped because there was insufficient packet memory (SRAM) on the VIP.
- **queue average**—The average queue length.
- **mark weight**—The probability of a packet being dropped when the average queue size is at the maximum threshold. In Example 8-15, 1/512 means one out of every 512 packets is dropped when the average queue is at the maximum threshold.
- **max available buffers**—Number of buffers allocated in SRAM for storing packets in the outbound VIP's SRAM.
- **min threshold**—Average queue depth at which RED begins to mark (drop) packets for this precedence level. Also represents the number of packets in the RED queue.
- **max threshold**—Average queue depth beyond which RED marks (drops) all packets. This value also represents the number of packets in the RED queue.

Note   The default values for the min and max threshold are calculated based on the value of the output queue length for the interface. Remember, this output queue is not the interface output hold queue, but rather the interface transmit queue on the VIP.

The min threshold for the precedence queue 0 is set to half the output queue length. The interval between the min-threshold for precedence 0 and the max-threshold is divided into eight values, and each value is assigned as the min-threshold for the remaining precedences. Precedence 0 has the lowest min-threshold and precedence 7 gets the highest min-threshold.

If a majority of the traffic on a link doesn't react to packet drops (UDP, for example), then RED cannot help in any way.

Selective Packet Discard

When the input queue of an interface fills up with traffic destined to the router, there's a good chance that the next packet dropped will be important to the state of the network itself—a routing protocol update or a link keepalive, for instance. Selective Packet Discard (SPD) allows IOS to prioritize traffic that is important to the network's stability when an interface's input queue is congested.

Essentially, any packet recognized by IOS as being important to the stability of the network is given preferential treatment during the process of queuing it on the input queue. SPD is available on all Cisco routers.

The command **show ip spd** shows SPD details, as demonstrated in Example 8-16.

Example 8-16 **show ip spd** *Displays SPD Details*

```
Router#show ip spd
Current mode: normal.
Queue min/max thresholds: 73/74, Headroom: 100
IP normal queue: 8, priority queue: 0.
SPD special drop mode: none
```

Lower precedence packets are dropped when the queue size reaches *min threshold*. The number of packets allowed to be enqueued over the normal input hold queue is the *headroom*.

Other QoS Features

There are many QoS features in IOS not covered in this chapter—an entire book can be written on just these features. Some of the other QoS features offered in IOS include the following:

- **Committed Access Rate (CAR)**—A popular rate-limiting feature used for policing the traffic rate inbound or outbound on an interface. CAR often is thought of as a traffic-shaping feature, but it's not, because CAR doesn't shape traffic.

- **Generic Traffic Shaping (GTS)**—A traffic-shaping feature used to smooth out traffic outbound on a interface.

- **Resource Reservation Protocol (RSVP)**—A QoS signaling mechanism used for resource reservation.

Summary

This chapter covered the implementation of various QoS mechanisms within Cisco IOS. There are two general mechanisms employed to ensure that traffic streams receive the level of service they require—*congestion management* and *congestion avoidance*. Congestion management schemes covered include priority queuing, custom queuing, various forms of weighted fair queuing, and MDRR. RED is the congestion avoidance technique discussed.

NetFlow Switching

Although many people think of NetFlow as a switching path, it isn't; instead, it enables several key applications that customers can use for billing, traffic monitoring, and traffic profiling. Although NetFlow provides traffic accounting and feature acceleration services, packet switching is still performed by process switching, fast switching, optimum switching, or CEF. Therefore, NetFlow can be applied with other switching methods.

A *flow* is defined as a unidirectional sequence of packets between given source and destination endpoints. A flow in the context of NetFlow is defined as the combination of the following fields:

- Source IP address
- Destination IP address
- Source TCP/UDP application port number
- Destination TCP/UDP application port number
- IP protocol type
- IP ToS (Type of Service)
- Input logical interface

When NetFlow is configured on an interface, only packets that arrive into the interface are accounted by NetFlow. NetFlow does not account for packets that are going out an interface. The following steps illustrate the packet path for an IP packet arriving into a NetFlow-enabled interface:

Step 1   A flow lookup is done in the flow cache (the definition of what constitutes a flow is defined later).

Step 2   If this is the first packet for this flow, a new flow entry is created. If this is not the first packet belonging to a flow, the statistics for the flow are updated in the flow cache entry.

Step 3   If there are any input features (input access lists, for example) and this is the first packet for a flow, the access list is checked to make sure the packet is permitted or denied. Access list checking for all subsequent packets for the flow is bypassed.

Step 4 A lookup of the destination address is done in the CEF, optimum switching, fast switching, or routing table. If the destination lookup is successful, the packet has the new Layer 2 encapsulation for transmission on the outbound interface.

Step 5 An output feature check is performed (output access list, for example) for the first packet for a flow. Access list checking for all subsequent packets for the flow is bypassed.

Step 6 The packet is transmitted to the outbound interface.

The NetFlow feature is turned on by the interface level configuration command **ip route-cache flow**. The NetFlow cache is stored in the main memory in non-distributed platforms and on the Line Card main memory in the 7500 VIP cards and the GSR. As packets of the same flow arrive into the interface, the traffic statistic counters are incremented for that flow.

Flow Cache Maintenance

The size and the number of entries in the flow cache are platform dependent. Table A-1 lists the default values.

Table A-1 *Flow Cache Entry Default Values*

Platform	Default Cache Entries	Default Memory for NetFlow Cache
AS5800, 4x00, 3600, 2600, 2500, 1600, 1400	4000	256 KB
7200, RSP7000	64,000	4 MB
VIP with 16 MB DRAM	2000	128 KB
VIP with 32 MB DRAM	32,000	2 MB
VIP with 64 MB DRAM	64,000	4 MB
VIP with 128 MB DRAM	128,000	8 MB

Each time a new flow is added to the NetFlow cache, the number of available NetFlow cache entries is checked. If only a few free flows remain, NetFlow attempts to age 30 of the existing flows using an accelerated timeout. If only one free flow remains, NetFlow automatically ages 30 existing flows regardless of their age. The intent is to ensure free flow entries always are available.

The aging process includes the following:

- Flows that have been idle for 15 seconds are expired and removed from the cache.

- Long-lived flows (more than 30 minutes by default) are expired and removed from the cache. The flow expiration parameter is user configurable.

- TCP flows that have reached the end of byte stream (FIN) or that have been reset (RST) are expired from the cache.

Example A-1 demonstrates the output of the **show ip cache verbose flow** command, which displays details about the NetFlow cache.

Example A-1 **show ip cache verbose flow** *Command Output Displays NetFlow Cache Details*

```
router#sh ip cache verbose flow
IP packet size distribution (5693M total packets):
   1-32    64    96   128   160   192   224   256   288   320   352   384   416   448   480
   .000  .135  .166  .100  .066  .051  .039  .033  .028  .024  .021  .019  .017  .015  .013

   512   544   576  1024  1536  2048  2560  3072  3584  4096  4608
   .012  .011  .068  .065  .108  .000  .000  .000  .000  .000  .000


IP Flow Switching Cache, 2228352 bytes
   6005 active, 26763 inactive, 134383926 added
   1347994477 ager polls, 0 flow alloc failures
   last clearing of statistics never
Protocol         Total    Flows   Packets Bytes  Packets Active(Sec) Idle(Sec)
--------         Flows    /Sec     /Flow  /Pkt    /Sec    /Flow      /Flow
TCP-Telnet        1248     0.0         3    40     0.0      0.5       16.6
TCP-FTP             10     0.0         6    46     0.0      4.3       11.5
TCP-FTPD             2     0.0      1011    40     0.0     26.8        5.9
TCP-WWW            490     0.0         8   313     0.0      4.5       13.2
TCP-SMTP         14045     0.0        16   363     0.0      0.5       14.8
TCP-other     105635036   29.1        53   363  1560.5     51.8       15.7
UDP-DNS         593992     0.1         1    66     0.1      0.0       16.8
UDP-NTP         286608     0.0         1    76     0.0      0.1       16.7
UDP-other     25237407     6.9         1    83    10.4      0.1       16.8
ICMP           2558041     0.7         1    59     0.8      0.4       16.7
Total:        134326879    37.0       42   361  1572.1     40.7       15.9

SrcIf          SrcIPaddress     DstIf           DstIPaddress     Pr TOS Flgs  Pkts
Port Msk AS                     Port Msk AS     NextHop             B/Pk Active
Gi1/0/0        63.75.60.227     Gi8/0/0         24.129.29.189    06 00   18      2
06BC /0   0                     062F /0   0     0.0.0.0                  48    2.0
```

The first section of the output in Example A-1 displays the packet size distribution percentages by packet size. Other notable fields include the following:

- **Pr**—The IP Protocol Field (for example, TCP = 6; UDP = 17) byte.

- **TOS**—Type of Service byte in the IP header.

- **Flgs**—The flags field contains the logical OR of the TCP flags for all packets of a given TCP flow. This field is undefined for non-TCP flows.

- **AS**—In the BGP autonomous system number field, a value of 0 for the AS number can be due to several reasons:

  — Traffic destined to the router.

  — Flows that are not routable.

  — Traffic local to the AS (in other words, traffic that is only Intra-AS).

  — Asymmetric routing. If a demand-based cache scheme (fast, optimum switching) is used as the switching method, then the source or the destination IP address cannot be in the route-cache due to asymmetric routing. CEF is topology driven and not data driven; therefore, CEF fixes this problem.

  — **peer-as** or **origin-as** has not explicitly been configured. **ip flow-export version 5 peer-as | origin-as** must be explicitly configured to enable the export and the collection of AS numbers.

Flow Export

Flow data is exported in UDP datagrams periodically (once per second) or as soon as a full UDP datagram of expired flows is available. The size of each flow record depends on the NetFlow version. Four versions of NetFlow Export currently are supported:

- **Version 1 (v1)**—Version 1 format was the original format supported in the initial Cisco IOS software releases containing NetFlow functionality.

- **Version 5 (v5)**—The Version 5 format added Border Gateway Protocol (BGP) autonomous system information and flow sequence numbers.

- **Version 7 (v7)**—The Version 7 format is an enhancement that adds NetFlow support for Cisco Catalyst 5000 series switches equipped with a NetFlow feature card (NFFC). Version 7 is supported only by the Catalyst 5000 NFFC.

- **Version 8 (v8)**—Version 8 is the format used to export aggregated NetFlow statistics via the Router-Based NetFlow Aggregation feature; this version also provides total flow sequence numbers.

Versions 2 through 4 and Version 6 either were not released or are not supported.

For a Version 1 datagram, up to 24 flows can be sent in a single UDP datagram of approximately 1200 bytes. For a Version 5 datagram, up to 30 flows can be sent in a single UDP datagram of approximately 1500 bytes. For a Version 7 datagram, up to 28 flows can be sent in a single UDP datagram of approximately 1500 bytes. Obviously, the flow collector application should support the flow version that is being exported from the router.

Router-Based Flow Aggregation Export (RBA)

Flow export from a busy interface with large numbers of flows can generate a very significant amount of NetFlow traffic. The RBA scheme (NetFlow Version 8) addresses this issue by aggregating the flows on the router without exporting the individual flows. As of this writing, IOS supports five NetFlow aggregation schemes:

- **Autonomous System aggregation scheme**—Provides significant NetFlow export data volume reduction and generates autonomous system–to–autonomous system traffic flow data. This aggregation scheme groups data flows with the same source Border Gateway Protocol (BGP) autonomous system, the destination BGP autonomous system, the input interface, and the output interface.

- **Destination Prefix aggregation scheme**—Generates data so you can examine the destinations of network traffic passing through a NetFlow-enabled device. This aggregation scheme groups data flows with the same destination prefix, destination prefix mask, destination BGP autonomous system, and output interface.

- **Prefix aggregation scheme**—Generates data so you can examine the sources and the destinations of network traffic passing through a NetFlow-enabled device. This aggregation scheme groups data flows with the same source prefix, destination prefix, source prefix mask, destination prefix mask, source BGP autonomous system, destination BGP autonomous system, input interface, and output interface.

- **Protocol Port aggregation scheme**—Generates data so you can examine network usage by traffic type. This aggregation scheme groups data flows with the same IP protocol, source port number, and destination port number when applicable.

- **Source Prefix aggregation scheme**—Generates data so you can examine the sources of network traffic passing through a NetFlow-enabled device. This aggregation scheme groups data flows with the same source prefix, source prefix mask, source BGP autonomous system, and input interface.

Each aggregation scheme uses its own cache, the size of which is configurable (default 4096 entries).

For more information on the NetFlow aggregation schemes, visit CCO (www.cisco.com) and search for "NetFlow aggregation."

INDEX

Symbols

A

B

C

D

N

Q

R

S

U

V

W–Z

Cisco Career Certifications

Building Cisco Remote Access Networks

Cisco Systems, Inc., edited by Catherine Paquet

1-57870-091-4 • AVAILABLE NOW

Based on the Cisco Systems instructor-led course available worldwide, *Building Cisco Remote Access Networks* teaches you how to design, set up, configure, maintain, and scale a remote access network using Cisco products. In addition, *Building Cisco Remote Access Networks* provides chapter-ending questions to help you assess your understanding of key concepts and start you down the path for attaining your CCNP or CCDP certification.

Building Scalable Cisco Networks

Cisco Systems, Inc., edited by Catherine Paquet and Diane Teare

1-57870-228-3 • AVAILABLE OCTOBER 2000

Based on the Cisco Systems instructor-led course available worldwide, *Building Scalable Cisco Networks* teaches you advanced router configuration. As the replacement for the Advanced Cisco Router Configuration (ACRC) course, BSCN is one of four new courses recommended by Cisco for CCNP and CCDP preparation. If you are pursuing CCNP or CCDP certification, this book helps you with strong and accurate early study material by covering routing principles, extended IP addresses, single- and multiple-area OSPF, EIGRP, BGP, and scalability implementation.

Building Cisco Multilayer Switched Networks

Cisco Systems, Inc., edited by Karen Webb

1-57870-093-0 • AVAILABLE NOW

Based on the Cisco Systems instructor-led course available worldwide, *Building Cisco Multilayer Switched Networks* teaches you how to build and manage campus networks using multilayer switching technologies. As the replacement for the Cisco LAN Switch Configuration (CLSC) course, BCMSN is one of four new courses recommended by Cisco for CCNP and CCDP preparation. If you are pursuing CCNP or CCDP certification, this book helps you with strong and accurate early study material.

Interconnecting Cisco Network Devices

Cisco Systems, Inc., edited by Steve McQuerry

1-57870-111-2 • AVAILABLE NOW

Based on the Cisco course taught worldwide, *Interconnecting Cisco Network Devices* teaches you how to configure Cisco switches and routers in multi-protocol internetworks. ICND is the primary course recommended by Cisco Systems for CCNA #640-507 preparation. If you are pursuing CCNA certification, this book is an excellent starting point for your study.

CISCO SYSTEMS

CISCO PRESS®

www.ciscopress.com

CCIE Professional Development

Large-Scale IP Network Solutions

Khalid Raza, CCIE, and Mark Turner

1-57870-084-1 • AVAILABLE NOW

Network engineers can find solutions as their IP networks grow in size and complexity. Examine all the major IP protocols in-depth and learn about scalability, migration planning, network management, and security for large-scale networks.

Advanced IP Network Design

Alvaro Retana, CCIE, Don Slice, CCIE, and Russ White, CCIE

1-57870-097-3 • AVAILABLE NOW

Network engineers and managers can use these case studies, which highlight various network design goals, to explore issues including protocol choice, network stability, and growth. This book also includes theoretical discussion on advanced design topics.

Cisco LAN Switching

Kennedy Clark, CCIE; Kevin Hamilton, CCIE

1-57870-094-9 • AVAILABLE NOW

This volume provides an in-depth analysis of Cisco LAN switching technologies, architectures, and deployments, including unique coverage of Catalyst network design essentials. Network designs and configuration examples are incorporated throughout to demonstrate the principles and enable easy translation of the material into practice in production networks.

Routing TCP/IP, Volume I

Jeff Doyle, CCIE

1-57870-041-8 • AVAILABLE NOW

This book takes the reader from a basic understanding of routers and routing protocols through a detailed examination of each of the IP interior routing protocols. Learn techniques for designing networks that maximize the efficiency of the protocol being used. Exercises and review questions provide core study for the CCIE Routing and Switching exam.

Cisco Press Solutions

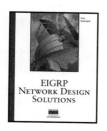

EIGRP Network Design Solutions
Ivan Pepelnjak, CCIE

1-57870-165-1 • AVAILABLE NOW

EIGRP Network Design Solutions uses case studies and real-world configuration examples to help you gain an in-depth understanding of the issues involved in designing, deploying, and managing EIGRP-based networks. This book details proper designs that can be used to build large and scalable EIGRP-based networks, and it documents possible ways each EIGRP feature can be used in network design, implementation, troubleshooting, and monitoring.

Cisco IOS Releases: The Complete Reference
Mack Coulibaly

1-57870-179-1 • AVAILABLE NOW

This book is the first comprehensive guide to the more than three dozen types of Cisco IOS releases being used today on enterprise and service provider networks. You will learn to select the best Cisco IOS release for your network and to predict the quality and stability of a particular release. With that knowledge, you'll be able to design, implement, and manage world-class network infrastructures powered by Cisco IOS software.

OpenCable™ Architecture
Michael Adams

1-57870-135-x • AVAILABLE NOW

Whether you're a television, data communications, or telecommunications professional or simply an interested business person, this book will help you understand the technical and business issues surrounding interactive television services. It will also provide you with an inside look at the combined efforts of the cable, data and consumer electronics industries' efforts to develop those new services.

Enhanced IP Services for Cisco Networks
Donald C. Lee, CCIE

1-57870-106-6 • AVAILABLE NOW

This is a guide to improving your network's capabilities by understanding the new enabling and advanced Cisco IOS services that build more scalable, intelligent, and secure networks. Learn the technical details necessary to deploy Quality of Service, VPN technologies, IPsec, the IOS firewall, and IOS Intrusion Detection. These services will allow you to extend the network to new frontiers securely, protect your network from attacks, and increase the sophistication of network services.

CISCO SYSTEMS

CISCO PRESS

www.ciscopress.com

Cisco Press Solutions

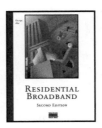

Residential Broadband, Second Edition
George Abe

1-57870-177-5 • AVAILABLE NOW

This book provides a comprehensive, accessible introduction to the topics surrounding high-speed networks to the home. It is written for anyone seeking a broad-based familiarity with the issues of residential broadband. You will learn about the services that are driving the market, the technical issues shaping the evolution, and the network with the home and how it connects to the access network.

Voice over IP Fundamentals
Jonathan Davidson and Jim Peters

1-57870-168-6 • AVAILABLE NOW

This book will provide you with a thorough introduction to the voice and data technology. You will learn how the telephony infrastructure was built and how it works today. You will also gain an understanding of the major concepts concerning voice and data networking, transmission of voice over data, and IP signaling protocols used to interwork with current telephony systems.

Top-Down Network Design
Priscilla Oppenheimer

1-57870-069-8 • AVAILABLE NOW

Building reliable, secure, and manageable networks is every network professional's goal. This practical guide teaches you a systematic method for network design that can be applied to campus LANs, remote-access networks, WAN links, and large-scale internetworks. Learn how to analyze business and technical requirements, examine traffic flow and Quality of Service requirements, and select protocols and technologies based on performance goals.